The Powhatan Landscape

SOCIETY AND ECOLOGY IN ISLAND AND COASTAL ARCHAEOLOGY

UNIVERSITY PRESS OF FLORIDA

Florida A&M University, Tallahassee
Florida Atlantic University, Boca Raton
Florida Gulf Coast University, Ft. Myers
Florida International University, Miami
Florida State University, Tallahassee
New College of Florida, Sarasota
University of Central Florida, Orlando
University of Florida, Gainesville
University of North Florida, Jacksonville
University of South Florida, Tampa
University of West Florida, Pensacola

Society and Ecology in Island and Coastal Archaeology
EDITED BY VICTOR D. THOMPSON

The settlement and occupation of islands, coastlines, and archipelagoes can be traced deep into the human past. From the voyaging and seafaring peoples of the Oceania to the Mesolithic fisher-hunter-gatherers of coastal Ireland, to coastal salt production among Maya traders, the range of variation found in these societies over time is boundless. Yet, they share a commonality that links them all together—their dependence upon seas, coasts, and estuaries for life and prosperity. Thus, in all these cultures there is a fundamental link between society and the ecology of islands coasts. Books in this series explore the nature of humanity's relationship to these environments from a global perspective. Topics in this series would range from edited volumes to single case studies covering the archaeology of initial migrations, seafaring, insularity, trade, societal complexity and collapse, early village life, aquaculture, and historical ecology, among others along islands and coasts.

The
Powhatan Landscape

An Archaeological History
of the Algonquian Chesapeake

Martin D. Gallivan

Foreword by Victor D. Thompson

UNIVERSITY PRESS OF FLORIDA

Gainesville / Tallahassee / Tampa / Boca Raton
Pensacola / Orlando / Miami / Jacksonville / Ft. Myers / Sarasota

This book may be available in an electronic edition.

First cloth printing, 2016
First paperback printing, 2018

23 22 21 20 19 18   6 5 4 3 2 1

Names: Gallivan, Martin D., 1968– author. | Thompson, Victor D., author of
foreword.
Title: The Powhatan landscape : an archaeological history of the Algonquian
Chesapeake / Martin D. Gallivan ; foreword by Victor D. Thompson.
Other titles: Society and ecology in island and coastal archaeology.
Description: Gainesville : University Press of Florida, [2016] | Series:
Society and ecology in island and coastal archaeology | Includes
bibliographical references and index.
Identifiers: LCCN 2016015362 | ISBN 9780813062860 (cloth)
ISBN 9780813064901 (pbk.)
Subjects: LCSH: Powhatan Indians—History. | Powhatan Indians—Social life
and customs. | Indians of North America—Chesapeake Bay Region (Md. and
Va.)—History. | Indians of North America—Chesapeake Bay Region (Md. and
Va.)—Social life and customs. | Chesapeake Bay Region (Md. and
Va.)—History. | Chesapeake Bay Region (Md. and Va.)—Social life and
customs.
Classification: LCC E99.P85 G36 2016 | DDC 975.5004/97347—dc23
LC record available at https://lccn.loc.gov/2016015362

The University Press of Florida is the scholarly publishing agency for the State University
System of Florida, comprising Florida A&M University, Florida Atlantic University, Florida
Gulf Coast University, Florida International University, Florida State University, New College
of Florida, University of Central Florida, University of Florida, University of North Florida,
University of South Florida, and University of West Florida.

University Press of Florida
15 Northwest 15th Street
Gainesville, FL 32611-2079
http://upress.ufl.edu

To Lila, the best seven-year-old dirt archaeologist I know.

To Liam, who promised to read it even if nobody else would.

To Mona, who never had a doubt, even when I did.

To Catherine, the best teacher I ever had.

And to John, who inspired it all.

Contents

Figures

Tables

Foreword

Martin Gallivan's book is the first volume in the University Press of Florida's Society and Ecology in Island and Coastal Archaeology series. This series focuses on several core themes related to the nature of how people came to dwell along the islands and coastlines of the distant and recent past. Indeed, the settlement and occupation of islands, coastlines, and archipelagoes can be traced deep into human history and likely played a core role in the shaping of human societies. Thus, an understanding of how people adapted, viewed, experienced, and became one with such places lends fundamental insights into human societies. Books in the series explore the commonalities of the entangled histories of people who came to live in these regions.

Today, over 40 percent of the world's population lives within 100km of coasts, and in countries such as the United States, the percentage of the population that lives in these areas is on the rise. Understanding the changing nature of humanity's connection with islands and coastlines provides important historical lessons for the future of such relationships. As more and more people move into these environments, greater challenges face those of us who study the histories of these areas, as development for housing, businesses, and the like erases the record that archaeologists depend upon for clues. Added to the issues of increased development is the present and coming loss of land (and archaeological sites) due to the projected sea-level rise accompanying the end of the twenty-first century.

In a very real sense, we are in a race against the rising tide of the global seas and an increasing demand for land in these areas. Thus, it seems that in our current situation there is a need now more than ever to understand the history of our species with respect to coastal environments—to help us contemplate what kind of future is important to us. To understand such questions effectively, we must go beyond simply examining such histories in purely economic terms, but rather take a more nuanced view to understand how socially as well as emotionally people became connected to such landscapes. This is exactly what Gallivan's volume does for one of the most famous estuaries along the Atlantic Coast—the Chesapeake.

Long before the waters of the Chesapeake bordered the modern capital of Washington, D.C., a different political power called it home—Powhatan. Gallivan's volume is a tour de force archaeological synthesis and reinterpretation of the greater Powhatan landscape. This landscape and the peoples whose histories were so intertwined with it form a central part of the story of the colonial efforts of the British. However, unlike other scholarly works, which tend to disembody these peoples from not only their own histories but also from the landscape itself, Gallivan takes a refreshing look at how longer-term histories and relationships structure not only the moment of contact but the longer temporal rhythms of history, focusing on the changing relationships that Algonquian-speaking peoples had with the Chesapeake and its surrounding lands.

Drawing on different but complementary theories that link to historical ecology, placemaking, landscape anthropology, and the like, Gallivan weaves each of these theoretical frameworks into a broader narrative. The product of this melding of theories, with its specific gaze on the Powhatan landscape, is a highly readable interpretative framework for Native societies of the Eastern Woodlands. Gallivan's main point is that we need to consider the deep histories that structure the societies of the Chesapeake interactions with the coming of the Europeans. This important perspective results in a reinterpretation of the events of contact, as well as both the ultimate and proximate reasons for the way in which these histories played out. As Gallivan shows, the Tsenacomacoh's landscape is a web of complex relationships and is, in part, a product of Algonquian social practices from AD 100 up through the Chesapeake's colonial history.

Following Gallivan's introduction to the region and his outline of Tsenacomacoh's landscape in theoretical terms, the subsequent chapters in this volume go on to link the broader concepts of these higher-level theories, particularly the ideas of dwelling and placemaking, with the available data on the region. While some of the ideas presented are nuanced,

Gallivan deftly unpacks these concepts so that they are understandable and can be readily linked to historical and archaeological evidence. He accomplishes this by drawing on a variety of perspectives. For example, he provides a deep discussion of the landscape as viewed from historic documents and maps, as well as ethnohistory. He uses this departure point to provide a discussion of how the broader world was perceived by early colonists. Gallivan uses this to link his perspective of a "deep time gaze" to begin to understand the world of Powhatan.

In the volume the Chesapeake estuary not only plays a prominent role in the analysis but is itself an actor in the unfolding of the various relationships explored by Gallivan. From this perspective, the estuary is not simply the backdrop upon which Virginia Algonquians moved and gathered food. Instead, the estuary was critical in how communities related to one another, and as Gallivan points out, it served as the very basis for community names and identity. The picture that emerges from this treatment is a landscape connected and defined by its waterways. These relationships, as the author shows, permeated both political and social life. This viewpoint takes the reader beyond other studies that tend to offer more bounded perspectives for estuarine groups, and it illustrates the centrality of the estuaries. In the Chesapeake, water was not always a social or political boundary.

While Gallivan explores social and political dimensions of the landscape, he does not neglect the bounty of the Chesapeake's estuaries and the role they played among the Virginia Algonquians. Specifically, he considers the nature of ethnogenesis in the region and draws together linguistic, ethnohistoric, and archaeological information to examine how use of aquatic resources played into notions of identity, and how the consumption of such resources varied in the region and shifted through time. Related to this is the adoption of maize-based economies in the region and how they articulated with the transition from fisher-foraging to more agricultural endeavors across the landscape.

Gallivan's final chapters and the epilogue bring the discussion back around to the idea of place making and dwelling that are introduced at the start of the volume. He shows the durable and transposable meanings that places had among the Native communities of the colonial Chesapeake landscape. He demonstrates that despite the ruptures, disjunctions, and ultimate displacement of so many Native peoples of this region, these groups continued to link their spatial practices to important places on the landscape. They did this by returning over and over again to persistent places for the burial of the dead, communal feasts, and social and religious ceremonies to reify identity and a sense of community—with both the living and the ancestors. This conclusion demonstrates the value of the approach taken in the volume by showing how a deeper understanding of historical moments can be achieved by considering their context within the distant past. Finally, in the epilogue, Gallivan discusses the meaning that his, along with his colleagues,' ongoing research is more than simply academic and has real implications for the modern descendants of the Native communities of the Chesapeake. This ending shows the connection and the importance that archaeology can have for groups, and that working together—or as David Hurst Thomas says, "partnering up"—is an important component of archaeological research.

Gallivan's book is a wonderful inaugural volume for the Society and Ecology in Island and Coastal Archaeology series. Its unique articulation of complementary theoretical perspectives provides the reader with insight into the history of these communities' relationships with the broader aquatic Chesapeake landscape. This work is foundational and will certainly be important as we explore the nature of colonial encounters and engagements in other coastal and island regions of the world.

Victor D. Thompson
University of Georgia

Acknowledgments

This book is the end point of a lengthy trip that started in central Virginia and flowed eastward through Tidewater Virginia. The initial idea to create an archaeological history of the Powhatan landscape began about twenty-five years ago in a dusty, pale blue Suburban driven around the Virginia piedmont by Jeffrey Hantman. Conversations with Jeff and with other University of Virginia colleagues, including Michael Klein and Stephen Plog, have shaped my approach to the Native past in fundamental ways.

My education as an anthropologist later shifted eastward with an appointment to the faculty at William and Mary. My most important partnership at the college has been with Danielle Moretti-Langholtz. Danielle vouched for me with the Virginia Indian community and showed me what a civically engaged anthropology looks like. Through their example and advice, William and Mary colleagues—including Neil Norman, Matt Liebmann, Katie Bragdon, Audrey Horning, Mary Voigt, Fred Smith, Bill Fisher, Brad Weiss, Jonathan Glasser, Marley Brown, Jenny Kahn, Michelle Lelièvre, and Barbara King—have each taught me how to be a better scholar. I am particularly indebted to Shannon Mahoney and Michael Blakey of the William and Mary Institute for Historical Biology, who partnered with me to study the Chickahominy River Survey collection.

Scores of William and Mary students working along the Chickahominy River, at Kiskiak, and at Werowocomoco have contributed countless hours in the field and laboratory, generating the evidence used here. Among these, I am particularly grateful to Buck Woodard, Ashley Spivey, Anna Hayden, Christopher Shephard, Jessica Herlich, and Jessica Jenkins. I also thank Patrick Johnson, whose patient editing of an early draft of the manuscript improved my writing considerably.

The Werowocomoco site represents the centerpiece of this book, and the investigations conducted there involved numerous colleagues, students, and supporters. Our investigations at Werowocomoco were initially spurred on by Lynn Ripley's discovery of American Indian artifacts while walking her property along Purtan Bay. Lynn and Bob Ripley have been instrumental in the success of the archaeological research at Werowocomoco ever since, welcoming into their home the Werowocomoco Research Group, Virginia Indians, William and Mary field school students, and interested visitors by the busload. I am especially grateful for their hospitality and support over the years.

My partners in the Werowocomoco Research Group—Randy Turner, Dave Brown, Thane Harpole, and Danielle Moretti-Langholtz—have each been critical to the project from the outset. The research group is much more than the sum of its parts, and I count myself fortunate to have been a part of the team. Randy Turner, former director of the Virginia Department of Historic Resources Tidewater Regional Office, was the first to recognize the significance of Lynn Ripley's discoveries and to envision what a Werowocomoco project might entail. David Brown and Thane Harpole of the Fairfield Foundation have played a largely unheralded role as the driving force behind Werowocomoco's archaeology. Both have given tremendously of their time, energy, and expertise to ensure that the fieldwork accords with the discipline's best practices. Drawing on years of relationship building and unparalleled diplomatic skills, Danielle Moretti-Langholtz of William and Mary's American Indian Resource Center set the research team on a course of collaborative archaeology that has yielded tremendous rewards.

Much of the credit for the research at Kiskiak and related sites on the Naval Weapons Station goes to colleagues at the William and Mary Center for Archaeological Research, including former director Dennis Blanton and former project archaeologist John Underwood. Civilian archaeologists with the U.S. Navy, particularly Bruce Larson and Susan Ritter, facilitated this research in a model partnership between a federal agency and an academic institution.

Conversations with Powhatan scholars Margaret Williamson and Helen Rountree have greatly improved my understanding of the Native past in

Tidewater Virginia. Likewise, Stephen Potter's work along the Potomac River inspired the approach followed here. Discussions with Stephen and his review of the draft manuscript have improved my scholarship considerably. Justine McKnight's keen archaeobotanical analyses have been critical to my perspective since we first met in the 1990s. Even earlier than this, William and Mary professors Norman Barka and Ben McCary had the vision to develop the Chickahominy River Survey as the study of a riverine landscape at a time when most research focused only on a single site.

I may never be able to settle my considerable debt of gratitude to Virginia's Native community. Virginia Indians have contributed considerably to the research at Chickahominy, Kiskiak, and especially Werowocomoco. The members of Werowocomoco's Virginia Indian Advisory Board have given generously of their time to meet with the researchers, to serve as liaisons to the Indian community, and to offer thoughtful guidance. Advisory Board members have included Jeff Brown (Pamunkey, now deceased), Chief Mark Custalow (Mattaponi), Kerry Canaday (Chickahominy), Lee Lockamy (Nansemond), Chief Anne Richardson (Rappahannock), Reggie Tupponce (Upper Mattaponi, now deceased), and ex-officio advisors Chief Steve Adkins (Chickahominy), Chief Ken Adams (Upper Mattaponi). Members of the Virginia Indian community have also joined the Werowocomoco field crew, including Jeff Brown, Ashley Spivey, James Krigsvold, Gloria Custalow, and Ethan Brown. Conversations with Jeff, including a memorable one during a trip around Purtan Bay in his skiff, changed my perspective on the Powhatan past. Now a William and Mary PhD candidate, Ashley has since assumed a leadership role in the nascent Indigenous archaeology of the Chesapeake. I am particularly grateful to Ashley who reviewed several iterations of this book and offered advice with her customary intellect and grace.

I thank Wayne Adkins, First Assistant Chief of the Chickahominy Tribe, whose prudent guidance regarding the Chickahominy River Survey study guaranteed that project's success. Crucial advice on the Kiskiak research has come from former chief Kevin Brown (Pamunkey) and from Chief Mark Custalow (Mattaponi).

A sincere thanks goes to manuscript reviewers Stephen Potter and Julia King and the staff of the University Press of Florida (UPF). I am especially grateful to Victor Thompson, creator and editor of UPF's Society and Ecology in Island and Coastal Archaeology series. I thank UPF director

Meredith Babb for her steady (and patient) guidance throughout the publication process. Copy editor Lisa Williams also has my gratitude for her keen and discerning eye.

Grant funding for the research discussed in this book came from a National Endowment for the Humanities Collaborative Research Grant, a National Park Service Save America's Treasures Grant, the Virginia Foundation for the Humanities, the Federal 2007 Jamestown Commemoration Commission, and the Colonial Dames of America. This book was written with fellowship support from the National Endowment for the Humanities. Critical support has come from the College of William and Mary and the Department of Historic Resources. I thank these institutions and all of these individuals for helping to make the voyage a success.

Glossary of Algonquian Words

Accomac (AA-koh-maak). "Other side town"; Virginia Algonquian town.

Appamattuck (aa-poh-MAA-tuhk). "Trap-fishing river"; river and Virginia Algonquian town.

Chickahominy (chihk-uh-HAW-muh-nee). "Coarse-pounded corn people"; river and unified Virginia Algonquian communities living on it.

Kiskiak (KIHS-kee-aak). "Wide land" or "High place"; Virginia Algonquian town.

Kuscarawaok (kuhs-kah-RAH-wawk). "Place of making shell beads"; Virginia Algonquian town.

Macocanaco (MAH-koh-kah-NAH-koh). "Gourd field"; Virginia Algonquian town.

Mamanatowick (muh-mahn-uh-TOH-wihk). Paramount chief, infused with spiritual power.

Manitou (MAH-nee-too). Spiritual power.

Mattahunt (MAAT-uh-huhnt). "Place at the end of the stream"; Virginia Algonquian town.

Mattaponi (MAAT-uh-poh-niy). "Stopping place on the path"; river and Virginia Algonquian town.

Opechancanough (oh-pee-KAAN-kuh-noo). Pamunkey chief and brother to Powhatan.

Orapax (AW-ruh-paaks). "Deserted water place"; Virginia Algonquian town and temple.

Pamunkey (puh-MUHN-kee). "Sloping hill"; river and Virginia Algonquian town.

Paspahegh (PAAS-puh-hay). "At the mouth"; Virginia Algonquian town.

Patawomeck (paat-uh-WOH-mihk). "To bring again they come and go"; river and Virginia Algonquian town.

Pawtuxent (puh-TUHKS-uhnt). "At the rapids"; river and Virginia Algonquian town.

Pissacoack (pihs-AAK-oh-aak). "Muddy place"; Virginia Algonquian town.

Powhatan (POW-uh-taan or POH-uh-tawn). "Hill of priestly divination"; Wahunsenacawh's natal town; Algonquian name for James River; term applied to Virginia Algonquians' tributary to Wahunsenacawh; label for Wahunsenacawh's chiefdom.

Quioccosuk (kwee-AWK-uh-haw-suhk). Minor god; priest.

Rassawek (RAAS-uh-wehk). "In-between place"; Virginia Algonquian hunting camp.

Secowocomoco (SEH-koh-wuh-KOH-muh-koh). "Enclosure at the outlet"; Virginia Algonquian town.

Tassantass (TAHS-uhn-tahs). Stranger; term applied to English colonists.

Tsenacomacoh (sehn-uh-kuh-MAH-kah). "Land that was dwelt upon closely together" or "a nearby dwelling-place"; the Virginia coastal plain.

Uttamussak (OOT-uh-moo-sahk). Virginia Algonquian town of temples on the Pamunkey River.

Wahunsenacawh (wah-hoon-SEHN-uh-kah). Paramount chief in Tsenacomacoh; also known as Powhatan.

Warraskoyac (waw-rihs-KOY-ahk). "Point of land"; Virginia Algonquian town.

Weanock (WAY-uh-nahk). "Place around which the river winds itself"; Virginia Algonquian town.

Weroance (WAYR-uh-ahns). Commander or chief.

Werowocomoco (WAYR-uh-wah-KOH-muh-koh). "Place of the antler wearers"; Virginia Algonquian town and center place of the Powhatan chiefdom.

Wighcomoco (wiy-KOH-muh-koh). "Pleasant place"; name for two Virginia Algonquian towns.

Winsack (WIHN-sahk). "Pleasant place near the river mouth"; Virginia Algonquian town.

Yihakin (yih-HAY-kihn). Sapling-framed Algonquian house.

Youghtanund (YAW-tuh-nuund). Virginia Algonquian town.

Prologue

December 12, 1607

Two hundred armed men waited quietly along the swampy headwaters of the Chickahominy River, closely following the stranger captain's progress upstream.[1] Hidden along the cold river bank, they watched as the short, bearded Englishman passed by the town of Mattahunt—a place named for the "End of the stream."[2] The American Indians following Captain Smith that day came from six towns located along rivers that flow into the Chesapeake Bay. They were led by Opechancanough (oh-pee-KAAN-kuh-noo), the chief of the Pamunkey and brother to the paramount chief, Powhatan (POH-uh-taan). Powhatan claimed authority over a large portion of the Tidewater region. This area, Tsenacomacoh (sehn-uh-kuh-MAH-kah), was centered on the James and York, rivers known then as the Powhatan and the Pamunkey.[3] Lined with marshes and swamps that rise and fall with the tides, the Powhatan, Pamunkey, and other rivers in the region transition from freshwater to brackish to salt water as they flow southeast to the Chesapeake Bay. The term *Powhatan*, then, referred variously to a man, the town where he was born, a tidal river, a political territory in Tidewater Virginia, and a paramount chiefdom with as many as 15,000 adherents.

By 1607 Powhatan had earned the title Mamanatowick (muh-mahn-uh-TOH-wihk). As such, he was filled with *manitou* (MAH-nee-too), the Algonquian term for the spirit force that infused certain people, objects, and places on the landscape. Manifested in the marvelous, the beautiful, and the dangerous, *manitou* hints at a Virginia Algonquian understand-

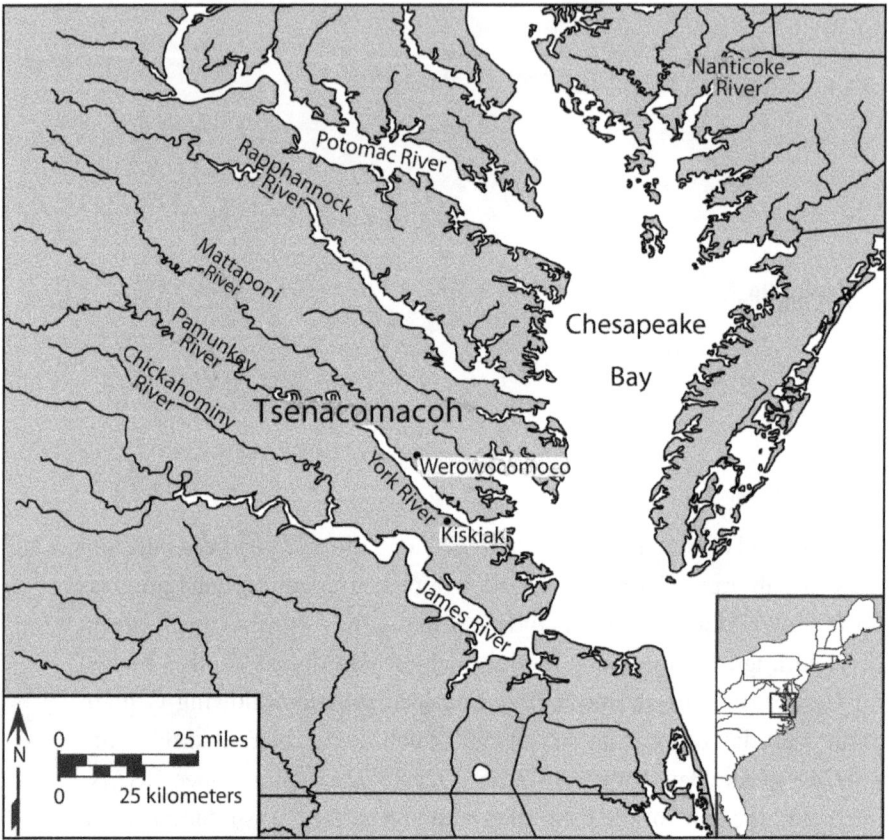

Figure P.1. Map of Tsenacomacoh.

ing of the world without the same distinctions between culture and nature, the animate and inanimate, the powerful and passive drawn by the
English colonists like Smith.[4] Smith reported that Virginia Algonquians
viewed Powhatan not only as a king but also as half god.[5] The Powhatan
chiefdom, though, had been forged recently by warfare and was fraught
with divisions in 1607. Three of the six groups accompanying Opechancanough came from core communities of the chiefdom. Two others—the
Paspahegh and Kiskiak—had been incorporated into the chiefdom more
recently by violent conquest. The Chickahominy, the formidable "Coarse-
pounded Corn People" remained independent of Powhatan's authority,
though they periodically allied with him, as they did in late 1607.[6] Despite
the overwhelming attention paid by historians to the Powhatan and James

Fort leadership, the early-seventeenth-century Chesapeake was populated by a number of powerful and populous Native communities.[7]

Smith traveled with two other Englishmen in a dugout canoe paddled by Chickahominy guides. As the Virginia Company's "cape merchant," Smith was responsible for securing supplies, an effort he began on three previous trips to Chickahominy towns.[8] Along the way, Smith experienced, mapped, and described the Virginia Algonquian landscape more extensively than any other Englishman to date. Twenty miles above Apocant, the last Chickahominy town on the river, Smith put ashore to eat. With the fire burning and the pot boiling, the captain instructed his men to keep their pieces lit and to fire a warning shot at the first sign of Native visitors. He then walked a short distance to take in his surroundings.

With Smith separated from his men, Opechancanough's forces attacked. One group killed the Englishmen waiting by the canoe. The main force surrounded Smith. He fought back, firing a pistol several times before being struck by an arrow to the leg. Outnumbered and outmaneuvered, the English captain fell into the cold mud of the Chickahominy swamp and surrendered.

During the following weeks, Opechancanough brought the captive Smith by dugout canoe and on foot along a winding pathway through Tsenacomacoh, ending at the town of Werowocomoco (WAYR-uh-wah-KOH-muh-koh), Powhatan's principal residence and the central town of the chiefdom. Smith's writings of events at Werowocomoco have been transformed into evocative narratives focused on his near-death experience and rescue there by Powhatan's daughter Pocahontas.[9]

In fact, the tale of Pocahontas' rescue has come to play a prominent role in America's origin stories. As such, the Smith rescue has become what ethnohistorian Ray Fogelson has termed an "epitomizing event" in modern historiography that condensed, encapsulated, and dramatized longer-term processes of American colonial history.[10] Built around the story of a celebrated "Indian princess" whose friendship with Smith and marriage to colonist John Rolfe afforded the English at James Fort a tenuous peace in the Chesapeake and a toehold in North America, the rescue story has contributed to master narratives behind the struggle to "plant" English civilization on American shores.[11]

Rather than start with Smith's rescue and a story centered on James Fort, a better point of departure for considering Virginia Algonquian culture and history begins instead with an event that occurred earlier in Smith's month-long captivity.[12] Brought to Opechancanough's town on the Pamunkey neck, Smith was placed before a fire within a temple. Priests entered, began an invocation, and surrounded the fire with a circle of corn meal. They then encircled the corn meal with two rings of corn kernels while alternating invocations and songs. The priests continued this ceremony for three days, eventually adding sticks between the kernels. Smith described the event as a "divination" meant to foretell his future, specifically whether he and the English intended any harm. He understood the figure on the temple floor as a rendering of the Powhatan world: the circle of meal depicted Tsenacomacoh, the maize kernels represented the edges of the ocean, and the sticks stood for the colonists. Recent interpretations suggest that the priests' diagram conveyed principles of cosmology, processes of incorporation, and the colonists' profound otherness.[13] Rather than simply a divination, the ceremony was more likely a means of redefining Smith in order to absorb him and the English colonists into Tsenacomacoh.

As an Algonquian map designed to effect a change in the world through ritual performance, the divination diagram drew upon Virginia Algonquian tropes and the authority of priests to define and remake the world. The Pamunkey priests represented Tsenacomacoh as a circle of refined corn surrounding a fiery center. Two outer rings of unprocessed maize kernels signified Tsenacomacoh's boundaries. Depicted as sticks, the colonists had crossed into Tsenacomacoh yet remained something apart from it. Smith was not initially told what the fire signified, though he later learned that the town of Werowocomoco represented the hub of the Powhatan tributary network and the center of a multitiered, paramount chiefdom.[14]

Elements of the divination ceremony—circular arrangements, concentric boundaries, maize, a central fire—appear in other Virginia Algonquian settings before and after European contact, highlighting their importance for these communities. They appear in collective burials known as ossuaries, in concentric ditch features constructed at chiefly centers, in dance circles used in public ceremonies, and in maps depicting the Native landscape. As anthropologist Margaret Williamson has pointed out, circles provided a basis for Powhatan social categories that emphasized relationships between center and periphery.[15] Similarly, the dichotomy of inside and outside evidently served as an organizing principle in Powhatan society. The early colonial-era effort to incorporate the English into the Powhatan circle, ethnohistorian Frederic Gleach has suggested, required that the colonists first be refined and civilized.[16]

John Smith's original published account of his captivity omits any references to the divination ceremony, shifting this event instead to a subsequent discussion of indigenous religious practices.[17] Historians have generally followed Smith's lead by excluding the divination from their narratives. Referenced briefly, if at all, in most accounts of the colonial Chesapeake, the divination ceremony constitutes a "nonevent" in historical scholarship, since it receives little, if any, attention in colonial histories as they are recounted today.[18]

The American Indian past is, of course, full of events that are recognized, defined, and valued locally and differentially. Some episodes may not be considered significant in a local context; others may be intentionally forgotten by Native communities reconfigured by the colonial process; still others were so traumatic as to be denied. Framed in this way, events play a prominent role in a society's collective memory and in its forgetting.[19] Algonquian locations, including Werowocomoco and the towns along the Pamunkey Neck, today might also be thought of as "nonplaces."[20] Once-powerful towns and temples enmeshed in a network of meaningful Native places, they have been disconnected from one another, erased by colonial dispossession, forgotten by settler communities, and ignored by the modern American heritage industry. The nonevents omitted from historians' accounts served as the basis for Ray Fogelson's "ethno-ethnohistorical" approach to American Indian history.[21] Reliant on Native societies' own theories of the past as embedded in cosmology, ceremonies, and oral traditions, such an approach is intended to bring overlooked histories to light.[22]

The divination, a nonevent in what is now a nonplace, serves as a point of departure for this study of the changing landscapes of Tsenacomacoh. Centered on the James and York Rivers in Tidewater Virginia, *Tsenacomacoh* has been translated as the "land that was dwelt upon" [*ahkamikwi*] "closely together" [*tcīn*].[23] *Tsenacomacoh* includes the Algonquian term for "dwelling house" or "house site," so that historical linguist James Geary suggested that *Tsenacomacoh* may be glossed as "a nearby dwelling-place."[24] The place-name Tsenacomacoh calls to mind questions regarding the specific ways that Algonquian communities *dwelled* in Tidewater Virginia. Tsenacomacoh was rife with locations such as the "Hill of priestly divination" (Powhatan) and pathways that included the Potomac River

("To bring again they go and come").[25] Such place-names shaped Virginia Algonquians' orientations to the local setting and were in turn shaped by the Chesapeake's eventful past before and after European contact. The ways Virginia Algonquians named and mapped these places provide entry points for understanding their sense of place, the culturally and historically specific attachments to an area shared by those dwelling there.[26] *Placemaking*, the practices whereby locations are named, constructed, and instilled with significance, is as often as not also a process of *history making*, as stories from the past are gathered from the landscape and attached to locations.[27]

Landscape may be defined and understood in a number of different ways. A landscape may be thought of as a region that is explored and mapped or painted, with an eye toward accurately capturing its natural features, built environments, and geographic order. Alternatively, a landscape may be understood through the lens of someone living there, as a layer of meaning blanketing topological features with specific forms of knowledge and power. Both of these dimensions of landscape, objective and subjective, coalesce in lived experiences that involve moving along pathways and encountering places firsthand. The organizing features of a landscape come to be understood best by those dwelling *in* a landscape (i.e., inhabiting an area) and by those dwelling *on* a landscape (i.e., reflecting upon its salience).[28]

How did landscapes—defined in the broadest terms to include natural settings as well as built environments, representations of spaces, and experiences of places—contribute to the making of Tsenacomacoh and the unmaking of the Powhatan chiefdom? What role did maize and horticultural towns, political centers, sacred locations, and valued objects play in this landscape? Do maps, settlement arrangements, and burial traditions point us toward Virginia Algonquian modes of dwelling and of making history? Might a deeper history of Tsenacomacoh's spaces, places, and pathways bring to the fore silences in the way colonial histories are recounted today?

In the following chapters I develop the argument that our attentiveness to colonial history in the Chesapeake, with its emphasis on documented events involving prominent leaders, has concealed a deeper, indigenous past predicated on dwelling in Tsenacomacoh. The archaeological and ethnohistorical records, along with descendant communities' oral traditions and oral histories, provide evidence that the colonial-era Powhatan chiefdom was rooted in an older Virginia Algonquian landscape that began to coalesce as early as two thousand years ago. This Algonquian landscape was not simply a *stage* upon which Powhatan acquired power or the ecological *setting* that provided valued resources to be exploited by Native chiefs or by European colonists. Rather, Tsenacomacoh's landscape profoundly shaped and was shaped by Algonquian social practices from AD 100 through 1607, and throughout the subsequent history of the Chesapeake.

Chapter 1

Dwelling in Tsenacomacoh

When the Virginia Company established James Fort in 1607, the English colonists settled amidst the Powhatan chiefdom, a powerful polity of Algonquian-speakers centered on the James and York Rivers.[1]

Beginning with the construction of James Fort, the history of Native societies in the Chesapeake has been framed largely by colonists' firsthand accounts produced for European audiences. Such stories often tell us more about the seventeenth-century conceptions of literate Europeans than they do about the people they seek to explain. Today scholars rely heavily on colonists' accounts, often projecting a static "ethnographic present" into the precontact past. Where change has been the focus of study, archaeologists have long favored cultural ecological models. These approaches typically offer only a narrow opening for Native agency, American Indians' capacity to shape their own histories. Cultural ecological interpretations often assume that forces driving social changes in the Chesapeake were primarily adaptive or political, that is, to make the greatest use of the environment or to achieve dominance over the widest area.

This book aims at a different perspective on the Virginia Algonquian past by foregrounding the archaeology of Native settlements from the second through the seventeenth centuries AD. The primary goal is to shift the frame of reference from English accounts of the colonial era toward a longer narrative describing Virginia Algonquians' construction of places, communities, and connections in between. In this shift, archaeology serves as a method for developing a deep history of a Native landscape and a basis for reassessing colonial-era documents.[2] With its access to regional-scale patterns, material practices, built environments, and a Native past beyond European archives, archaeology has much to offer in this regard.

Reorienting the Archaeology of the Chesapeake

The move toward an archaeological history of Algonquian places responds, in part, to the "spatial turn" in the humanities and social sciences, scholarship that emphasizes the often-overlooked spatial dimensions of human experience.[3] *Spatiality*—the effect that space has on people's perceptions, practices, and interactions—has in recent years become a focus of inquiry in disciplines ranging from art history to neuroscience. With the spatial turn, researchers have directed their inquiries toward the spatiality of human life, giving *space* and *place* the same attention that has long been paid to *time* and *history* and to *social relations* and *society*.[4] Lived spaces are not simply a neutral backdrop that can be neatly captured by an objective geometry or universal Cartesian logic, with its x, y, and z dimensions. Rather, as French sociologist Henri Lefebvre put it, each society has its own way of making space collectively, as the product of interactions among people.[5] In this understanding of space as a social product, *places* are created through acts of naming and the distinctive histories associated with particular locations.[6] Places acquire their significance in relation to other locations and connective pathways in a broader landscape.[7]

As a network of spaces connected by people's activities, landscapes include not only settlements, activity areas, and natural places. Landscapes also incorporate *memories* acquired, as Julian Thomas put it, "through the closeness and affinity that [people] have developed for some locations, and through the important events, festivals, calamities, and surprises which have drawn other spots to their attention, causing them to be remembered."[8] In this way, landscapes combine geography with a sense of the past. Built environments are frequently reworked, though rebuilding is often influenced by the constraints and possibilities of previous construction.[9] As a result, some locations retain their importance through time as *persistent places*. These enduring locations, including Athens, Cairo, Quito, and Cahokia, serve as reservoirs of accumulated history.[10]

Archaeologists have in recent years begun to pay closer attention to conversations among geographers, sociologists, anthropologists, and environmental historians about space and place, resulting in archaeologies of landscape that differ from what came before. Of course, archaeologists have had considerable success unpacking settlement patterns and tracing human adaptations to natural environments for more than a century.[11] More recently, though, understandings of regional settings as a either a passive backdrop or the principal determinant of change have given way to more subtle notions of social space and its *active* role in the human past.[12] Emerging from the recent archaeologies of landscape are two key concerns: how people turn spaces into meaningful places, and how cultural memories are shaped through histories of placemaking.[13]

The resulting archaeologies of landscape vary considerably in their orientations and even their definitions of basic terms. Several approaches, though, seek to integrate evidence concerning both the physical environments that people inhabit and the meaningful locations in which they lived their lives.[14] Inherent tensions exist between *objective* characterizations of topographic features and ecological settings, on the one hand, and efforts to recover evidence bearing on *subjective* experiences of a place. Various archaeological schools of thought emphasize distinct orientations toward space and place. A remaining challenge is to find approaches that move beyond facile dichotomies and bring together different aspects of landscapes in compelling ways.

Archaeological studies framed in terms of historical ecology, for example, take landscapes (rather than sites or social groups) as the primary focus of inquiry. Historical ecologists understand landscapes as objective, physical forms modified by people such that human intentions and actions may be read from them.[15] Seeking to rectify the tendency of a previous generation of *cultural* ecologists to overlook or downplay human intentionality, *historical* ecologists understand landscapes as a product of the interplay between cultural acts and acts of nature in a particular setting.[16] There is no *cultural* landscape distinct from *natural* landscape in historical ecology—only landscape, a socionatural artifact that records the fusion of nature and history, biotic communities and human societies.[17] Historical ecology considers processes that transform landscapes on multiple scales and the ways these transformations are understood locally.[18] Historical ecologists frequently emphasize that settlement and subsistence practices are not necessarily adaptive or even sustainable, as demonstrated by recent climate instability and its destructive impacts. Landscapes are, instead, viewed as tangible manifestations of human and environmental history as they intertwine. For historical ecologists, landscapes record both *intentional* acts and *unintentional* consequences, revealing humans' role in the modification of ecosystems and the ways natural processes influence human history.

Historical ecological approaches have, for example, challenged the assumption that the Amazon's ecological parameters defined the pre-Columbian societies living there.[19] By tracing the construction of earthworks, the management of forests, and the enhancement of soils, researchers have argued persuasively that the late prehistoric Amazon was composed of "saturated anthropogenic landscapes," engineered and managed for centuries.[20] Such landscapes signal the *contingency* of the Amazonian past, which includes diverse and unpredictable histories dependent on a complicated blend of socionatural factors.

Other scholars, including those influenced by ideas drawn from phenomenological philosophy, turn toward the meaningful dimension of space. Phenomenology, the study of human experience, emphasizes structures of perception and consciousness. A research tradition rooted in the twentieth-century philosophy of Edmund Husserl, Martin Heidegger, and Maurice Merleau-Ponty, phenomenology examines the ways spaces and objects were experienced from a first-person perspective.[21] Heidegger's approach focused on people's regular engagement with the world around them, suggesting a phenomenology aimed at the meanings embedded in everyday life.[22] In this approach, human experience is understood in terms of a notion of "dwelling."[23] For Heidegger, to dwell in a house is not simply to spend time there. Dwelling means to belong, to be content and at home, to have a sense of place.

Tim Ingold has built on these ideas by developing a "dwelling perspective" on landscape that seeks to bridge the gap between humans as social persons and as biological organisms.[24] Echoing ideas from historical ecology, Ingold suggests that what we refer to as "the environment" might be better understood as a tangle of pathways that continually intertwine then unravel. People do not *occupy* the world as something apart from it, rather "they *inhabit* it, and in so doing—in threading their own paths through the meshwork—they contribute to its ever-evolving weave."[25] In this approach meaning is "gathered" from a landscape as people perform shared tasks that orient them to specific places and to one another. The dwelling perspective emphasizes, above all, movement within social space. In Ingold's formulation, the process of working out meanings through activity unfolds within a "taskscape"—the interlocking of related tasks performed regularly by a community. Landscapes bear witness to the passing of time and possess a chronological dimension—a "temporality"—since they are formed through the accumulation of past taskscapes.[26] Landscapes are inscribed with enduring physical marks (ruins, monuments, pathways, rock art) generated by past taskscapes that influence people's experiences of the world. Rather than simply adapting to our surroundings, we collect meanings from these signs, reading the stories they tell.

The dwelling perspective is oriented toward the daily practices through which people come into relations with one another, with meaningful places, and with things. This approach offers a language for describing landscapes as the product of natural processes and the culturally specific ways people navigate the world. In settings containing rich documentary sources and analysis, including the Algonquian Chesapeake, an archaeology informed by a dwelling perspective may illuminate the ways places were established and transformed within a specific cultural tradition. A number of studies along these lines have emerged from a "Southwest school" of landscape archaeology that combines historical ethnography and a serious engagement with contemporary Native American communities.[27] Such methods have highlighted Native communities' diverse understandings of landscape, expressed through oral traditions and oriented by stories of mobility and placemaking.[28] In an example of this approach, James Snead draws on "deep mapping" of archaeological sites and contemporary indigenous perspectives to interrogate the historical process of "becoming" Pueblo.[29] Mobility—social movement through space—emerges as a defining feature of Puebloan life in this study, no less important to the regional landscape than emplacement in fixed locations inhabited for generations.

After a period of historical scholarship oriented toward large-scale studies of the Atlantic world, a number of Americanist historians have also pivoted toward "grounded histories" of particular places and landscapes in early colonial North America.[30] Some of this research has been influenced by William Cronon's innovative environmental history of New England, a study of the entwined social and natural "changes in the land" that resulted from English settlement in this region.[31] Others draw from Richard White's account of the "middle ground" that emerged in the Great Lakes area as both a colonial-era meeting place and a process of negotiation tied to the local politics of village life.[32] In the Chesapeake, interdisciplinary teams have developed rich histories of the ecosystem keyed to temporal scales ranging from the geological time scale to the two-year period of John Smith's Chesapeake voyages.[33] Such studies foreground local knowledge and a powerful sense of place, orientations that have proven to be more important to some historical developments than transatlantic linkages or imperial strategies.[34]

A Deeper Historical Anthropology of Algonquian Landscapes

Between 2003 and 2010 my colleagues in the Werowocomoco Research Group and I conducted excavations at the central Powhatan town of Werowocomoco.[35] These investigations revealed a long, complicated, and unexpected "biography" of a Native place, prompting questions about the town's changing spatial configuration and about Werowocomoco's role in a broader landscape of Native places.[36] Werowocomoco lacks the colossal architecture of Stonehenge or the standing ruins of Chaco Canyon. Still, the history of dwelling in a place that became the Powhatan political center suggests that factors other than archaeological visibility were behind the town's significance in the Virginia Algonquian world. The Werowocomoco investigations, including a reassessment of related documentary sources, opened up a new avenue for pursuing a deep history in the Chesapeake across the historic/prehistoric divide.

During the same period, several of my colleagues and I realized that the results of the Chickahominy River Survey, conducted by William and Mary archaeologists four decades prior, remained unanalyzed and unreported at the college.[37] The collection contains archaeological materials and human remains from Native sites along the Chickahominy River dating from the third through the seventeenth century AD.[38] After a period of close and careful consultation with the contemporary Chickahominy community, we worked collaboratively with the tribe, the William and Mary Institute for Historical Biology, and the college's American Indian Resource Center to assess the collection. The survey highlights the history of a riverine landscape of connected places that gave rise to the "Coarse-pounded Corn People."[39]

In addition to the archaeological investigations at Werowocomoco and Chickahominy, a third focus of the research considered in this study centers on Kiskiak, a Virginia Algonquian town on the lower York River. In

1607 Kiskiak was a political center subsumed within the Powhatan chief-dom following its conquest by the paramount chief. Today, Kiskiak, along with dozens of other Native sites in the vicinity, is part of the Naval Weapons Station Yorktown (NWSY). Archaeological survey and testing by the William and Mary Center for Archaeological Research at NWSY has uncovered a rich record of intact, deeply stratified sites around Indian Field Creek, including shell-midden sites that document the beginnings of an estuarine-oriented landscape in coastal Virginia. This archaeological record traces the historical ecology of Algonquian communities that reshaped the local landscape for centuries.

Drawing evidence from these three places, this study centers on the lower James and York Rivers. The Chesapeake region encompasses a much broader area than this, stretching north to the lower Susquehanna River valley and across the bay to the Eastern Shore. Algonquian-speaking groups in this broad area that drains into the Chesapeake Bay shared a similar cultural history and many social practices, though the landscape history developed in this study focuses on the Powhatan core along the James and York.

My effort to develop an archaeological history of landscape in this area also responds to important conversations in North American archaeology. Jeffrey Hantman has demonstrated that the Chesapeake's early colonial history can be understood best in the context of a regional political economy set in motion well before 1607 involving flows of highly valued trade items, which included copper.[40] Influenced by this study and similar research, Kent Lightfoot issued a call in 1995 for a reconfiguration of historical anthropology that spans the Contact period.[41] A growing number of studies have risen to this challenge, taking advantage of archaeology's unique temporal baseline that crosses the divide between prehistory and history.[42] In a related vein, Charles Cobb has critiqued the scholarly practice of placing American Indians into a "savage slot" as archetypes of simple, static societies against which to contrast the global dynamics of the contemporary world.[43] Cobb has urged archaeologists to confront this practice by developing a deeper historical anthropology that traces Native American communities as they migrated, created cultural links over long distances, and continuously redefined social spaces. Such dynamic processes of displacement and emplacement, typically associated with the globalized, postcolonial present, are in fact prominent parts of Native North America's precontact past.

A deeper historical anthropology of Algonquian landscapes in the Chesapeake also responds to collaborative efforts that have included members of today's Pamunkey, Chickahominy, Eastern Chickahominy, Mattaponi, Upper Mattaponi, Rappahannock, and Nansemond tribes.[44] Based on their own oral histories and oral traditions, members of these communities have demanded studies that challenge triumphalist colonial narratives hinging on Native defeat, assimilation, and abandonment.[45] The effort to "flip the script" from one centered on colonial-era personalities and American master narratives toward local forms of knowledge and deeper histories of place responds to these contemporary Virginia Indian priorities. My colleagues and I have partnered with members of Virginia's Native communities, a number of whom have urged us to orient our research in this direction by examining developments older than, distinct from, and counter to the colonial master narratives that originate in John Smith's account of his "rescue" and that dominate today's conversations about the Native past in the Chesapeake.

My colleagues in the Virginia Indian community have also explained how a focusing on the deeper *past* opens new possibilities for the *future* of their communities. "Let them have Jamestown," our Mattaponi advisor Mark Custalow once insisted, "Werowocomoco is ours." As the research team used archaeological survey and archival work to confirm the location of Werowocomoco on the York River's Purtan Bay, Mattaponi historian Linwood Custalow let us know that decades earlier his grandfather told him the site was Werowocomoco. The wider appreciation of the town's deep past that followed investigations at the site has sparked small, but significant, changes in the ways the region's colonial history is represented at local heritage parks and in Virginia's public school curriculum.[46]

The effort to work collaboratively with scholars in academia and with other Native communities has not always been a simple one for tribal communities in the Chesapeake. "It was a hard decision to make," Chickahominy chief Stephen Adkins told us after we asked whether his community would support a study of the Chickahominy River Survey collection, including its human remains: "Those remains are somebody's loved one: Would I want someone to disturb my mom's remains? But we thought we would be remiss if we didn't do some work with these remains that would help point us to a better place in the future." Periodic disagreements resulting from collaborative historical research with different stakeholders may be inevitable, though the friction is not always centered on relationships between descendant communities and scholars or property owners. During one particularly contentious meeting of the Virginia Indian Advisory Board regarding the Werowocomoco project, the Pamunkey representative pointed out that the Chickahominy were not a part of the Powhatan chiefdom in 1607. "The only way Chickahominy might be found at Werowocomoco," Jeff Brown insisted, "would be as a row of heads on stakes."

Writing the histories of Native societies in the Chesapeake is no longer a straightforward matter of scholarly authority. For archaeologists who choose to engage descendant communities, uplifting and paternalistic "outreach" is no longer enough. Truly collaborative research in the Chesapeake, indeed in all places of colonial violence and dispossession, must confront uncomfortable and painful pasts that diverge from accepted historical narratives.[47] Contemporary Virginia Indian communities have in recent years insisted on a place at the table during discussions of colonial history in the Chesapeake. They have developed their own tribal language and heritage programs and intertribal coalitions. Some have coordinated their research and activism with scholars in academia, seeking to expand and to recast understanding of the Native past.[48]

With several important exceptions, including Helen Rountree's formative work on the Powhatan and studies of recent Virginia Indian history by Frederic Gleach, Danielle Moretti-Langholtz, and Sam Cook, most accounts of Native societies in the Chesapeake focus on a brief window between the construction of James Fort in 1607 and Bacon's Rebellion in 1676.[49] In keeping with what Vine Deloria labeled the "cameo" theory of history, American Indians appear early in accounts of the colonial Chesapeake and then quickly fade from view.[50] The resulting narrative of contact, conflict, dispossession, and disappearance conceals key parts of the Native past and limits the ways Virginia's Indian communities may link the past to the present and the present to the future.

One reason that Native history in the Chesapeake faces these constraints is the reliance on the firsthand accounts of Englishmen who lived during the earliest years of the colony at James Fort. Studies aimed at the Native past in the Chesapeake—indeed, including this book—draw heavily from such accounts, though the narratives are read in several different ways.

Anthropologists often seek to reconstruct an ethnographic present on the eve of contact that encapsulates the social organization of Native societies—"upstreaming" from the colonial era documents toward the deeper past.[51] Some historians, on the other hand, have emphasized a "downstream" approach to the narrative flow of events surrounding early European settlement, in an effort to extricate the histories of Native communities and Anglo-Indian interest groups that are often overshadowed by European imperial perspectives.[52] Archaeologists typically draw upon descriptions of Native societies from the colonial archive to illuminate aspects of the prehistoric past.[53] This direct historical approach has been used to illuminate precontact developments, including the settlement of towns, the adoption of horticulture, and the emergence of chiefly political structures. Archaeological studies of chiefly societies in the Chesapeake—including the Powhatan, Monacan, Piscataway, Patawomeck, and Nanticoke—often emphasize cultural adaptations whereby the estuarine-oriented hunter-gatherer communities increased in population, developed circumscribed social networks, and started raising maize.[54]

Lewis Binford's dissertation provided the foundations for such efforts by combining ethnohistorical interpretation, settlement patterns, and ecological parameters.[55] In a series of influential publications emphasizing environmental variability, demography, and neo-evolutionary models, E. Randolph Turner linked Powhatan ethnohistory to Tidewater archaeology on a regional scale.[56] Stephen Potter's subsequent study of Algonquian cultural development in the Potomac valley remains the model for tracing the cultural ecology of a particular Native community in the Chesapeake.[57] Potter has combined archaeological survey data with archival research to construct a history of the Chicacoans across the prehistoric–colonial divide.

Still others read the colonists' accounts through the lens of recent ideas in historical anthropology. These approaches start with the premise that Native actions during the colonial era accorded with deeply rooted cultural orders, and that several layers of interpretation that include language, political economy, and cosmology need to be considered when assessing early encounters.[58] Margaret Williamson's *Powhatan Lords of Life and Death*, for example, probes the relationship between chiefly power and priestly authority, demonstrating ways that Powhatan ritual and cosmology framed twofold structures of leadership, or a "dual sovereignty."[59] Frederic Gleach's study of the Powhatan identifies culturally informed strategies of Virginia Algonquians and English colonists, suggesting that both sought to "civilize" the other.[60] In a similar vein, Seth Mallios' *Deadly Politics of Giving* recasts early colonial history in the Chesapeake through the lens of trade relations and an Algonquian moral economy of gift-giving.[61] Mallios' economic anthropology, Gleach's analytical frame, and Williamson's structuralist interpretation each inform the approach I follow in this study.

Public discussions of the colonial-era Chesapeake generally focus attention on Jamestown, overshadowing the archaeology and history of Native communities beyond the settlement.[62] Recent excavations at the site of James Fort, for example, have been widely covered in the media, particularly during the 2007 quadricentennial celebrations of the colony's establishment. The news coverage has often emphasized the banal or the macabre, with stories veering from a single, peculiar artifact to grisly tales of death and cannibalism.[63] Such stories invariably catch the public's attention, though they often distract from Jamestown's more complicated colonial process of violence, shifting economic relationships, and transculturation.[64] The effort to frame Jamestown as an icon of heroic American history has, in fact, obscured the colonists' contradictory motivations and experiences while rendering the Native presence all but invisible.[65] Jamestown's eventual success could be described as fluky, rather than inevitable—born out of horrific trauma and contingent on fortuitous twists of fate.[66] Indeed, even referring to the settlement as "Jamestown" implies a substantial and enduring community that has long persisted on the James River. In fact, Jamestown was smaller than Werowocomoco in 1607 and lasted less than a century as an occupied place. The settlement all but vanished after the colonial capital moved to Williamsburg (then Middle Plantation) in 1699.

When Native societies are included in discussions of James Fort's history, the terms are usually set by European voices. As Michael Klein and Doug Sanford have observed, "the snapshot of Virginia Indians presented in the map and writings of John Smith" has "dominated anthropological reconstructions of the Native American world" in the Chesapeake.[67] The valorization of James Fort has, in fact, obscured the histories of Native groups beyond the Powhatan core, concealing Algonquian, Siouan, and Iroquoian communities' varied responses to colonialism in the process.

Within recent years, though, new historical scholarship focused on the Chesapeake has begun to broaden this focus.[68] At the same time, new forms of collaborative archaeology have also appeared in the region, largely in response to contemporary American Indians' insistence that they be included in discussions of the Native past.[69] This recent and tentative development in the Chesapeake lags behind changes in archaeological practice adopted in other parts of North America.[70] Since the Commonwealth recognized three additional tribes in 2010, Virginia has eleven state-recognized tribes, and several of these groups have become involved with archaeological projects.[71] Maryland now has two groups that are officially recognized as indigenous tribes.[72] The state of Delaware recognized the Nanticoke by statute during the nineteenth century, and the tribe has genealogical ties to the Lenape and the Nanticoke Lenni-Lenape of Delaware and southern New Jersey.[73] The Nanticoke and Lenape tribes have become involved in public archaeology and successful cultural resource management projects, some of which started with antagonistic relations between Native leaders and archaeologists.[74]

Only one of these groups, the Pamunkey, has received federal acknowledgment that they are indeed American Indians, and then only recently. The absence of federal recognition has complicated indigenous communities' efforts to gain access to and influence over archaeological research in the Chesapeake. Federal acknowledgment represents a standing central to the consultation processes under the Native Americans Graves Protection and Repatriation Act and the National Historic Preservation Act. The Pamunkey received recognition from the federal government only in July 2015, despite their long history along the river that bears their name.[75] Treaties signed by the English in 1646 and 1677 guaranteed a Pamunkey homeland on the Pamunkey Neck, and tribal members have lived on reservation lands there for over three centuries. Even with this long history as a tribal community, a last-minute challenge by an anti-gambling organization threatened to reverse Pamunkey acknowledgment before a review board affirmed the decision to recognize the tribe in January 2016.[76]

Despite the obstacles facing Virginia Indian communities, concerted efforts by Native groups have resulted in repatriation and reburial of archaeologically excavated remains in Maryland and Delaware, beginning in the 1980s.[77] During the past decade the remains of more than a hundred individuals have been reburied in Virginia in accordance with the wishes of several tribes.[78] Each of these reburials involved significant collaboration between Native and archaeological communities.

Making and Unmaking Place in Tsenacomacoh

Seeking to build on efforts that deepen knowledge of the Native past in the Chesapeake, this book draws from a reassessment of early colonial documents and from three archaeological studies: the Werowocomoco project, the Chickahominy River Survey, and recent research focused on the town of Kiskiak.[79] In addition, I consider evidence and interpretation from historical linguistics, bioarchaeology, archaeobotany, and excavations at other Native settlements.

This book has six additional chapters, organized loosely around a model of social space proposed by spatial theorist Henri Lefebvre.[80] Lefebvre suggested that social spaces may be studied best along three axes: spatial *representations*, spatial *practices*, and the spatial *imaginary*. Representations of space—including the depictions of specific territories found in maps—offer accounts of the organizational structure of social space from a particular vantage. Spatial practices entail the ways people inhabit and move within space in everyday life, including their productive activities, exchange relations, and consumption habits. The spatial imaginary, what Lefebvre also termed the meaningful dimension of space, draws from everyday spatial practices and from representations of space. As demonstrated in other archaeological studies of spatiality, Lefebvre's conceptual triad challenges and complicates simple dichotomies of objective space versus subjective place.[81] The model provides a framework useful for organizing the archaeological history of Tsenacomacoh—the Virginia Algonquian term for the Tidewater region—considered from a dwelling perspective.

Chapter 2, "Mapping the Terrain," considers the ways that Virginia Algonquian communities constructed places and made history, beginning with disparate and contradictory *representations of space* recorded in colonial-era maps. Contrasting cartographic depictions of the Chesapeake colonial landscape highlight the distinct icons and tropes through which Natives and newcomers represented the world in which they dwelled. While the colonial historiography typically foregrounds early encounters understood from the perspective of English and Powhatan leaders, these maps illustrate how Tsenacomacoh's past may be understood as a longer and deeper narrative keyed to geographic spaces, meaningful places, and a broadly inclusive notion of landscape.

Chapter 3, "Placemaking in the Algonquian Chesapeake," considers Virginia Algonquian place-names, concluding that Tsenacomacoh was a landscape that was understood and labeled from the vantage of a canoe. Place-names typically referenced navigation along rivers and highlighted locations for fishing and for gathering wetland plants. Such *representations of space* hint that Tsenacomacoh was constructed on an estuarine landscape initially inhabited by mobile foragers and fishers. The rivers, streams, and embayed waters of the Chesapeake estuary provided the primary pathways connecting places in this setting. Algonquian place-names framed travel through Tsenacomacoh's waterscape, resulting in naming practices keyed to the dynamic interface between dry land and tidal water.

Chapter 4, "Arrival in the Wide Land," considers how the Virginia Algonquian landscape first coalesced as a result of population movements and social interaction involving different communities of forager-fishers during the early centuries AD. As documented within sites on the Naval Weapons Station Yorktown, the archaeology of the Middle Woodland period (500 BC–AD 900) records the appearance of new settlement forms, subsistence practices, and a ceramic tradition shared across a broad swath of the coastal Middle Atlantic. Linguistic studies raise the possibility that these developments resulted from the rapid replacement of indigenous foragers by newly arrived Algonquian speakers. The archaeological record on the James-York peninsula, by contrast, documents the coexistence for several centuries of communities from distinct traditions. The archaeology of interior encampments and of riverine settlements with shell middens points toward seasonal movement between places where forager-fishers gathered for events that involved feasting, exchange, and intermarriage. These *spatial practices* introduced during the second century AD signaled an emphasis on estuarine settings that has oriented Native history in the region to the present day.

Chapter 5, "The Coarse-Pounded Corn People," focuses on archaeological investigations along the Chickahominy River and a history of residential settlements, subsistence practices, and burial grounds during the Middle to Late Woodland transition. In the sixth century AD, groups along the Chickahominy began to bury the deceased in communal ossuaries located in the drainage's swampy interior. During the Late Woodland period (AD 900–1500), new places were established along the Chickahominy with the construction of dispersed farmsteads, burial grounds, and a palisaded compound. In this history of placemaking, we see evidence of the *spatial practices* whereby forager-fishers became the Chickahominy. As is apparent from colonial accounts of the Chickahominy, the "Coarse-pounded Corn People," a horticultural economy was a part of this process. Analysis of skeletal remains and bone chemistry from the Chickahominy provides a basis for considering the history of maize-based horticulture in the region.

Chapter 6, "The Place of the Antler Wearers," considers Werowocomo-co's role in the Virginia Algonquian *spatial imaginary* and political history. Shortly after its establishment as a sizable town circa AD 1200, Werowo-comoco's residents reconfigured the settlement's spaces, constructing a residential area along the river and an interior zone marked by a series of trenches. A biography of place and a close reading of colonial-era accounts suggest that Werowocomoco was reconfigured and redefined several times as a ritualized location. As a town that marked the transition from a hor-ticultural taskscape to hunting camps during the feasts and sacrifices of autumn, Werowocomoco anchored the annual cycle. The construction of earthworks and elite architecture within Werowocomoco made reference to construction episodes centuries earlier, suggesting that the town's spatial history also influenced Powhatan's decision to center his chiefdom there during the sixteenth century.

Chapter 7, "Persistent Places in Colonial Tsenacomacoh," addresses the enduring power of place in the Virginia Algonquian spatial imaginary. Re-sistance to colonists' encroachment on traditional lands, burial grounds, and sacred spaces took the form of coordinated revolts in 1622 and 1644. These uprisings resulted in English retaliation and further Native loss of life and land. Yet archaeological evidence from this period indicates that Virginia Algonquians returned to persistent places to bury ancestors, sac-rifice animals, and inter objects, even after the residential population had departed. The continuation of such practices in the shatter zone of colonial Tsenacomacoh contradicts a narrative of abandonment, acculturation, and disappearance.[82] Instead, these postcolonial commemorations within pre-colonial places highlight lasting ties to ancestors and homeland.

In recent years Native communities in the region have reclaimed a more prominent place on the Chesapeake landscape and a greater role in repre-sentations of their pasts. Virginia and Maryland tribes have achieved state recognition, partnered with federal and state agencies, reburied ancestors, created indigenous archaeology programs, and prevented the destruction of traditional cultural properties by residential development and dam construction.

Yet even as American Indian tribes in the Chesapeake move beyond the difficult history of the colonial era, the early-seventeenth-century colonial narrative still frames the publicly acceptable ways these communities may discuss their past, present, and future. For Native communities in the Chesapeake, the rethought and reinterpreted landscape represents a powerful basis from which to contest narratives and government policies that have denied their existence. My goal with this book is to add to this conversation by offering other reference points in a deeper history of Tsenacomacoh's landscape.

Chapter 2

Mapping the Terrain

A year after John Smith's capture on the Chickahominy and return to James Fort, Powhatan, better known today as Wahunsenacawh (wah-hoon-SEHN-uh-kah), invited Smith and other English leaders to visit him at Werowocomoco.[1] When the colonists arrived, Wahunsenacawh demanded that Smith and his men lay down their weapons, noting that as his "subjects," this was expected. Smith, who clearly did not share Wahunsenacawh's sense of Powhatan sovereign authority, shifted the conversation with an offer to subjugate the Monacan and Susquehannock on behalf of Wahunsenacawh. Apparently content with the offer, Wahunsenacawh reminded Smith that he was now a Powhatan *weroance* (WAYR-oh-ahns), the local Algonquian term for commander or captain. The colonists were no longer to be considered *Tassantasses* (TAHS-uhn-tahs-ehs [strangers]) or *Paspaheghs* (the town closest to James Fort), but *Powhatans*. As Powhatan's people, the colonists would be provided gifts of corn, women, and land. "The next day," wrote Smith, "the King conducted mee to the River, shewwe me his Canowes, and described unto me how hee sent them over the Baye, for tribute Beades, and also what Countries paid him Beads, Copper, or Skins."[2]

Efforts to represent the Chesapeake cultural landscape, including Wahunsenacawh's account of the Powhatan tributary economy, figure prominently in the early documentary record. In fact, the best known of these comes not from Wahunsenacawh but from John Smith's *Map of Virginia*, described as the fountainhead of ethnographic information regarding the Indians who inhabited the Chesapeake Bay area.[3] A meticulous representation of the lower Chesapeake estuary and the social geography on land,

Smith's map illustrates a colonial effort to capture Tsenacomacoh through a cartographic idiom familiar to English audiences. Smith's *Map* transforms Tsenacomacoh into Virginia by collapsing details of the region's settled spaces, by placing powerful Native groups on the periphery and out of focus, and by removing any ambiguity regarding chiefly sovereignty in the Powhatan world. Wahunsenacawh's February 1608 discussion of his "countries" provides an alternative representation of this cultural landscape. In this rendering, the movement of canoes across the estuary traced flows of gifts from the edges of the world to Werowocomoco at its center and outward again to communities subsumed within the Powhatan orbit. While the English planned to colonize Virginia, extract commodities, and generate profits for London, Wahunsenacawh sought to incorporate the Tassantasses within an expanding political economy based on tributary flows and centered on Werowocomoco.

Smith's map and Wahunsenacawh's geographic discourse were by no means the only representations of social space in the Chesapeake produced during the early seventeenth century. Virginia Algonquians generated maps on several occasions described in colonists' accounts, demonstrating their expansive geographic knowledge in the process. In James Fort's early days, the colonists relied on a chart of the James River drawn by a local guide.[4] Colonist Henry Norwood reported that an Eastern Shore weroance used a stick in 1649 to sketch a detailed map of Native settlements to the south. The weroance drew circles to depict towns, a convention shared by Native groups throughout the Southeast.[5] Circles played a role in maps used in ceremonial settings as well. An anonymous colonial author noted that seventeenth-century Powhatan conjurors raised storms by "drawing circles, and muttering words, by making a dreadful howling and using strange gestures and various rites, upon which the wind ariseth."[6] Other maps of Tsenacomacoh, discussed below, appear in the circular diagram of Smith's "Divination" and in "Powhatan's Mantle." One of the few organic artifacts remaining from this era, Powhatan's Mantle includes a mix of elements that is difficult to interpret today. In its imagery, though, are indications that Powhatan's Mantle made claims regarding sovereignty by depicting Tsenacomacoh's political landscape from a chiefly perspective.

As a hinge around which systems of meaning pivot, a map provides an entry point into the way social spaces were understood.[7] The following chapter considers the Chesapeake cultural landscape from several cartographic perspectives, starting with maps produced by English colonists, then turning to others drawn by Virginia Algonquians. The conventions, icons, and visual tropes embedded in these maps orient us toward Virginia Algonquian and English conceptions of the Chesapeake landscape and toward the ways these conceptions became enmeshed at contact. The English colonial maps and narrative accounts are, of course, biased, incomplete, and colonialist in their aims. Nonetheless, read carefully and critically, they offer an alternative frame for considering Algonquian representations of landscape and the region's archaeological record. Differences in the two English maps discussed below reveal alternative conceptions of Virginia at different moments in the colonial process. Differences in the two Native maps considered here highlight chiefs' and priests' distinct orientations to Tsenacomacoh.

Smith's Map of Virginia

Smith's widely celebrated *Map of Virginia* went through at least eleven revisions and multiple printings during the early seventeenth century.[8] Numerous scholars have probed the *Map* for signs of English colonial rhetoric and for Native political organization at the moment of contact.[9] The *Map of Virginia* and the accompanying *Description of the Country, the Commodities, People, Government, and Religion* were published together in 1612, three years after Smith returned to England, and four years after the publication of his initial narrative, *A True Relation*. Working with engraver William Hole, Smith based the map in part on his own extensive voyages around the Chesapeake. The *Map of Virginia*, though, was more than simply firsthand reportage. Much of the imagery for the map was drawn from Theodor de Bry's earlier engravings of Algonquian landscapes surrounding the failed Roanoke Colony on North Carolina's Outer Banks. Originally published in 1588, the de Bry engravings accompanied Thomas Harriot's *A Briefe and True Report of the New Found Land of Virginia*.[10] Those engravings, in turn, copied from Roanoke colonist John White's vivid watercolors of the coastal settings and Algonquian people surrounding the Roanoke Colony. Thus, the *Map of Virginia* represented, in part, a facsimile of a facsimile. Moreover, the failed Roanoke Colony to the south provided key visual and textual references for Smith, strongly influencing the way we perceive Jamestown today. "The rest," Smith noted, "was had by information of the Savages, and are set downe, according to their instructions."[11]

Figure 2.1. Inset from John Smith's *Map of Virginia*. Library of Congress.

Historian April Lee Hatfield has perceptively noted that Smith may, in fact, have drawn his *Map* and written his *Description* with Spanish colonial strategies in mind.[12] At times Spanish colonists cultivated an understanding of Native political and military institutions in order to transform them to serve Spanish colonial aims. In framing the Chesapeake as dominated and controlled by the powerful "emperor" Powhatan and a secondary tier of leaders occupying "king's houses," a similar colonial strategy might be possible for the English. Smith's map was at least as reliant on Native geographic expertise as it was on the European surveying technologies he employed, so much so that the map recorded the inescapable connectedness of colonizer and colonized during this period.

Smith's *Map* and his published accounts drew from his experiences during the colony's tumultuous initial years. Intermittent contacts between American Indians and Europeans during the shadowy sixteenth century had already influenced Virginia Algonquians' perceptions of the English colonists and, likewise, English colonists' expectations of the Native inhabitants.[13] In addition to poorly documented visits by European vessels during this century, close, and ultimately violent, encounters surrounded the failed Spanish Jesuit mission to Virginia of 1570–1571 and the unsuccessful Roanoke Colony of the 1580s.[14] Four decades into this period of sporadic contact, 104 English men and boys began constructing James Fort near the Native town of Paspahegh on May 14, 1607.[15] Over the next half century the colony struggled with starvation, infighting, and unstable leadership. Relations with diverse Native groups alternated between alliance and violence, tolerance and manipulation, cohabitation and apartheid. Eventually the colonists identified Orinoco tobacco monoculture as the commercial basis for a successful royal colony built upon the labor of indentured servants and, by the end of the seventeenth century, the labor of enslaved Africans. The Virginia colony expanded outward from James Fort, consuming Native lands in the process. Virginia Algonquians' resistance to this gradual invasion, including coordinated revolts in 1622 and 1644, ultimately collapsed alongside the Powhatan chiefdom.

During the colony's initial years, though, that outcome seemed far from likely. On numerous occasions, Wahunsenacawh and other Native leaders held the upper hand. Heavily reliant on Native food stores and on unreliable supplies from England, the colonists struggled against disease, disorganization, and death. Smith's four published accounts of his experiences in Virginia from 1607 to 1609 describe events that swing wildly from the heroic to the comedic to the horrific.[16] Historians' sense of the veracity of these accounts has shifted over time, though in recent decades researchers have followed Philip Barbour's lead in viewing Smith as a mostly reliable witness, if one prone to self-aggrandizement.[17] Fellow colonist George Percy, who clashed with Smith during James Fort's tumultuous early years, published his "Trewe Relacyon" in 1625 as an explicit rebuttal to Smith's version of events.[18] Smith was, in fact, reasonably well prepared to play a leadership role in the colony and to survive in the early colonial Chesapeake. He originally left England in 1596 at age 16 to volunteer in France with forces battling for Dutch independence from Spain. Four years later he joined Austrian forces to fight the Ottoman Turks. Promoted to "captain" while fighting in Hungary, Smith was later wounded in battle, captured, and sold as a slave to the Turks. Smith's narrative of this experience recounts his escape by beating his owner to death before making his way back to England in 1604.[19] The consensus view of most historians is that Smith embellished his accounts for dramatic effect. This is implied by the four separate instances in which young women appeared and saved him at moments of peril, with the most famous of these occurring at Werowocomoco.[20] Despite indications that he inflated his own importance and misconstrued elements of Powhatan society, he emerges as a savvy culture broker capable of adapting to novel circumstances.

Smith's *Map of Virginia* depicts the Chesapeake region from the vantage of those arriving via the "Virginia Sea" (i.e., the Atlantic), with west (rather than north) at the top. An engraving of Powhatan (i.e., Wahunsenacawh) seated on an elevated platform in his house at Werowocomoco and another engraving of a "Gyant like" Susquehannock bowman flank the coastal territory labeled "Powhatan." This busy landscape of settlements and waterways included "ordinary houses" and "kings' houses," each with its own icon, spread along the rivers flowing into the Chesapeake Bay, including the Powhatan (James), Pamunkey (York), Rappahannock, and Potomac. King's towns were represented by a sapling-framed house, or *yihakin*, while settlements labeled as ordinary houses mimicked the Native convention of depicting Native places with circles. Other Native groups, including the Chowan, Mangoag, Monacan, Mannahoac, and Susquehannock, surrounded the Powhatan. The enigmatic Massawomeck were depicted some distance to the northwest on a large body of water. Each of these groups lay beyond the crosses on the map marking the limits of areas where Smith had traveled. Smith's knowledge of the landscape beyond the crosses came solely from Native informants. Like the Powhatan, each of the groups beyond the crosses was mapped with at least one king's house.

The *Description* that accompanied the map starts with a summary of the region's geographic features and the names of its principal Native towns.[21] Smith had learned a modicum of the local Virginia Algonquian dialects on trade missions and while a captive at Werowocomoco. He provides a sense of the area's demographic structure by enumerating men of fighting age in each community. The area was, in Smith's estimation, not particularly populous, with but 5,000 residents (and only 500 men of fighting age) within 60 miles of James Fort. Indeed, the population distribution he provides for the broader region includes few towns with more than 100 warriors, or a total of about 300–350 residents if we follow his ratio of about 3.33 people per warrior. Finding Smith's counts mostly credible, archaeologists have arrived at an overall estimated population of 12,000–15,000 Algonquian speakers for Virginia's Tidewater region, a value keyed to Smith's warrior estimates of roughly 4,000 for the region.[22] The Virginia Tidewater, or Coastal Plain region, represents the area from the Atlantic Coast to the Fall Zone, the natural border with the Piedmont. Streams passing through the Fall Zone flow through the resistant igneous and metamorphic rocks of the Piedmont and drop to sea level, creating rapids or falls.

Smith's population figures for each Coastal Plain community, ranging from 20 to 300 warriors, likely applied to a principal town plus related outlying settlements. Powhatan towns, Smith noted, were located along tidal rivers and close to freshwater springs.[23] Houses were constructed with a framework of bent saplings and woven matting for walls and a roof. Towns reportedly included from two to 100 houses with between six and 20 residents living in each house. Virginia Algonquian houses were constructed in and around horticultural plots, which ranged in size from small garden areas to larger fields. The highest population densities appeared on the Pamunkey Neck, the area between the Pamunkey and Mattaponi Rivers, and just south of this along the Chickahominy River. This distribution indicates that these areas in the inner Coastal Plain were home to large, concentrated populations of Virginia Algonquians, while some of the most important places on the Powhatan landscape, including Werowocomoco, held fewer residents.

One element of the Virginia Algonquian cultural landscape that repeatedly struck Smith and other colonists was the extensive forest clearing around residential towns. Writing in the unstandardized orthography of the day, Smith noted that "neare their habitations is little small wood or old trees on the ground [i.e., debris from forest clearing and immature regrowth] by reason of their burning of them for fire. So that a man may gallop a horse amongst these woods any waie, but where the creekes or Rivers shall hinder."[24] William Strachey similarly remarked, "Those Indians, as it may well appeare, [are] better husbands [i.e., farmers] than in any parte ells that we have observed, which is the reason that so much ground is there clieried and opened, enough, with little labour, alreaddy prepared, to receave corne."[25] Echoing Smith's descriptions, Strachey added that most

Figure 2.2. Demographic profile of Algonquian-speaking communities in the Chesapeake region. Circle size is keyed to John Smith's (1986d) warrior counts.

towns consisted of a scatter of houses situated along a hill or an elevated river terrace, a placement that provided residents with ideal sight lines toward anyone approaching from the water.[26] Such descriptions point toward Virginia Algonquians' forest management practices, horticultural practices, and town planning. Like other Native societies in the Eastern Woodlands, the Virginia Algonquians set fire to forests in order to drive deer and other animals toward hunters, further altering the landscape surrounding settlements.[27] Once English colonists succeeded in forcing Virginia Algonquians from their towns in the opening decades of the seventeenth century, the colonists often established their own initial agricultural settlements on old "Indian fields," as these riverine terraces were already cleared of trees and possessed highly productive soils.[28]

Smith's *Description* closes with discussions of Native social domains in terms that, along with the writings of fellow colonists William Strachey, Henry Spelman, George Percy, and Gabriel Archer, have come to define Powhatan history and culture.[29] Smith summarizes the annual settlement round, which involved group movement from riverine towns inhabited during the spring through fall to interior hunting camps used during the late fall and winter months. He describes garden horticulture and related women's work, men's labor that was focused on hunting and fishing, and weroances' consultations with priests over warfare, religion, and governance. In addition to winter, spring, and summer, the Virginia Algonquian year was divided according to the earing of corn, Nepinough (NEHP-ihn-aw), and the corn harvest, Taquitock (TACK-wih-tawk). September through November was reserved for the "chiefe Feasts and sacrifice" held in the region's principal towns after the annual harvest. "The greatest labor they take," Smith emphasizes here, "is in planting their corne."[30]

Smith also reports here that the Native groups west of the Fall Zone, the Monacan and Mannahoac, were "many different in language" and "barbarous," "living for the most part of wild beasts and fruits."[31] Beyond the fragmentary knowledge the colonists gained about the Monacan and Mannahoac during James Fort's early years, the documentary record offers only limited references to these Piedmont groups during the following century.[32] Researchers have concluded that the Monacan and Mannahoac likely spoke Siouan dialects related to those of the Saponi, Tutelo, Occaneechi, and Mohetan, though we have a vocabulary only for the Tutelo.[33] Drawing on the Piedmont's archaeological record and from colonial accounts, Jeffrey Hantman has demonstrated that Smith's brief reference to the Monacan and Mannahoac misconstrued fundamental elements of their subsistence practices and political structures. Smith also overlooked the influential role that the Monacan played in the regional political economy as a source of copper.[34] Smith had little direct experience of Virginia's interior and no knowledge of the languages spoken there, learning most of what he did report about the Monacan and Mannahoac "by relation" from Algonquian-speaking informants. Rather than an accurate summary of Monacan and Mannahoac society, the *Map of Virginia* and the *Description* instead offer a clearer sense of how the Virginia Algonquians saw themselves in opposition to Siouan-speaking outsiders: as maize eaters who spoke mutually intelligible Algonquian dialects.

The *Map of Virginia* also provides a summary of Virginia Algonquian settlement patterns and the institutional structures of the Powhatan chiefdom. Weroances administered the region from their "kings' houses," while "ordinary houses" lacked such political leaders and paid tribute to them. Tribute, particularly the shell beads, copper, and deerskins mentioned above by Wahunsenacawh, flowed from commoners to weroances and from weroances to Wahunsenacawh.[35] These materials figured prominently in elite clothing and body adornment, constituting a material expression of chiefly social status. Weroances dominated the exchange networks through which these materials moved.

The Zuñiga Chart

While the Zuñiga Chart is not as well known as Smith's *Map of Virginia*, it offers a clearer sense of the events and social connections shaping the colonial-era Chesapeake than can be drawn from the *Map of Virginia* alone. Technically a "chart" rather than a map, in modern English terms, the document provides shoreline details critical for riverine navigation rather than specific features on land. The Zuñiga Chart was first discovered in the Archivo General de Simancas accompanying a September 1608 letter to King Philip III from Don Pedro de Zuñiga, Spain's ambassador to England, informing the Spanish king of developments at James Fort.[36] First published in 1890 in Alexander Brown's *The Genesis of the United States*, the chart appears to be a copy of a map that John Smith sent to England along with his *True Relation* in 1608.[37] Instructed by the Spanish Council for War in the Indies to investigate England's colonial efforts in the Chesapeake, Zuñiga wrote a series of short letters documenting the intelligence he obtained about the Virginia Company's efforts.[38] Zuñiga sent his chart to King Philip with a brief letter dated September 10, 1608.[39] The chart's original source remains unclear, though colonists John Smith and Nathaniel Powell are both possible candidates as the chart's creator.[40] References to "Captaine Powel's *Map*" appear in later sources, and Powell appears to have authored the "Diarie of the second voyage in discovering the bay" sent to England by Christopher Newport in 1608.[41] Either copied by an agent working for the Spanish at James Fort or intercepted by Zuñiga's mole in London, the Zuñiga Chart provided the Spanish King Philip with important information on the English colonial effort in the Chesapeake.

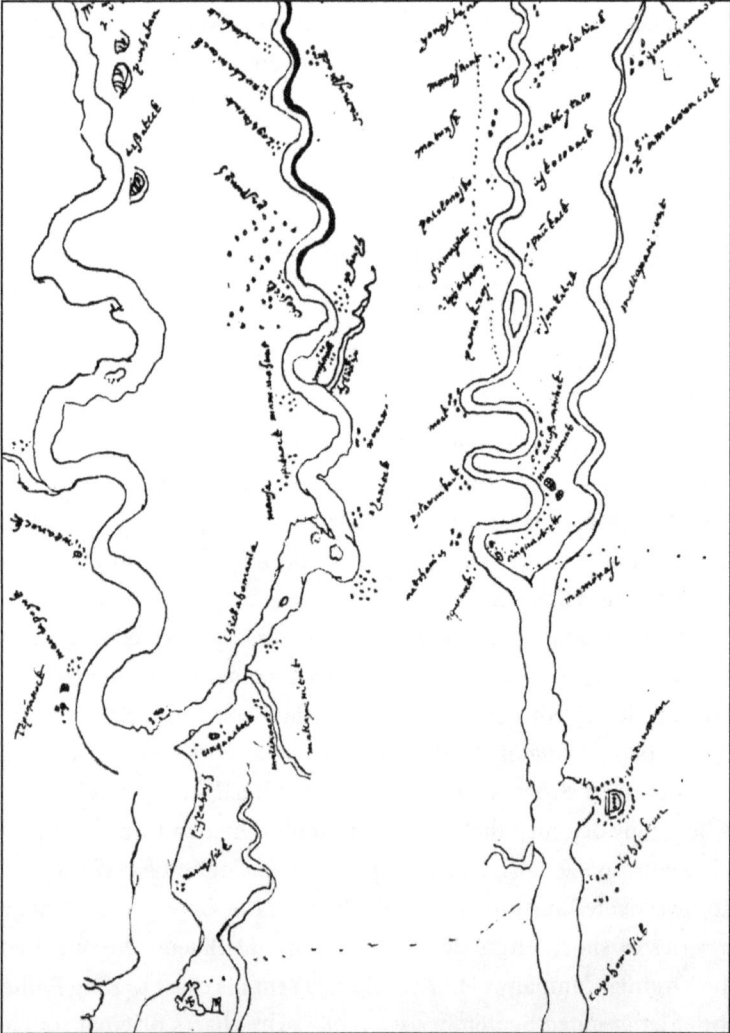

Figure 2.3. Inset from the Zuñiga Chart. Adapted from Brown 1890:184.

At the time Spain claimed possession of the Americas in their entirety, and Jamestown's Protestant colonists posed a threat to Catholic Spain's imperial designs. Concerned about the danger posed by a potential English pirate base on America's Atlantic coast, Zuñiga gathered considerable intelligence on the English colony in Virginia from 1606 to 1608. This information included a chart accurately depicting the location and layout of James Fort, the numbers of settlers there, the names of the colony's leaders, and information on London's Privy Council deliberations about the settlement.[42] Zuñiga's intelligence gathering apparently relied on at least one well-placed source. He wrote in September 1607 that he "had found a person of confidence by which to penetrate all that will occur in the Council concerning what they call Virginia."[43]

Like the *Map of Virginia,* the Zuñiga Chart represents Tsenacomacoh from an Atlantic perspective, with west at the top. The chart includes the Neuse, Pamlico, and Roanoke Rivers of the Albemarle drainage as well as the James, York, Rappahannock, and Potomac Rivers of the Chesapeake. The cartographer chose to represent both James Fort and Werowocomoco prominently on the chart. The fort appears as a three-sided structure with round bastions at the corners. At Werowocomoco the cartographer added an unusual set of markings that appear as 17 dots surrounding a double "D"-shaped pattern. Within the two "Ds" are three additional dots. The significance of this diagram is unclear, but its large size clearly conveys Werowocomoco's importance alongside James Fort.

Annotation on the chart near the Neuse River notes, "Here remayeth 4 men clothed that came from roonock to oconohowan." On the Pamlico River: "Here the king of paspahegh reported our men to be and went to se." The Powhatan/James extends to the western edge of the chart: "Here the salt water beatethe into the rier amongst their rocks being the south sea." At the headwaters of the Chickahominy, the chart is annotated as follows: "20 miles above this C. S. was taken," and dotted lines trace the route along which C.S. (i.e., Captain Smith) was conducted during his captivity and travel back to James Fort. Additional notation on the chart includes scattered dots that represent dispersed house locations within Virginia Algonquian towns.

The Zuñiga Chart was clearly drawn by someone more familiar with the Powhatan core along the Powhatan/James and Pamunkey/York than with areas beyond these rivers. It was produced by someone knowledgeable enough of the Chesapeake estuary to facilitate riverine navigation, in contrast with the London engraver's depiction of the same region in the formal *Map of Virginia*. The Zuñiga Chart reflects John Smith's (or perhaps Nathaniel Powell's) recordation of a Chesapeake landscape as experienced firsthand. The chaotic mix of dots, blobs, and odd marks on the Zuñiga Chart traces an effort to characterize a landscape of dispersed Native towns and community forms with which the colonists were unfamiliar.[44] Recent excavations at the site have demonstrated that the sketch of the three-sided James Fort is, in fact, the only accurate rendering of its footprint during the colony's early days to survive in the archive.[45]

The annotation about men from Roanoke refers to survivors of the Roanoke Colony who may have moved northward in order to shelter with Native groups near the mouth of the James River. The reference to "our men" on the Pamlico hints that, decades after their disappearance from Roanoke, some survivors still lived in Carolina Algonquian communities. The English misconception that the James offered a short passage to a western sea still persisted when the cartographer produced this chart. Together these notes highlight the colonists' fragmentary knowledge of the regional geography and of the colonial contacts that preceded the construction of James Fort. The Zuñiga Chart offers no indications that the English were aware of the failed Jesuit mission of 1570–71, exposing limits to their knowledge of the Chesapeake landscape and its history of Native–European interaction.

Along the dotted pathway that constitutes Smith's captivity route, the imagery at Werowocomoco is, at first glance, difficult to parse. The D-shaped enclosure may, in fact, depict Wahunsenacawh's large house there, reported by Smith to be longer than any others—over a hundred feet in length.[46] Another possibility, one that appears more likely, given the evidence at hand, is that the enclosure and dots at Werowocomoco depict the actual footprint of the town. This would be consistent with the drawing of James Fort and the depiction of other towns, such as Kiskiak on the York, which are represented as a scatter of dots denoting houses lining the riverfront. The distribution of dots at Kiskiak matches the site's archaeological record and parallels the configuration of other Contact-period towns with houses dispersed along elevated riverine terraces. As detailed in chapter 6, the double D-shaped enclosure at Werowocomoco also corresponds roughly with earthworks identified at the site that were in use between the thirteenth and early seventeenth century.

The historical record indicates that Smith's *Map of Virginia* likely evolved out of a version of the Zuñiga Chart, though the *Map* had changed considerably as it was standardized according to the formal cartographic style of early-seventeenth-century England. Where Smith had experienced the Chesapeake landscape while passing through it (as indicated by the captivity trail on the Zuñiga Chart), the formalized *Map of Virginia* effectively obscured events leading to its creation. This concealment parallels a broader colonial process: beginning in the fifteenth century, European colonists' narrative accounts of new places were replaced by maps, documents that "colonized" social space in the process.[47] Named places associated with varied topologies, histories, and memories were conflated through their inclusion on the same flat plane. Whereas tours involve firsthand narratives of those moving through a territory, maps depict a stable and enduring configuration of places.

Smith's *Map of Virginia* achieves this totalizing vision of a territory by excluding the narrative elements and settlement diversity contained in the earlier Zuñiga Chart, details that prove valuable in understanding the Native landscape of Tsenacomacoh circa 1607. The *Map of Virginia* presents an iconography of powerful "houses" surrounded by tributary settlements. The Zuñiga Chart, by contrast, depicts Werowocomoco differently than other Native settlements: it appears as a unique town with a series of concentric figures, including dots and D-shapes surrounding other dots. Similar circular enclosures appear in other Algonquian maps, suggesting that the Zuñiga Chart actually incorporated Native mapmaking conventions and iconography in its representation of a prominent Native town.

In fact, the Zuñiga Chart combines elements of a tour—a narrative account of moving through a territory—with the conventions of a map depicting European and Algonquian iconography in a blended, or hybridized, spatial order. Literary critic William Boelhower has pointed out that the Zuñiga Chart was likely meant to be read in conjunction with Smith's *True Relation*.[48] Boelhower understands the Zuñiga Chart's key feature as the dotted line between Werowocomoco and James Fort. This line marked a "gift path" that traced the tenuous social nexus between the colonists and Wahunsenacawh in Jamestown's earliest days. The colonists' earliest interactions with Wahunsenacawh and other Native leaders highlight a political economy in which gift giving played a prominent role. The arrival of English colonists within a Native town generally began with ritual speeches, gifts, tobacco, and a shared feast, even in 1607 when Smith was Wahunse-nacawh's captive.

Gift exchange typically includes three obligations: giving, the necessary initial step for creating a social relationship; receiving, for refusing to receive is to reject the social bond; and reciprocating, in order to demonstrate good faith and respect.[49] John Smith's accounts hint that he grasped the subtleties of such obligations better than most of his countrymen. Starting with the realization that Tsenacomacoh's political economy was organized around gift giving, Seth Mallios' analysis of exchange involving Jamestown colonists, the Spanish Jesuit mission, and the Roanoke Colony points out that Europeans repeatedly violated indigenous gift-exchange principles.[50] In the process, European newcomers provoked the "deadly politics" of Native retribution. The failure of other European colonists to understand the obligations of gift giving in the Algonquian world explains some of the violence surrounding the Spanish Jesuit mission at Ajacan, the Roanoke Colony, and the Jamestown Colony.

Wahunsenacawh used his canoe fleet to illustrate the regional political linkages in Tsenacomacoh's tributary economy. The most highly valued objects moving through these estuarine and riverine pathways—shell beads and copper—were brought from the edges of Tsenacomacoh to its center. Shell bead production was concentrated in locations such as Kuscarawaok (kuhs-kah-RAH-wawk), literally "Place of making shell beads," located on the Eastern Shore and along the Atlantic fringes of Wahunsenacawh's influence.[51] While shell flowed from the east, red copper moved in the opposite direction, coming from west of Tsenacomacoh near the Blue Ridge Mountains or from the northwest and more distant sources along the Great Lakes. These materials flowed into chiefs' storehouses and, from there on to Werowocomoco through tributary networks, then outward through the politics of gift giving.

Powhatan's Mantle

John Smith reported that those living in Tsenacomacoh imagined the world to be flat and round, like a "trencher," with the Powhatans in the middle.[52] "Powhatan's Mantle," a deerskin garment dating to the early seventeenth century, offers a representation of Tsenacomacoh that was evidently keyed to such circular depictions of Virginia Algonquian communities. Consisting of four sewn deerskins ornamented with circular discs of *Marginella* shell bead, the mantle appears to have been both a sleeveless cloak and a map. Archaeologist Gregory Waselkov's comparison of the mantle to other Native maps from the colonial Southeast remains the most thorough assessment of this artifact.[53] Waselkov notes that circles representing social groups, from the level of small villages to entire tribal confederacies, were widely shared features of these southeastern Indian maps.[54]

Viewed in the broader context of Native cartography, Powhatan's Mantle appears as an expression of Powhatan sovereignty in Tsenacomacoh. Sovereignty, the political regimes and territorial claims that emerge from

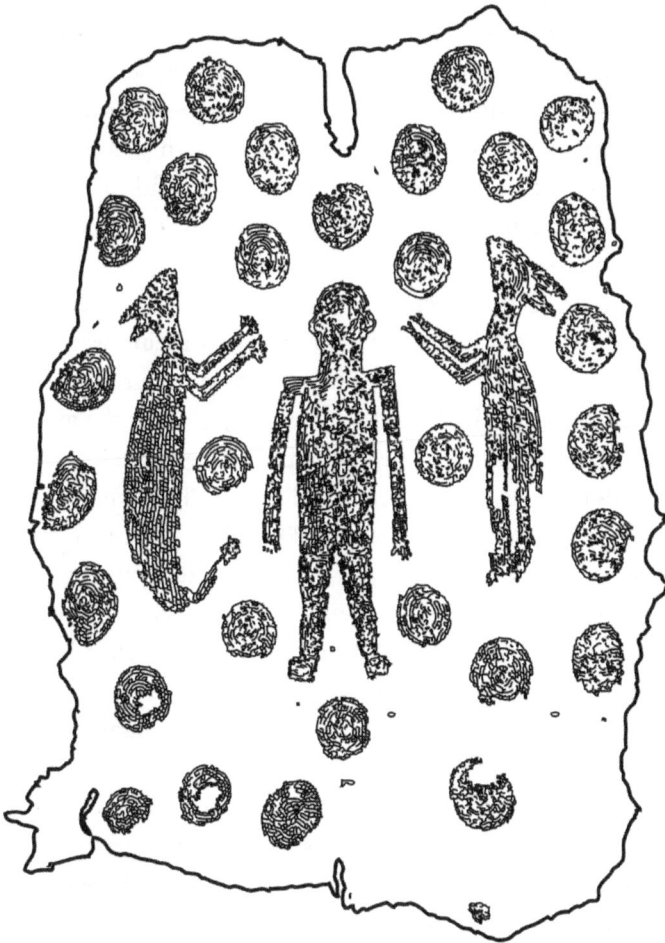

Figure 2.4. Powhatan's Mantle. Adapted from Waselkov et al. 2006:454.

negotiations between authorities and subjects, was a frequent topic in the Jamestown colonists' discussions of the Powhatan chiefdom.[55] Wahunsena-cawh's authority rested at once on his centrality to tributary networks, on his military prowess, and on his divine-like status as Mamanatowick. As Mamanatowick, Wahunsenacawh was filled with *manitou*, the spirit force that infused powerful people, objects, and places on the landscape. The early colonial accounts also highlight his strategic use of kinship to cement ties with prominent lineages across the Tidewater region. Wahunsenacawh reportedly had dozens of wives, and he placed relatives in leadership positions after conquering and incorporating towns within his expanding chiefdom. His influence straddled what Margaret Williamson has referred to as a "dual sovereignty" in the Virginia Algonquian world: priests possessed the ultimate *authority* to ordain strategic actions and to declare war, while weroances held the complementary *power* to make tactical decisions and to enact plans, including confronting visiting Englishmen or leading men into battle.[56] As Mamanatowick, Wahunsenacawh possessed the priestly authority to define a "Powhatan" political order, while as a weroance he exercised the chiefly power to bring it into existence through warfare, trade, and marriage.

The mantle, measuring an impressive 235 cm by 160 cm (about eight by five feet) is currently housed in Oxford's Ashmolean Museum as part of the Tradescant Collection, a seventeenth-century cabinet of curiosities donated to the Oxford Museum by Elias Ashmole in 1677.[57] How the mantle arrived in England is not entirely clear, though it has been catalogued as part of the collection since 1656, when it was listed as "Pohatan, King of Virginia's habit all embroidered with shells, or Roanoke."[58] There are some indications in the early Jamestown accounts that the mantle may have been a gift from Wahunsenacawh to Captain Christopher Newport.[59] Alternatively, the mantle may have been stolen from a Powhatan temple, where it was stored alongside the remains of deceased chiefs.

The garment is decorated with a large, square-shouldered human figure surrounded by two animal figures and thirty-four circular disks of *Marginella* shell beads, a few of which have worn away over time. Given the prominent role that shell beads and deerskins played in Powhatan tributary networks, the media of Powhatan's Mantle were in all likelihood part of its message. The smaller animal to the right of the human appears to represent a deer with cloven hooves, while the animal on the left with five digits and a long tail may depict a cougar or a wolf.[60] Smith's description of Wahunsenacawh's storehouse at Orapax echoes some of this animal imagery, linking it to his chiefly lineage and to an important place in the Powhatan landscape: "At the 4 corners of this house stand 4 Images as Sentinells; one of a Dragon, another a Beare, the three like a Leopard, and the fourth like a giantlike man: all made evill favordly, according to their best workmanship."[61] Several of the figures on Powhatan's Mantle were similar to those at the corners of the treasury, including the leopard and the giant. Deer figured prominently in Virginia Algonquian subsistence, in tributary relations, and in origin stories.

Might the central images of the cougar/wolf, giant human, and deer reference important Virginia Algonquian social categories? Perhaps clan totems or the names of moieties fundamental to the Powhatan chiefdom's origins? A clan consists of a group of people united by actual or perceived kinship and descent, while moieties divide a community into two halves. The use of animal categories as classificatory devices for clans has a rich history in Algonquian-speaking societies from the Atlantic Coast to the Great Lakes and into the northern forest.[62] In some areas, Algonquian totems denoted animals' ownership of foraging tracts, signaling a multi-generation linkage between a clan and a specific place.[63] Danielle Moretti-Langholtz and Buck Woodard have argued persuasively from the early colonial accounts that the Chickahominy were organized into moieties.[64] The Algonquian-speaking Lenape of the nearby Delaware Valley were divided into three clans, Wolf, Turtle, and Turkey.[65] The Cherokee clan system originally had seven clans, including Deer and Wolf.[66] While there are indications in the Jamestown accounts that Wahunsenacawh used marriage and descent to extend his reach and to expand his chiefly lineage, few details regarding Virginia Algonquian kinship structure were recorded in the colonial-era accounts or in oral traditions. The significance of the central figures in Powhatan's Mantle remains, then, frustratingly out of reach.

There are, however, somewhat stronger indications that the pattern of shell discs sewn into the mantle represented Native communities within a map of the Powhatan polity, as archaeologist E. Randolph Turner first pointed out.[67] Colonist William Strachey wrote that Wahunsenacawh's "petty weroances in all may be in number, about three or fower and thirty," matching the number of shell discs on the mantle.[68] Since circles were commonly used to depict social groups in the Native Southeast, the mantle's discs may in fact reference the 34 towns Wahunsenacawh claimed as tributaries. The discs are arranged around the animal and human figures on the mantle in four roughly vertical columns. This grouping calls to mind the distribution of weroances along the four principal waterways in the region—the James, York, Rappahannock, and Potomac. However, the placement of the discs does not accord in any obvious way with town locations along these rivers.

The Powhatan chiefdom's formative history occurred during the sixteenth century, prior to the arrival of the English colonists at James Fort. Of these thirty-four places within the Powhatan political realm, as Wahunsenacawh explained to Smith, "Some countries he hath, which have been his ancestors, and came unto him by inheritance, as the countrie called Powhatan, Arrohateck, Appamatuck, Pamunkey, Youghtanund, and Mattaponi. All the rest of his Territories expressed in the Map, they report have beene his severall conquests."[69] The six original communities that Wahunsenacawh references here were all located well west of the Chesapeake Bay in Virginia's inner Coastal Plain. Drawing in part from this colonial account, researchers have long pointed to the inner Coastal Plain as the area that most likely gave rise to the Powhatan chiefdom.[70] Archaeological and ethnohistorical evidence supports this interpretation, with the inner Coastal Plain's population density, intermittent warfare, and trade relations with the Monacan all likely playing a role in the origins of the polity. The inner Coastal Plain towns of Powhatan, Arrohateck, and Appamatuck were situated on the James River, while Pamunkey, Youghtanund, and Mattaponi refer to inner Coastal Plain locations within the York River drainage.

Combining these colonial accounts with the archaeological evidence, Lewis Binford has suggested that the Powhatan chiefdom was built upon an older alliance between Algonquian communities on the York and James Rivers, and other scholars have followed Binford in this interpretation.[71] During the centuries immediately prior to Jamestown's settlement, communities on the James and York produced two different types of ceramics— simple-stamped Gaston ceramics for the James and the fabric-impressed ceramics of the Townsend series on the York.[72] Located in the York River drainage, Werowocomoco's archaeological record is dominated by fabric-impressed Townsend ceramics for most of its history. Both simple-stamped and fabric-impressed pottery began to occur at the site during the late sixteenth and early seventeenth century, when Wahunsenacawh moved to Werowocomoco and the Powhatan chiefdom coalesced around the town.

This archaeological pattern may in fact relate to the political alliance between James and York River groups at the roots of the Powhatan chiefdom.

Together the archaeological patterns and documentary evidence of the Powhatan chiefdom's beginnings raise the possibility that Powhatan's Mantle references elements of the polity's origins and structure. The mantle may record the union of Virginia Algonquian lineages or clans at the beginnings of the Powhatan chiefdom and related claims to sovereignty over 34 towns and weroances across Tsenacomacoh. In the absence of further oral tradition, documentary sources, or archaeological evidence tying the two animal figures on Powhatan's Mantle to the two ceramic traditions at the origins of the Powhatan chiefdom, though, the links between these remain tentative.

Divination Ceremony

As a representation of Tsenacomacoh's political landscape from a chiefly vantage, Powhatan's Mantle offers a static rendition of a fixed order. By contrast, the divination ceremony was the ephemeral product of a dynamic performance, enacted by the Pamunkey priests, who created a ritual map over several days.[73]

The divination was described by Smith in two different publications, his *True Relation* and his *Generall Historie*. The later version, excerpted below, offers the greatest detail:

> Not long after, early in a morning a great fire was made in a long house, and a mat spread on the one side, as on the other, on the one they caused him [i.e., Smith] to sit, and all the guard went out of the house, and presently came skipping in a great grim fellow, all painted over with coale. . . . With most strange gestures and passions he began his invocation, and environed the fire with a circle of meale; which done, three more such like devils came rushing in with the like antique tricks, painted halfe blacke, halfe red . . . and then came in three more as ugly as the rest; with red eyes, and white stroakes over their blacke faces, at last they all sat downe right against him; three of them on the one hand of the chiefe Priest, and three on the other.
>
> Then all with their rattles began a song, which ended, the chiefe Priest layd downe five wheat cornes [i.e., corn kernels]: then . . . he

Figure 2.5. Diagram of John Smith's divination ceremony. Drawing by Brian Heinsman.

began a short Oration: at the conclusion they all gave a short groane; and then layd down three graines more. After that, began their song againe, and then another Oration, ever laying downe so many cornes as before, till they had twice incirculed the fire; that done, they tooke a bunch of little stickes prepared for that purpose, continuing still their devotion, and at the end of every song and Oration, they layd downe a sticke betwixt the divisions of Corne. Till night, neither he nor they did either eate or drinke, and then they feasted merrily, with the best provisions they could make. Three dayes they used this Ceremony; the meaning whereof they told him, was to know if he intended them well or no. The circle of meale signified their Country, the circles of corne the bounds of the Sea, and the stickes his Country.[74]

The divination ceremony was held in Opechancanough's town of Mena-capunt (muh-NAH-suh-puunt), one of four closely clustered king's houses that formed the Pamunkey homeland and a core area of the Powhatan chiefdom. Over the course of three days, three groups of priests from Pamunkey entered the temple where Smith was forced to sit. The priests then conducted a ceremony that involved singing, oration, and the creation of a concentric diagram around a fire. The diagram included three circles of corn, the first one made from processed cornmeal and the other two from corn kernels. Sticks, "prepared for that purpose," were added between the kernels after each prayer.

The diagram offers yet another representation of social space within Tsenacomacoh, this one created and performed by Pamunkey priests. Sacred practitioners in the Powhatan world included priests and conjurors. Both were considered by Virginia Algonquians to be *quioccosuks* (kwee-AW-kuh-suhks), an Algonquian term translated as "the just" or "the upright ones."[75] Where conjurors forecast enemies' plans, identified thieves, and found items that were lost, priests were closely tied to weroances and to Powhatan governance. Priests tended temples where the bodies of deceased weroances dwelled and advised living weroances on matters of strategic importance.[76] As quioccosuks, priests and chiefs had been initiated into the world of sacred knowledge through their completion of the Huskanaw rite of passage. Priests made sacrifices to spirits, including the powerful god Okee, and in the process maintained balance in the world by keeping dangerous outside forces in check.[77]

Unlike the other three maps discussed above, the divination diagram was not designed to be seen publically and was instead performed and embodied by religious specialists in an isolated temple. Rather than a statement of colonial designs or a claim of regional sovereignty, the figure appears as a cosmogram—a flat geometric figure depicting the universe, regarded as an ordered system. Frederic Gleach has argued persuasively that the divination ceremony may be more fully understood as but one element of a protracted rite of passage.[78] Smith was initially separated from his old status when he was captured on the Chickahominy, held in a transitional state as he was conducted through the Chesapeake landscape, and reintegrated into a new status as a Powhatan weroance at Werowocomoco. As part of this process, the divination ceremony was evidently designed to incorporate Smith into the Virginia Algonquian world through the mimetic (i.e., imitative) process of map making. Gleach identifies parallels between the Powhatan divination and the Big House ceremony, or *Gamwing*, a social gathering of the Lenape Indians who formerly resided in the Delaware Valley. Both the divination and the Gamwing were Algonquian rituals centered on mimesis and ritually prepared maps to effect a change in the universe. Concentric pathways were traced by participants in the Gamwing and by priests in the divination.

In fact, just as circular imagery appeared often in Native maps of the Southeast, the Jamestown narratives frequently document the creation of circles in Virginia Algonquian social settings, particularly in ceremonial or diplomatic contexts.[79] Colonist William Strachey described circular dances with which Native groups greeted English visitors.[80] Colonist George Percy noted that at the rising and setting of the sun, Virginia Algonquians created a round disc of dried tobacco in order to pray, "making many Devil-lish gestures with a Hellish noise foming at the mouth, staring with their eyes, wagging their heads and hands in such a fashion and deformitie as it was monstrous to behold."[81] Henry Spelman, who lived with the Patawom-eck and learned their language, reported that priests periodically brought people into the woods, lit a ring of fire, and offered to sacrifice children.[82] A circle of posts with carved faces surrounded temples and dance grounds.[83] The map at the center of Smith's divination ceremony appears to draw upon these circular icons and bounding metaphors.

The second prominent element of the divination ceremony involves the use of corn. Assuming that Smith accurately understood and reported the significance of the three corn circles around the fire, a key difference may be seen in that the corn meal that "signified their Country" was processed into corn meal, while the corn kernels that referenced areas beyond Tse-nacomacoh remained unprocessed. The processed corn orients the map toward Tsenacomacoh and the fire at its center. The third element in the divination referenced in Smith's account, the sticks, apparently depicted the colonists—something completely apart from the corn-based world of Tsenacomacoh. Sticks, especially those that are "prepared for that purpose" reappear in a variety of Eastern Algonquian ceremonial settings.[84]

Smith's brief report on the ceremony, framed in terms of which ele-ments of the diagram "signified" specific meanings, apparently relied on the Pamunkey priests themselves. While much of Smith's interpretation of the divination ceremony seems convincing, our understanding of the divi-nation diagram and of other maps of Tsenacomacoh would benefit from a richer understanding of their signs, understood as the relationship be-tween a signifier (such as a circle or sticks) and a signified (such as Tsena-comacoh or the English).

The semiotic framework developed by Charles Peirce provides a terminology useful for considering the meanings of such signs.[85] Peirce described three central typologies of the sign, the best known of which highlights the relationship between a signifier and the signified.[86] This relationship may be completely arbitrary or *symbolic*. Alternatively, a signifier may point in the direction of the signified as an *index*, much as a weathervane points in the direction of the wind. Finally, a sign may convey meaning through conventional resemblance between the signifier and signified as an *icon*, much like the image of a recycle bin on a computer desktop. Some signs involve more than one of these modes of signification. Pierce's typology is particularly useful in archaeological settings, as it highlights relationships between objects and meanings that may be more accessible because they are indexical or iconic, and not necessary solely arbitrary or symbolic. An advocate of Peircean semiotics, Robert Preucel has recently issued a programmatic call for a "pragmatic" archaeology committed to understanding the culturally and historically specific ways in which signs mediate social relations: "Signs function not simply to represent social reality, but also to create it and effect changes in that reality."[87]

This analytical framework offers language to extend our interpretations of Tsenacomacoh's maps. The divination diagram included several signifiers. The most prominent of these were circles, one made from processed corn, others from unprocessed corn. From the vantage of the Pamunkey priests, the circles in the divination seem to have been symbolic, iconic, and indexical all at once. The use of a circle to depict Virginia Algonquian communities is, in part, built on an arbitrary relationship between the signifier (the circle) and an abstract or imagined signified (Tsenacomacoh). Some settlements within the Chesapeake—notably those with palisades or ditch enclosures—also bore a formal resemblance to the circles in the diagram. It is this iconic relation between circles and settlements that reappears as a widespread convention within other maps in the region, including in the shell discs of Powhatan's Mantle. Theodor De Bry's engraved map showing Algonquian settlements in the area surrounding the Roanoke Colony depicts all Native settlements as circular palisaded enclosures, even though archaeological research indicates that many were not, in fact, surrounded by stockades as depicted.[88] Circular enclosures also appear on Smith's *Map of Virginia* as icons for "ordinary houses," or settlements lacking a weroance. The other icon included on the *Map of Virginia*, the king's house, offers imagery that would in all likelihood be familiar to audiences in England, where manor houses constructed in the medieval era still dominated the rural seventeenth-century landscape.[89]

Indexical signs also appear in the Zuñiga Chart and the *Map of Virginia*. The line of the captivity route on the Zuñiga Chart orients the reader of Smith's *True Relation* to his movement through the Tidewater landscape during Jamestown's early months. His route to Jamestown also indexes the relationship he forged with Wahunsenacawh through the Powhatan gift economy. These indexical signs and the early colonial history they reference disappear on the later *Map of Virginia*, replaced with a large, ornate compass rose engraved amidst the "Virginia Sea" that points in 32 directions. The extending lines link the Chesapeake shoreline to a precise instrument of European cartography. The nautical charts emerging from this mapmaking tradition had by the seventeenth century encompassed much of the globe, illustrating colonial efforts to capture and redefine landscapes in Africa, Asia, and the Americas.

Perhaps most important for understanding the Virginia Algonquian world, indexical elements also appear in the divination diagram. The Pamunkey priests' construction of the map moved outward from a central fire to a circle of processed corn meal to rings of unprocessed corn kernels. Based on Smith's understanding of the diagram, the unprocessed maize around the corn meal pointed beyond the Virginia Algonquian world toward the "bounds of the sea" and to Native groups outside Tsenacomacoh. The "barbarous" Monacans to the west were marked as different from those living in Tsenacomacoh in that they did not eat maize (at least insofar as was erroneously reported by Virginia Algonquians). As strangers from beyond the edges of the sea, the English were represented as similarly barbarous. Maize's indexicality pointed outward from the center, in a geographic direction and toward a scale ranging from refined to unrefined. In this way, maize appears alongside concentric circles as an important basis for representing Algonquian social categories.

Chiefly Geographies

The four maps discussed above offer different perspectives on Tsenacomacoh/Virginia, highlighting distinct cartographic conventions and iconography as well as differences in the ways these social spaces were represented.

With its settlement hierarchy composed of Werowocomoco, local chieftains' towns, and ordinary towns linked by tributary flows of valued wealth items, the Powhatan chiefdom as understood from the *Map of Virginia* fits comfortably within the neo-evolutionary model of a paramount chiefdom.[90] Powhatan's Mantle offers a parallel vision of the Powhatan polity, one that conveys claims of chiefly sovereignty via a local iconography and objects (i.e., deerskins and shell beads) that indexed social relations across the coastal region.

The Powhatan chiefdom, though, looks somewhat different from an archaeological perspective, as explored in subsequent chapters. Many of the classic archaeological indicators of other chiefdoms around the world either are absent or are present in fairly muted forms in the Chesapeake.[91] Chiefdoms, understood as kin-based societies in which a person's place in a kinship system determines his or her social status and political position, often come about as heads of lineages consolidate power.[92] Such leaders may do so by acquiring wealth, perhaps through strategies centered on flows of highly valuable "prestige goods."[93]

Alternatively, chiefs may rise to power by controlling staples through strategies that involve exerting influence over the means of production.[94] A settlement hierarchy of powerful chiefly centers and secondary administrative communities often results from these dynamics.[95] Other Native North American chiefdoms materialized chiefly ideologies through lavish displays of precious objects in ceremonial settings or by mobilizing labor to construct monumental settlements and ritualized spaces, particularly in the Mississippian world of the Southeast and Midcontinent.[96]

Documentary sources from the Chesapeake indicate that Wahunsenacawh consolidated power using at least some of these strategies, and chiefdom models are indeed useful in understanding Powhatan history and politics. Still, clear archaeological evidence for chiefly structures and related political practices is difficult to detect in the region. Shell beads and copper objects appear in the archaeological record, especially after AD 1200, though the frequencies with which these objects have been recovered suggest that the flows of such exotic materials were fairly modest in the Chesapeake. Monumental architecture in the form of long, concentric trench features is present at Werowocomoco, though such spaces are difficult to find within other regional settlements. In fact, a hierarchy of settlement sizes is difficult to detect in the Chesapeake. In short, the

Map of Virginia and Powhatan's Mantle both raise as many questions as they answer regarding the Powhatan chiefdom's origins and precontact dynamics.

When considered together, the Zuñiga Chart and the divination ceremony point toward possible answers to these questions by calling attention to political dynamics in the early seventeenth-century Chesapeake and by highlighting priestly authority structures that existed parallel to those of weroances. The Zuñiga Chart illustrates a political economy of tributary relations and gift giving that was still in flux and in the process of becoming in 1607. The Zuñiga Chart's gift path, drawn between Werowocomoco and Jamestown, indexed a political and economic alliance through which Wahunsenacawh sought to expand his recently formed tributary network and regional sovereignty.

The divination ceremony shows that sacred practitioners possessed authority of a different source, but perhaps comparable to that of powerful chiefs, including Opechancanough and Wahunsenacawh himself. Before Opechancanough presented Smith to Wahunsenacawh, he brought the colonist to a group of Pamunkey priests, organized according to their own hierarchical structure. The Pamunkey priests conducting the divination ceremony described by Smith, including a "chief priest" and six others, were from Uttamussak, a town of temples on the Pamunkey: "This place they count so holy as that but the Priestes and kings dare come into them."[97] Smith's understanding of the ceremony indicates that the divination involved an expression of the Pamunkey priests' authority, which in this case included the capacity to absorb Smith and the potentially dangerous outsiders into the Virginia Algonquian world of Tsenacomacoh.

The history of the early colonial Chesapeake suggests that chiefs and priests shared leadership in Tsenacomacoh. This social fact signals one significant way that the Powhatan polity differed from classic chiefdom models. The Powhatan chiefdom was not simply hierarchical. It was also "heterarchical," meaning that the relative importance of different power bases shifted in response to the changing circumstances of early colonial history.[98] A term first introduced into archaeology by historical ecologists, heterarchy provides a concept useful for understanding social settings organized by a set of interrelated institutions with fluctuating prominence. It appears that there was no single nexus of power in the Algonquian Chesapeake. Nor was there one single way to represent the social spaces of Tsenacomacoh. Powhatan's Mantle and the divination diagram each attempt a totalizing or all-encompassing vision of the Virginia Algonquian world, yet in the end each provides only a partial representation of Tsenacomacoh's cultural landscape. Similarly, scholars' discussions of the Native Chesapeake circa AD 1607 in terms of the Powhatan chiefdom often overlook important dimensions of this complex cultural landscape.

Chapter 3

Placemaking in the Algonquian Chesapeake

In 1610 English colonist Samuel Argall visited Patawomeck, a town on the northern fringes of the Powhatan world. While there, the weroance's brother recounted the Patawomeck creation story:

> We have (said he) five gods in all; our chief god appeares often unto us in the likeness of a mighty great hare; the other four have noe visible shape, but are indeed the four wynds which keepe the four corners of the earth (and then, with his hand, he seemed to quarter out the scytuations of the world). Our god, who takes upon him this shape of a hare, conceaved with himself how to people this great world, and with what kinde of creatures, and yt is true (said he) that at length he devised and made divers men and women, and made provision for them, to be kept up yet a while in a great bag.
>
> Nowe there were certaune spiritts, which he described to be like great giants, which came to the hare's dwelling-place (being towards the rising of the sun), and had perseveraunce [i.e., become aware] of the men and women which he had put into that great bagg, and they would have had them to eat, but the godlye hare reproved those canibal spiritts, and drove them awaye. . . .
>
> [T]he old man went on and said how that godlike hare made the water and the fish therein and the land and a great deare which should feed upon the land; at which assembled the other four gods envyous hereat from the east, the west, from the north, and south, and with

hunting pooles kild this great deare, dreast him, and, after they had feasted with him, departed againe, east, west, north, and south.

At which the other god, in despight [i.e., anger] for this their malice to him, tooke all the haires of the slaine deare, and spred them upon the earth, with many powerfull words and charmes, whereby every haire became a deare; and then he opened the great bag, wherein the men and the women were, and placed them upon the earth a man and a woman in one country and a man and a woman in another country, and so the world tooke his first begynning of mankind.[1]

The story describes a benevolent god—the Great Hare—and sacred winds blowing across a world without people. It was a place of water and fish, land and a great deer, as well as cannibalistic giants from the four directions. Before people arrived in this place, giants hunted the deer with spears. Once the giants killed the first deer, the Great Hare released the people from his bag and placed them in different areas. The giants disappeared, departing to the edges of the world.

The Patawomeck creation story represents a narrative of placemaking, the process of creating and representing a meaningful "place-world" through stories of "what happened here."[2] While few such stories of Virginia Algonquian placemaking persist today, Algonquian names of towns do provide a way to consider an indigenous sense of place in the Chesapeake. In tandem with the maps discussed previously, these place-names enhance our understanding of Virginia Algonquian representations of social space. Combined with an archaeological record that traces the establishment and reconfiguration of settlements across the region, the rough outlines of Virginia Algonquian placemaking in the deep past may be brought into view.

The names of Virginia Algonquian towns frequently end in "-omoco," a suffix that refers to a bounded enclosure or an encircled place.[3] Secowocomoco (SEH-koh-wuh-KOH-muh-koh), a settlement on the north side of the Potomac River, was the "Enclosure at the outlet." This "locative" ending in Virginia Algonquian echoes the iconic representation of Native towns as circumscribed spaces on the maps discussed previously. Other Virginia Algonquian place-names end in "-anient," meaning "on a path or trail." Mattapanient (or Mattaponi) was "Stopping place on the path."[4] Such labels highlight the polysynthetic structure of Algonquian languages whereby words may be formed out of a combination of several elements that serve as nouns, verbs, adjectives, and adverbs.[5] Statements that may take a number of words to say in English can often be expressed with a single word in Virginia Algonquian.

For many, and perhaps all, societies important cultural orientations are folded into place-names. In his study of White Mountain Apache place-names, Keith Basso concluded that "Apache constructions of place reach deeply into other cultural spheres, including conceptions of wisdom, no-tions of morality, politeness and tact in forms of spoken discourse, and certain conventional ways of imagining and interpreting the Apache tribal past."[6] For the Apache, past events are inextricably linked with places and their positions on the landscape. Apache place-names evoke stories handed down from ancestors, at times regarding the histories of clans and their at-tachments to place.

Basso's eloquent study of place-names relies on his rich ethnographic sensibility as well as a thorough understanding of Apache semantics (the linguistic study of meaning) and pragmatics (the ways in which context contributes to meaning). In contrast with Basso's study of a living Athabas-kan language, sources from the Chesapeake offer few discussions of how Algonquian places acquired their names. Stories of places have been passed down to today's Virginia Indians, though a colonial process of land loss has separated these communities from former homelands, constraining their access to, and links with, places associated with the precolonial past. Even with the considerable linguistic scholarship aimed at reconstructing East-ern Algonquian languages, current understanding of the dialects spoken in coastal Virginia during the colonial era is also limited.[7]

Still, seventeenth-century colonial maps and documentary accounts in-cluded a considerable list of place-names reported by Native residents in the Chesapeake whose meanings can be determined with some confidence today. As often as not, indigenous place-names in the Chesapeake seem topographic, describing the arrangement of natural features of the land-scape as well as movement through the Chesapeake estuary. Woven through Virginia Algonquian place-names are references to streams, wetlands, and fishing grounds as well as their connections with adjacent land and wild plants found there. Such naming practices appear, at first glance, to rely on a straightforward recording of natural features and spatial arrangements.

However, they also highlight the salience of a waterborne frame of reference that viewed places from the perspective of a canoe moving through the Chesapeake estuary. These conventions resulted in naming practices and an orientation to land and water that was fundamentally *relational*: Weanock (WAY-uh-nahk), a king's house on the James River, was the "Place around which the river winds itself"; Rassawek, a name assigned to a hunting camp in the interior, was the "In-between place." The list of Native place-names in the Chesapeake also throws into sharp relief the names of a handful of locations that diverged from naming practices centered on waterways and topographic relationships. A consideration of geographic names in the Chesapeake, particularly their typical configurations and the unusual outliers, opens a vista onto a Virginia Algonquian sense of place.

Table 3.1. Algonquian place-names in the Chesapeake

Name	Location	Meaning	Source	Alternative Meanings
Appamattuck	James	Trap-fishing river	Barbour 1971:286	
Chawopo	James	South still-water, tidal-water	Barbour 1971:287	
Chesapeake	James	People on the great river	Barbour 1971:287	
Kecoughtan	James	Great town	Barbour 1971:288	
Mattapanient	James, Patuxent, Mattaponi	Stopping place on the path; portage	Tooker 1904b:679	Barbour 1971:291—Junction of waters or Landing
Nansemond	James	The point or corner fishing-place	Tooker 1905a:63	
Paspahegh	James	At the mouth (outlet)	Barbour 1971:296	
Powhatan	James	Priest's village or hill	Barbour 1971:297	Tooker 1904a:467—Hill of divination
Quiyoughco-hannock	James	Gull river	Barbour 1971:298	
Rickahake	James	Sandy place	Barbour 1971:298	

continued

Name	Location	Meaning	Source	Alternative Meanings
Warraskoyac	James	Point of land	Tooker 1904b:679	
Weanock	James	Place around which the river winds itself	Trumbull 1870:48	
Chosick	Chickahominy	Pine-tree place	Barbour 1967:221	
Mamanahunt	Chickahominy	Swampy place	Barbour 1967:221	
Mattahunt	Chickahominy	At the end of the stream	Barbour 1967:222	
Apanaock	Chickahominy	Where the water widens out	Barbour 1971:285	
Appocant	Chickahominy	Place with abundant flag reeds	Barbour 1971:285	
Askakep	Chickahominy	At the swamp	Barbour 1971:286	
Attamuspinck	Chickahominy	Atamasco-lily swamp	Barbour 1971:286	
Chickahominy	Chickahominy	Coarse-pounded corn people	Tooker 1895a:261	
Cinquoteck	Chickahominy	Cold water place	Barbour 1967:221	
Manascosic	Chickahominy	At the little grassy island	Barbour 1971:291	
Mattinock	Chickahominy, Nansemond	Separated or cut-off island	Barbour 1967:221	
Mansa	Chickahominy	Island	Barbour 1967:221	
Orapax	Chickahominy	Deserted water place	Tooker 1904b:680	
Rassawek	Chickahominy, James R piedmont	In-between place	Barbour 1971:298	
Monacan	James R piedmont	People who dig the earth	Tooker 1895b:380	Barbour 1971:291— Digging stick
Monahassanough	James R piedmont	People who dig rock	Tooker 1895b:382	
Monasukapanough	James R piedmont	People who dig tubers	Tooker 1895b:383	

Name	Location	Meaning	Source	Alternative Meanings
Mowhemcho	James R piedmont	Those who gather fruit	Tooker 1895b:385	
Kupkipcock	York	Closed up	Barbour 1971:288	
Mamanahunt	York	Two sharing the same outlet	Barbour 1967:221	
Mamanassy	York	Junction	Barbour 1971:289	
Myghtuckpassu	York	Tree	Barbour 1971:292	
Pamunkey	York	Sloping hill	Barbour 1971:295	
Cantaunkack	York	Top of a hill; highest place	Tooker 1905a:63	
Capahowasick	York	Closed outlet	Barbour 1971:288	
Capahowasick	York	At the place of shelter	Tooker 1905a:63	
Kiskiak	York	Upland, high land	Barbour 1971:288	Tooker 1905a:63—Wide land, broad place
Werowocomoco	York	Place of the antler wearers	Tooker 1905b:525	Barbour 1971:302—Rich, royal place
Wighsakan	York	A bitter medicinal plant	Barbour 1971:302	
Parankatanck	Piankatank	Town on other side	Tooker 1894a:392	
Acquack	Rappahannock	On the other side	Barbour 1971:285	
Cawwontoll	Rappahannock	Pine-wood land	Barbour 1971:288	
Checopissowo	Rappahannock	Great mud	Barbour 1971:287	
Kapawnich	Rappahannock	Closed place	Barbour 1971:287	
Menaskunt	Rappahannock	Grassy island	Barbour 1971:291	
Nawacaten	Rappahannock	Hill	Barbour 1971:293	

continued

Name	Location	Meaning	Source	Alternative Meanings
Nawncutough	Rappahannock	Bend in-the-river place	Barbour 1971:293	
Opiscatumek	Rappahannock	At the branch of a stream	Barbour 1971:294	
Opiscopank	Rappahannock	Steam-bath place	Barbour 1971:294	
Oquomock	Rappahannock	Owl-place	Barbour 1971:295	
Pawcocomocac	Rappahannock	Pierced or broken ground	Barbour 1971:296	
Pissacoack	Rappahannock	Muddy place	Barbour 1971:296	
Pissaseck	Rappahannock	Muddy outlet	Barbour 1971:297	
Rappahannock	Rappahannock	Tidal river	Barbour 1971:298	
Secobeck	Rappahannock	Still-water outlet	Barbour 1971:299	
Winsack	Rappahannock	Pleasant place at river mouth	Barbour 1971:302	
Mannahoac	Rappahannock R piedmont	A very merry people	Tooker 1895b:386	
Hassinunga	Rappahannock R piedmont	People who dwell in caves	Tooker 1895b:387	
Massinacack	Rappahannock R piedmont	At the place of stones	Tooker 1895b:385	
Shakahonia	Rappahannock R piedmont	Stone people	Tooker 1895b:388	
Tanxsuntania	Rappahannock R piedmont	People of the little rivers	Tooker 1895b:388	
Assaomeck	Potomac	Middle fishing place	Barbour 1971:286	
Namassingakent	Potomac	Plenty of fish	Barbour 1971:293	
Namoraughquend	Potomac	Fishing place	Barbour 1971:293	
Onawmanient	Potomac	Path where they were led astray	Tooker 1904b:679	
Patawomeck	Potomac	To bring again they go and come	Tooker 1894b:178	Barbour 1971:296— Trading center

Name	Location	Meaning	Source	Alternative Meanings
Potopaco	Potomac	Bay village	Barbour 1971:297	
Quiyough	Potomac	Gulls village	Barbour 1971:298	
Secowocomoco	Potomac	Town at the outlet	Barbour 1971:299	
Tauxenent	Potomac	Little path	Tooker 1904b:679	
Acquaskac	Patuxent	Grassy place	Barbour 1971:285	
Acquintanacsuck	Patuxent	Canoe-people place	Barbour 1971:285	
Macocanaco	Patuxent	Gourd place or field	Barbour 1971:289	
Pawtuxent	Patuxent	At the rapids	Barbour 1971:296	
Accohannock	Bay	Other side river	Barbour 1971:285	
Accomac	Bay	Other side town	Barbour 1971:285	
Kuskarawaok	Bay	Place of making shell beads	Barbour 1971:288	
Nantaquack	Bay	Tidewater people	Barbour 1971:293	
Poquosin	Bay	Low, marshy ground at or near the widening	Tooker 1899:166	
Tockwough	Bay	Tuckahoe, edible round root	Barbour 1971:299	
Wighcomoco	Bay	Pleasant place	Barbour 1971:302	
Chawons	South	South country	Barbour 1971:287	
Mancoak	South	Rattlesnakes	Barbour 1971:289	
Susquehannock	Susquehannock	Muddy-stream place	Barbour 1971:299	
Pocoughtaonack	West	Fire people	Barbour 1971:297	
Quirank	West	Long hill	Barbour 1971:298	

Virginia Algonquian Place-Names

English colonists John Smith and William Strachey recorded words, phrases, and place-names in Virginia Algonquian, a language sometimes referred to as "Powhatan."[8] The interpretations they offer provide some of the earliest surviving records of any Algonquian language.[9] Smith's vocabulary included 46 words and English translations, as well as the numerals from one to ten, twenty to a hundred by tens, and a thousand.[10] Smith also recorded ten phrases, including the Virginia Algonquian for questions such as, "I am very hungry; what shall I eat?"[11] These short passages consist of a stripped-down version of the language, with words that are strung together in pidgin syntax.[12] Pidgins often arise out of language contact, allowing for communication by means of a grammatically simplified form of the language with a reduced vocabulary. A number of Algonquian pidgins appeared along North America's Atlantic coast as European colonists began to explore, colonize, and proselytize during the sixteenth and seventeenth centuries. As with other colonists reliant upon pidgins, John Smith's fluency in specific Native dialects was apparently limited.

Strachey's much more extensive dictionary (formally, the *Dictionarie of the Indian Language, for the Better Enabling of Such who shalbe Thither Ymployed*) offers English translations of about a thousand words and phrases.[13] The handwriting in Strachey's original manuscript is difficult to read. This adds some ambiguity to the lexicography (i.e., vocabulary) and phonology (i.e., sound system) he recorded. Strachey's dictionary nonetheless represents the primary source for all Virginia Algonquian linguistics, due to the extensive scope of his vocabulary and his effort to record Virginia Algonquian phonology with some precision.[14] Linguist Frank Siebert relied heavily on Strachey's dictionary in his effort to reconstitute Virginia Algonquian, concluding that Strachey's "ear for an exotic language appears to have been of a superior order."[15] Smith's and Strachey's word lists, as well as studies of related Algonquian languages, provide a basis for deciphering Virginia Algonquian place-names. This process involves seeking cognates (words that have the same linguistic derivation or root etymological origin) for a place-name in Virginia Algonquian and other Eastern Algonquian languages that point toward a meaning.

Several place-names in the Chesapeake stand out. Powhatan was a town on the James River near present-day Richmond. It was the name Wahunsenacawh drew from his birthplace and subsequently applied to his entire chiefdom. The English generally referred to Wahunsenacawh, the man, as Powhatan. John Smith assigned the name Powhatan to what is now the James River on his *Map of Virginia*, though it is not entirely clear whether Virginia Algonquians also used this name for the river. In short, the place-name Powhatan assumed a prominent role during the sixteenth century and in the early colonial Chesapeake. As a shorthand for the Algonquian-speaking peoples of coastal Virginia and the chiefdom that coalesced around them, Powhatan offered an appealing label for the colonists and remains so among scholars today. The term was also somewhat ambiguous in that it refers to a shifting array of geographic, personal, political, and social entities—something Wahunsenacawh apparently intended as he willed the Powhatan chiefdom into existence. Recall that after meeting John Smith and other English leaders at Werowocomoco, Wahunsenacawh insisted that the colonists should no longer be considered strangers (*Tassantasses*) or Paspaheghs (the town nearest James Fort), but *Powhatans*.[16]

Philip Barbour's study of Virginia Algonquian place-names suggests that the name Powhatan derived from a cognate of the Narragansett word *pouwaw*, "a priest," and Abenaki terms for "town" or "hill," such that Powhatan refers to the "Town or hill of priests."[17] Parallels in the Lenape word for "an interpreter of dreams" led William Tooker to offer a slightly different, though compatible, gloss on Powhatan as the "Hill of divination."[18]

Werowocomoco, another distinctive place-name in the Chesapeake and Wahunsenacawh's residence during the early seventeenth century, has been translated as the "Place of weroances," or simply the "King's house" in the colonists' idiom.[19] As detailed in chapter 6, there are indications in the archaeological record that Werowocomoco was an unusual town on the Virginia Algonquian landscape for at least three centuries prior to Wahunsenacawh's rise to power. The concentric earthworks constructed at the town beginning in the thirteenth century suggest that the settlement was an important center well before the Powhatan chiefdom coalesced.

Werowocomoco's etymology also points toward its distinctiveness. The Virginia Algonquian terms Werowocomoco and *weroance* were likely cognate to a Narragansett term (*wauontakick*) that refers to wise men or counselors, and a similar Lenape term (*wewoansu*) for the learned.[20] William Strachey's dictionary defines the Virginia Algonquian word *wawirak* as "hornes of a deare," and deer antlers appear on the heads of weroances and *cockarouses* (i.e., learned counselors) several times in the colonial accounts, particularly in diplomatic or ceremonial settings.[21] When greeting the colonists, the Rappahannock weroance wore a crown of deer hair festooned with two long feathers arranged to resemble antlers.[22] During the *Huskanaw,* a male rite of passage held in a weroance's town, boys danced along a large circular track and around a group of sacred practitioners painted black and wearing antlers on their heads.[23]

Wahunsenacawh evidently took the name of his birthplace (Powhatan) at the "Hill of priests" and moved to the "Place of the weroances," or the "Place of the antler-wearers" (Werowocomoco) as he assembled a regional chiefdom. As both Mamanatowick and paramount chief, Wahunsenacawh drew upon multiple sources of rule in the Algonquian world. Powhatan sovereignty rested on the authority of priestly divination and was implemented through the power of weroances who served as Wahunsenacawh's counselors.[24] The use of Powhatan as a name for Wahunsenacawh and his efforts to construct a regional polity under the Powhatan label were, no doubt, carefully considered. Wahunsenacawh's decision to shift his residential base to Werowocomoco, a town named for antler-wearing wise men and a place with a history of monumental architecture, was also important in the coalescence of the Powhatan chiefdom. In short, Virginia Algonquians expressed authority and power via names that included Powhatan and Werowocomoco. Wahunsenacawh's pathway to a paramount chiefly status appears to have drawn from his passage from Powhatan to Werowocomoco and from meanings associated with these places.

Unlike Powhatan and Werowocomoco, most Native place-names in Tidewater Virginia reference a riverine perspective keyed to the arrangement of waterways and their relationship to the land upon which a town was built. Figure 3.1 summarizes patterning in these names, listing the number of times common terms occur within the recorded place-names that have translations. Several tendencies emerge in this list. Roughly a quarter of the place-names reference streams or waterways, highlighting their locations along the low banks and bluffs adjacent to the Chesapeake's principal rivers.

Appamattuck, a king's house located in the James River drainage, refers to a "Trap-fishing river," while another king's house, Pawtuxent, was "At the rapids." As noted on the chart, a number of place-names highlight the relationship between land and water: Winsack was "Pleasant place near the river mouth," and Accomac was the "Other side town." Prominent towns

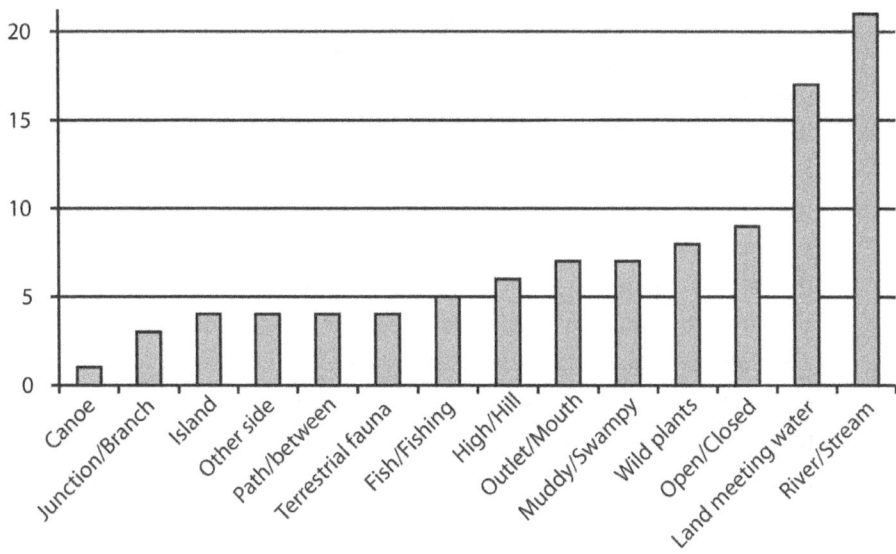

Figure 3.1. Frequency of terms used in Algonquian place-names in the Chesapeake region.

were often named for their appearance from the water: Pamunkey was a "Sloping hill," Warraskoyac, the "Point of land," Pissacoack, the "Muddy place." In fact, a relational or connective perspective runs through many such place-names in the Tidewater region, highlighting river outlets, open or closed waterways, and places in between, as well as junctions or branches in streams. Wild plants, fish, and terrestrial animals also appear often within these place-names, while domesticated plants almost never appear. References to towns or built environments are similarly rare.

Places located on the edges of the Tidewater region and beyond the Powhatan core often have labels that depart from the riverine tenor that runs through most Virginia Algonquian place-names. Located along Tsenacomacoh's northern fringe, Patawomeck, or Potomac, has been glossed simply as "Trading center," though a detailed linguistic assessment suggests a more complex derivation.[25] The first part of the name repeats the Virginia Algonquian term *patow*, defined in Strachey's dictionary as "to bring again." The second element of the name, "-om-," relates to a simple verb of motion in several Eastern Algonquian languages.[26] The final element (-eke) is a suffix applied to the plural form of verbs that refer to animate objects. Combining these elements, Patawomeck emerges as "To bring again they come and go."[27]

A powerful and populous community, the Patawomeck had a history of regional interaction and population movement with some parallels in this place-name. Studies of the Potomac River valley's archaeology and ethnohistory note that the region represented a meeting ground for Algonquian-, Iroquoian-, and Siouan-speaking groups whose interactions ranged from trading and alliance to open warfare.[28] Archaeological excavations at the Potomac Creek site, the settlement ancestral to Patawomeck, have traced the establishment of a town during the fourteenth century AD that was surrounded by a robust double palisade with stout rectangular bastions.[29] The Potomac Creek site housed several hundred residents whose settlement form, which was quite unusual in the coastal Potomac, suggests ties to the *north* and a possible homeland in the Susquehanna River drainage.[30] Potomac Creek ceramics, by contrast, offer hints of links to the *west*, in the Potomac River piedmont.[31] Further complicating Potomac Creek's history, Nanticoke and Piscataway oral traditions describe migration from the *east* into the Potomac River valley, originating on the Chesapeake Bay's Eastern Shore.[32] In fact, the archaeological and linguistic records indicate that all three of these directional influences may have shaped Potomac Creek's history. The town ceased to have defensive palisades during the fifteenth century, after becoming a regional cemetery. By the sixteenth century, Potomac Creek's residents established the town of Patawomeck along the stream-front nearby, continuing to use the old town—still encircled by concentric ditches—as a burial ground.[33] Patawomeck was located near the fall line and the Siouan-speaking Mannahoac to the west. The settlement was also within striking distance of the Iroquoian-speaking Susquehannock from the north. Starting in 1608, the English visited Patawomeck several times, and its residents were eager to develop trade relations with the colonists and an ally to counter Wahunsenacawh's growing influence.[34]

The place-names recorded for the Monacan and Mannahoac towns of the Piedmont appear to depart even more starkly from those to the east in the Coastal Plain. The archival record includes relatively few references to the Monacan or the Mannahoac.[35] The colonists at James Fort made only one poorly documented trip into the Virginia Piedmont, with the primary goal of discovering mines for precious metals.[36] The Monacan and Mannahoac are referenced briefly in Jamestown's records, primarily as enemies of the Powhatan who periodically crossed the fall line to raid in the Tidewater region. Following James Mooney's assessment of these groups in *The*

Siouan Tribes of the East, most historical linguists assign the Monacan and Mannahoac a Siouan affiliation distinct from Virginia Algonquian.[37] Even so, the names of towns John Smith mapped in the Virginia Piedmont appear to be Algonquian, rather than Siouan.[38] The name he assigned to the principal Monacan town, Rassawek, for example, is in fact a well-documented Algonquian term.[39]

Monacan has been translated as "People who dig the earth" or "Digging stick," and Monacan town names apparently have similar connotations as places where people dig rocks and tubers or gather fruit (see table 3.1).[40] Several Mannahoac town names appear to be associated with stone: the Hassinunga were "People who dwell in caves," the Massinacack lived "At the place of stone," and the Shakakonia were simply the "Stone people." Other places beyond Tsenacomacoh were also labeled by Virginia Algonquians using a distinct or outside frame of reference: Chowan, located south of the James on Smith's *Map of Virginia*, was simply "South country." Pocoughtaonack (POH-kaw-tah-OH-nahk), depicted on the Zuñiga Map at the head of the Rappahannock River, refers to "Fire people," and Wahunsenacawh described them as "a fierce nation that did eate men." On the whole, these places were labeled by Virginia Algonquians using terms quite different than those applied to Tidewater locations. These appellations rely on a starkly different sense of place than the place-names woven through the Virginia Tidewater.

The Chickahominy, located close to the center of the Powhatan world, have one of the few names applied by Virginia Algonquians collectively to a people and not a place. The colonists did not record a town named Chickahominy, and the term does not appear to be a place-name on the same order as Powhatan or Werowocomoco. Strachey's dictionary defines *Ushuccohomen* as "to beat corn into a meal," leading to the translation of Chickahominy as "Coarse-pounded corn people" or "Refined-corn people."[41] Corn produced by the Chickahominy helped to sustain the colony at James Fort during its earliest days. Like the names listed above for groups outside the Powhatan core, Chickahominy may have originated as a term applied by neighboring groups. Nonetheless, the Chickahominy people adopted this name to refer to themselves, at one point offering to relinquish it in order to be called *Tassantasses* in solidarity with the colonists at James Fort.[42] The name Chickahominy also stands apart from others in its reference to a horticultural product. With the exception of Macocanaco

(MAH-koh-kah-NAH-koh), a settlement on the Patuxent River whose name means "Gourd field," Chickahominy is the only name to appear in early colonial maps and accounts that refers to a domesticated plant.

Clearly, these place-names offer a rich and complex source regarding a sense of place in Tsenacomacoh, illustrating the ways Virginia Algonquians dwelled in the Tidewater region. Also striking is the repeated use of the same place-name to refer to different locations in the Chesapeake. As first noted by Buck Woodard, such repetition complicates the notion that social identity in the Powhatan chiefdom was defined strictly in terms of one's residence within a specific district.[43] John Smith described a Powhatan political landscape organized around such districts, composed of a weroance's village surrounded by tributary settlements. This settlement hierarchy still forms the basis of political models applied to the Powhatan chiefdom today.

And yet two king's houses were named Wighcomoco (wiy-KOH-muh-koh—"Pleasant place") and were situated on opposite sides of the Chesapeake Bay. Two others on the Rappahannock River were named Cuttawomen. Several additional place-names occur more than once on Smith's *Map of Virginia* and in various narrative accounts of the region's colonial history. Mattaponi ("Stopping place on the path") refers to different towns on the James and the Patuxent and to a tributary of the York River. The Algonquian name Rassawek was applied to the Monacan chiefly center and to a hunting camp in the inner Coastal Plain where Smith was held captive. No king's house named Pamunkey appears on Smith's *Map*, and instead four king's houses (Kupkipcock, Uttamussak, Menapucunt, and Cinquoteck) appear in the Pamunkey homeland on the neck between the Mattaponi and Youghtanund Rivers. One of these, Uttamussak, had no residents beyond the chief priests and served a sacred role quite different than that of weroances' towns. In short, most of these labels appear to be place-names, or *toponyms*, rather than *ethnonyms*, or social identities. The character of these places differed considerably, despite the standardized, two-part iconography of "king's houses" and "ordinary houses" portrayed on the *Map of Virginia*.

To the colonists these names were unfamiliar, difficult to pronounce, and even harder to parse. Such names were often used by colonists as a shorthand for political units within the Powhatan chiefdom. Today, the names on colonists' maps and in their accounts have become emblems for tribes assumed to have homogeneous regional identities and a unified political structure. This usage, though, seems incomplete, as it overlooks the prominent relationship between people, place, and landscape in Tsenacomacoh. Virginia Algonquian place-names instead highlight the manner in which places were situated geographically and perceived while traveling along the waterways through the region's landscape, perhaps more accurately understood as a *waterscape*. These representations of social space stand in sharp contrast to the names applied to American Indian peoples and places located immediately outside Tsenacomacoh.

A Virginia Algonquian sense of place that oriented those who dwelled in the Chesapeake appears to have a deep history, extending to a time before horticultural towns had been built. Rather than referencing domesticated plants or built spaces, Algonquian place-names in the Chesapeake emphasized the water's edge, wild plants, and wetland settings. Dwelling in Tsenacomacoh was evidently oriented less toward fixed places or built environments than to waterborne travel through the estuary. In fact, the Chesapeake estuary served not only as transportation corridor and source of food for Virginia Algonquians but also as a basis for naming communities and for defining their relationship to one another. Rather than as boundaries between the landforms emphasized on English maps of the colonial-era Chesapeake, waterways appear as central to Virginia Algonquians' social and political life.

Chapter 4

Arrival in the Wide Land

Following the heavy rains of Hurricane Floyd in September 1999, the earthen dam impounding Lake Powell near Williamsburg, Virginia, failed and collapsed in several places. With the dam breached, Mill Creek flowed once again to the James, as it had before the colonial era. In addition to creating transportation problems for local residents, the draining of the artificial lake exposed two American Indian sites.[1] Where most archaeological investigations in the area open only a small window onto a modest portion of a site, Hurricane Floyd laid bare two entire settlements dating to the Middle Woodland period (500 BC–AD 900). The archaeological record of these centuries highlights a history in which hunter-gatherers in the Chesapeake, perhaps better termed forager-fishers, adopted new subsistence practices and settlement patterns oriented toward estuarine settings.[2]

This chapter focuses on the mobility and placemaking of Native communities in the lower James and York River drainages during these Middle Woodland centuries. The Lake Powell sites 44JC1052 and 44JC1053 are in many ways typical of archaeological sites along the interior streams of the James-York peninsula dating to this period. Such small Middle Woodland encampments appear often along the freshwater creeks located upstream from the area's large tidal rivers.[3] The Lake Powell sites were, however, unusual in that their submersion by the colonial-era impounding of a small stream protected them from plow disturbance, while the draining of the lake exposed the living surfaces of two Native settlements. Our investigation of the sites revealed 23 rock clusters of varying sizes associated with concentrations of stone tools and ceramic sherds. Much of the pottery at the two sites came in the form of "pot drops"—the sherds from a single, broken vessel discarded in one place. These ceramics included varieties that archaeologists have classified into two distinct wares named Varina and Mockley. Pottery from both wares clustered around the large roasting platform at the center of site 44JC1052.

This distribution of ceramics within 44JC1052, and similar arrangements within other Middle Woodland sites on the James-York Peninsula, suggests that that these two pottery types were in use during the same occupations of these locations.[4] Mockley ceramics, tempered with crushed shell, and Varina ceramics, tempered with sand and stone, were both typically finished with cord-marked surface treatments. This shared surface treatment raises the possibility that both types of pottery were, in fact, produced by the same potters. However, subtle differences in the cordage impressed into the vessels indicate that Mockley and Varina ceramics were more likely the products of distinct learning networks of potters from different crafting traditions.[5]

The wooden paddles that Native potters used to finish ceramic vessels were wrapped with cords made from twined plant fibers. During the early colonial Chesapeake, the Native potters using such cord-wrapped paddles to produce pottery were primarily women.[6] While wooden paddles and other organic materials rarely survive in the region's archaeological record, the final twist direction of the cordage that Native potters used in ceramic production is preserved on sherd surfaces. Cordage twist direction was most likely the result of habits taught and learned by those within a crafting community.[7] Studies of Chesapeake ceramics have examined twist direction on the premise that shared ways of producing cordage highlight patterns in social networks and learning pools.[8]

The cordage impressed into Mockley ceramics recovered from the James-York peninsula was almost uniformly wound downward and to the right, resulting in an "S-twist" that is apparent in the impressed surfaces of Mockley vessels. Varina ceramics recovered from sites located in the interior of the peninsula, by contrast, were generally impressed with cordage twisted downward and to the left, resulting in a "Z-twist."[9] These regional differences in cordage twists suggest that the pattern was not simply the result of left- or right-handedness but was a product of distinct practices in different communities. Where both wares occur together, such as

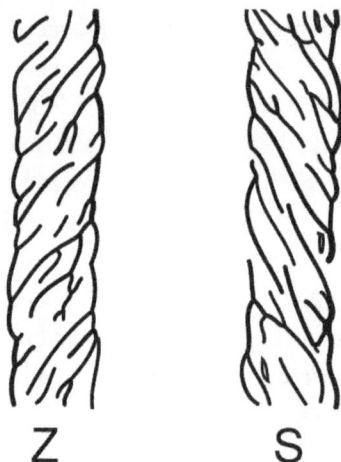

Figure 4.1. Z-twist and S-twist cordage.

within the 44JC1052 site, Varina vessels display a greater variety of cordage styles, including both S-twists and Z-twists in roughly even numbers. Mockley potters, by contrast, continued to rely on S-twist cordage within these settings.

As archaeologists often emphasize, pottery types rarely accord in any simple way with bounded social, linguistic, or political entities. Rather, the stylistic and functional attributes of pottery produced on a household scale generally result from learning and innovation within the domestic context of production.[10] In some settings, including the early colonial Chesapeake, this social learning process was framed by the ways Native women were recruited into a community of potters where they internalized a ceramic tradition and its standard operational sequence of steps.[11] Such communities typically shared dispositions guiding the choices considered appropriate in each production step, from the selection of clay and temper to the shapes of finished pots. Membership and recruitment in these communities were shaped by kinship networks, marriage practices, and residence rules.[12]

Understood in this way, Mockley and Varina ceramics, with their distinctive temper and cordage, were not simply markers of isolated hunter-gatherer bands or emblems of tightly bounded social groups. Instead, these ceramics highlight places of interaction and a cultural landscape composed of overlapping social networks. The Lake Powell sites and other sites on the James-York peninsula raise questions concerning the interaction that brought into contact different "communities of practice" associated with distinct material traditions, subsistence orientations, and settlement patterns. Communities of practice, such as those tied to the learning networks and routines of a pottery tradition, form around shared knowledge and expertise put into practice through creative or productive activity.[13] Rather than living completely separate lives in distinct parts of the peninsula, different forager-fisher communities residing between the James and York Rivers apparently had linked settlement rounds that brought them into regular contact.

Studies of hunter-gatherer societies have long emphasized the importance of gatherings that bring together different groups, events often centered on feasting and trade.[14] Such aggregation events typically hinge on the exchange of valued objects and the creation or reinforcement of alliances and kinship ties. Archaeologists often interpret such gatherings as a form of *adaptation* to environmental settings through the sharing of environmental information and marriage partners.[15] Gatherings may occur where different groups' movement across an area intersects or where rich subsistence resources draw several bands to assemble seasonally.[16] Such events create social and political links between hunter-gatherer groups, opening access to important resources and assistance in times of need.[17]

Recently, though, some researchers studying the archaeology of hunter-gatherer societies have begun to shift the interpretive focus to emphasize hunter-gatherers' *historical development*, rather than their adaptive behavior. Hunter-gatherer aggregation sites offer a setting for considering daily practices, cultural traditions, and even human agency in the histories of hunter-gatherer communities.[18] In some North American regions, including along the Atlantic and Gulf coasts, hunter-gatherer aggregation sites hosted gatherings of diverse groups fundamental to the continued existence of the society—its social reproduction.[19]

On the James-York peninsula, the evidence from the Middle Woodland period indicates that forager-fishers using Mockley and Varina pottery interacted regularly within interior encampments and in large estuarine settlements organized around shell middens. Shell-tempered Mockley ceramics occur most often in settlements concentrated along the region's principal rivers from AD 200 to AD 1000. Varina ceramics and similar wares tempered with sand and lithics have a longer history of usage, dating from 1200 BC, appearing most often within smaller sites dispersed more widely across the region.

Previously, archaeologists assumed that Mockley ceramics rapidly replaced the myriad, localized sand- and lithic-tempered wares produced in the Chesapeake before AD 200, including pottery labeled as Varina on the James-York peninsula.[20] Using the standard culture-historical model in which one "archaeological culture" replaces another in a linear sequence of phases, researchers previously relied on chronologies that overlooked evidence that some pottery types were used at the same time in Tidewater Virginia. An expanded suite of radiocarbon dates now indicates that pottery associated with *both* of these traditions appeared in the archaeological record circa AD 200 to 600, at times within the same occupations of a single location.

Mockley ceramics, some of the earliest shell-tempered pottery in North America, appeared on Middle Woodland sites in the Chesapeake region, to the south on the Albemarle Sound, and as far north as the Delaware

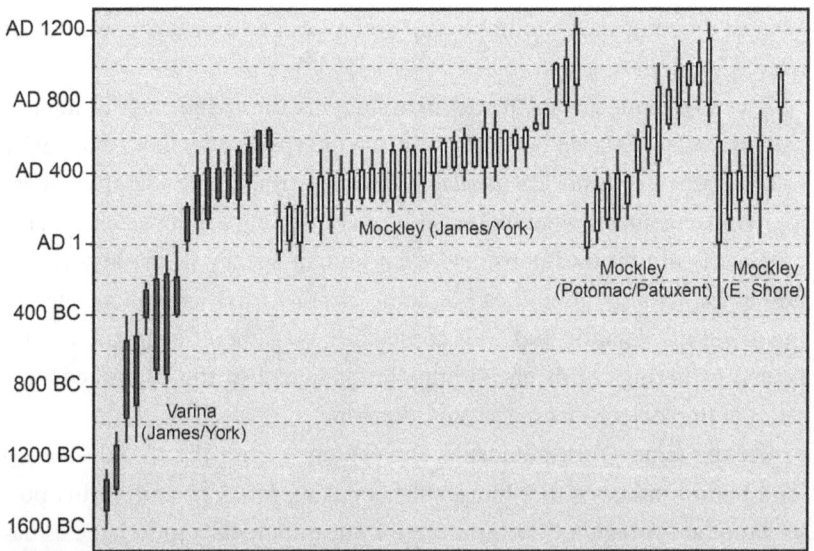

Figure 4.2. Calibrated radiocarbon dates for features containing Varina and Mockley ceramics. One-sigma range (box) and two-sigma range (lines) displayed.

Valley.[21] The most prominent Mockley settlements on the James-York peninsula were situated around shell middens—accumulations of trash left behind after the harvesting and processing of shellfish—or upriver, near seasonal runs of anadromous fish.[22] Some sites, such as those clustered along the broad mouth of Indian Field Creek on the York, contain rich deposits of oyster and clam shells within deeply stratified middens. Others, such as the Maycock's Point site located farther upstream on the James River, include deep middens containing freshwater shellfish, fish bones, and elaborately decorated ceramics that seem to have been used in feasting events.[23] Sites dominated by Varina ceramics, in contrast, were generally short-term settlements located in interior settings.[24] Deer bone and nutshell recovered from these sites highlight subsistence practices that differed markedly from those of Mockley settlements.

The archaeological record on the James-York peninsula points to the beginnings of Tsenacomacoh's Algonquian landscape in settings that gathered members of different forager-fisher communities, including along Lake Powell, around Indian Field Creek, and at Maycock's Point. Linguistic studies suggest that Eastern Algonquian speech communities spread across the Chesapeake during this period as the result of population movements of newcomers and language shifts within communities already residing in the area.[25] Algonquian dialects had spread from the Proto-Algonquian homeland near the present-day Great Lakes east to New England and Canada, then south along the Atlantic coast. The arrival of the Algonquian language in the Chesapeake and in the Albemarle Sound region was the final leg of this historical process.

While not all in agreement, interpretations of this language spread point to the arrival of Algonquian speech communities in the Chesapeake sometime between 500 BC and AD 900. Over the following centuries, Native communities in the coastal Chesapeake created persistent places organized around the harvesting of estuarine resources and during aggregation events, some of which involved forager-fishers from different communities of practice. By the close of the Middle Woodland period, Mockley ceramics were used across large, open social networks that stretched from the Albemarle Sound to the Delaware Valley. On the James-York peninsula, Algonquian-speaking communities subsequently constructed riverfront towns and an enduring cultural tradition within the "nearby dwelling place" that was Tsenacomacoh.

Foragers and Fishers in the Estuarine Chesapeake, AD 200–900

A number of archaeological studies in the Chesapeake, Delaware Valley, and coastal North Carolina have traced the development of estuarine-oriented settlement and subsistence in the Middle Woodland period.[26] During this period and in the subsequent Late Woodland centuries (AD 900–1500), "harvesters of the Chesapeake" created permanent base camps, increased in population, developed broad social networks, adopted horticulture, and established riverine villages and towns.[27] This path to village life may have become the dominant pattern in the Middle Woodland period, yet local factors shaped these developments in distinct ways.[28]

An archaeological survey conducted by the William and Mary Center for Archaeological Research (WMCAR) within the Naval Weapons Station Yorktown allows for consideration of the specific sequence on the James-York peninsula. Between 2000 and 2003 WMCAR archaeologists completed a systematic, shovel-test survey of 6,000 acres of this installation on the southwest bank of the York River, resulting in the most comprehensive database of settlement patterns in Tidewater Virginia.[29] Under the direction of Dennis Blanton, the program of survey at the Naval Weapons Station laid the groundwork for a study of Native settlement on the James-York peninsula. Like much of the lower Chesapeake estuarine region, the naval base consists of a series of terraces and upland ridges dissected by freshwater streams. On the NWSY these flow into three tidal creeks: Indian Field, Felgates, and King. The wetlands lining the lower, embayed portions of these creeks supported oyster (*Crassostrea virginica*) reefs and clam (*Mercenaria mercenaria*) beds during the late precontact and early colonial eras.

The 246 sites identified by the survey represent almost the entire span of the human past in eastern North America, from the Early Archaic (12,000 BC–10,500 BC) through the modern era. The sites dating before 1000 BC exhibited a distinct orientation toward higher elevations and interior locations, generally away from the York River and the three tidal creeks.[30] During the opening centuries of the Middle Woodland period (between 500 BC and AD 200) the number of sites identified on the NWSY increased significantly. The majority of these are small, single-component encampments in interior settings away from the tidal creeks and the York River. Diagnostic artifacts from this period include side- and corner-notched

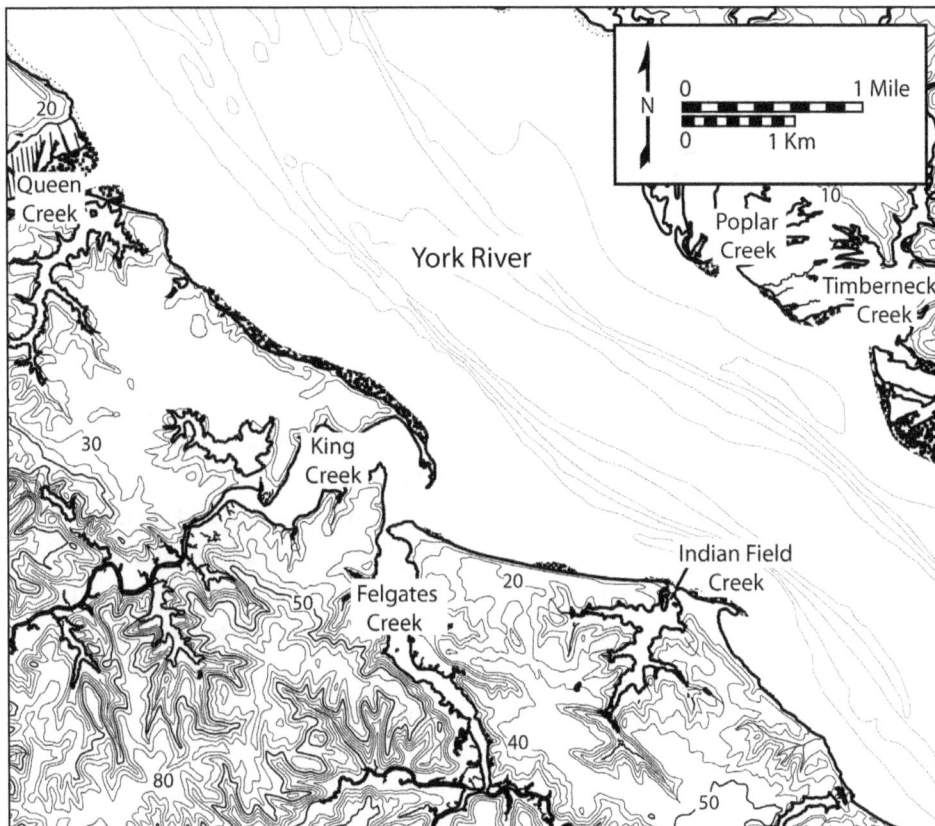

Figure 4.3. York River shoreline along the Naval Weapons Station Yorktown. Adapted from USGS 7.5-minute series, Clay Bank quadrangle.

projectile points as well as pottery tempered with sand or crushed stone and finished with cord-marked or net-impressed surface treatments. Names for these ceramics abound, in part because of localized differences in surface treatments and the temper added to clays prior to firing. On the James-York peninsula, the crushed-lithic-tempered ceramics with cord-marked or (less frequently) net-impressed surfaces from this period are often labeled as Varina ware. Other typological labels are applied to similar ceramics from this period, including Pope's Creek (sand-tempered and net-impressed or cord-marked) and Prince George (pebble-tempered and net- or fabric-impressed).[31] Given the variability within ceramic attributes from these centuries, though, such typological labels imply a level of standardization in pottery attributes that did not truly exist. Instead, ceramic production techniques and the communities of practice that shaped their distribution were apparently quite localized during the centuries between 500 BC and AD 200.

After AD 200, the number of sites along the York River and lower portions of the three tidal creeks matched the number of interior sites at the Naval Weapons Station, signaling a pivot toward an estuarine orientation that continued through contact. Circa AD 200, potters on the James-York peninsula began to produce a new ceramic type—Mockley. Tempered with crushed shell and cord-marked or net-impressed, Mockley ceramics rapidly appeared on estuarine and riverine sites across the coastal Chesapeake, south to the Albemarle Sound, east to the Eastern Shore, and north to the lower Delaware Valley.[32] While much of the cultural sequence that appears on the James-York peninsula prior to AD 200 has close parallels up and down the Atlantic seaboard, the "Mockley spread" signals the first Chesapeake-specific cultural pattern.[33] Stone projectile points associated with Mockley pottery differed from the notched styles typically found alongside Varina ceramics. "Selby Bay" or "Fox Creek" points associated with Mockley ceramics have a square stem or no stem at all. They were commonly made from rhyolite, a material found most often in outcrops located west of the coastal Chesapeake in the Piedmont.[34]

By the early centuries AD a shift in settlement focus toward estuarine settings had clearly developed on the Naval Weapons Station. Fewer sites dating from AD 200 to 900 were identified on the NWSY than during the previous Middle Woodland centuries, but those along the York River and the lower, embayed portions of the three tidal creeks were substantially larger than those of early periods. The density of ceramics, fire-cracked rock, and oyster shell also increased significantly during the Middle Woodland centuries of AD 200–900, particularly in sites with shell middens. Taken together, these patterns signal longer, repeated occupations of estuarine base camps by communities that produced Mockley ceramics.

The settlement pattern data from this period point to a seasonal round— or perhaps two connected seasonal rounds—scheduled to capitalize on the peak availability of productive staples such as shellfish, anadromous fish, mast (i.e., nuts), and deer.[35] Communities using primarily Mockley ceramics focused on the estuarine and riverine portions of this landscape. Places of seasonal aggregation containing dense concentrations of Mockley ceramics included locations in the lower, brackish portion of the estuary near oyster reefs and clam beds likely harvested during the fall and winter months. Other sites with Mockley ceramics were located upriver, marking spring and summer gatherings located near anadromous fish runs. While the settlement round of Mockley forager-fishers was aligned with the pathways of Chesapeake estuary, communities producing Varina pots made repeated use of interior encampments with ready access to mast and deer. Where these groups came into contact, the archaeological record hints that foods may have been exchanged as a result of what Dennis Blanton and Stevan Pullins have termed the "mutualism" of different hunter-gatherer groups.[36]

Studies of Middle Woodland ceramics point toward interaction between forager-fisher communities that eventually resulted in the development of new, larger social networks connected by the Middle Atlantic's riverine systems. Michael Klein's analysis of cordage twist patterns in the Potomac Valley, for example, identified a sequence of mixed and localized patterns prior to the appearance of Mockley ceramics, followed by broadly uniform (shell-tempered, S-twist) ceramics after AD 200.[37] This sequence suggests the emergence of loosely bounded learning networks and wide-open social interaction across the region after AD 200. A similar analysis by Anna Hayden found evidence that the Varina vessels made by foragers in the interior of the James-York peninsula retained Z-twist cordage even after S-twist Mockley ceramics came to dominate riverine settings.[38] Where both Varina and Mockley ceramics appeared together, Varina cordage displayed a mix of twist patterns. This cordage variability points to greater diversity in the practices of Varina-producing potters in settings where different communities came into contact. After AD 600, sand- and lithic-tempered Varina ceramics were no longer produced on the James-York peninsula, having been replaced by shell-tempered ceramics.

Studies of paleoclimate in the Chesapeake have identified a general pattern of warmer and wetter conditions during the Middle Woodland centuries, culminating in a local expression of the "Medieval Warm Period" circa AD 600 to 950. Based on recently collected paleoclimate data, this warm period occurred several centuries earlier than a similar warm interval in Europe.[39] The climate data considerably enhance our understanding of the environmental setting during this interval. One of the few systematic data sets tracking climate change in the region back to the Middle Wood-

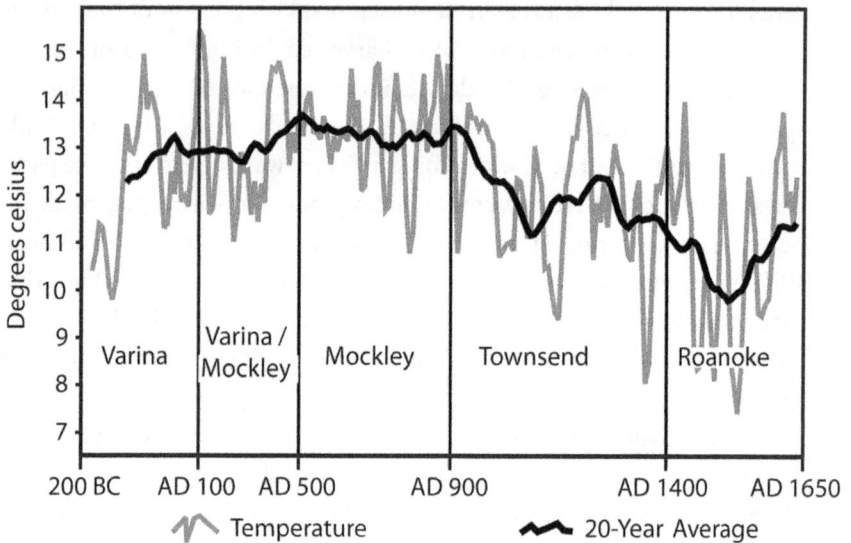

Figure 4.4. Estimated warm-season water temperature, degrees Celsius, and twenty-year average temperature, 200 BC–AD 1650. Data from Cronin et al. 2003 and Cronin et al. 2005.

land period comes from deep cores in the Chesapeake Bay. Researchers have found that shells contained within these cores provide proxy data for changing temperatures in their ratios of magnesium to calcium.

Based on these data, figure 4.4 records estimated spring water temperatures in the Chesapeake Bay, measured in degrees Celsius from the second century BC through the early seventeenth century. The Middle Woodland stands out as a period of generally rising and elevated temperatures. Temperatures peaked during the centuries after AD 500, when sites with solely Mockley ceramics supplanted those with mixed ceramic types on the NWSY. Warmer temperatures also led to the expansion of tidal wetlands in the lower Chesapeake estuary, including along Indian Field Creek. On the lower York, a straight, deep channel had previously limited the development of such environmental features and related shellfish beds before this warming trend took hold.

Virginia Indians focused their settlements on the York and lower portions of tributary streams, now embayed portions of the tidal estuary, through the period of colonial contact, even as temperatures declined. The use of shell-tempered ceramics also continued on the Naval Weapons Station and across the James-York peninsula through contact. The trend toward more focused settlement apparent in earlier centuries also persisted, as fewer, more intensively occupied sites occur within the NWSY, and especially along Indian Field Creek.

A Persistent Place on Indian Field Creek

By the sixteenth century, the town of Kiskiak starts to come into focus in the NWSY archaeological data, with evidence of architecture (in the form of post stains) and shallow sheet middens spread along the terraces overlooking Indian Field Creek. Early colonial-era maps, including Robert Tindall's 1608 *Draught of Virginia* and Smith's 1612 *Map of Virginia*, depict Kiskiak's location on the York River, known as the Pamunkey River to Smith, and as "Prince Henneri his River" to Tindall. Virginia Algonquian towns, including Kiskiak, were typically organized as dispersed communities spread along elevated riverine terraces, as depicted on the Zuñiga Map's illustration of Kiskiak.[40] Situated along the lower, embayed portion of Indian Field Creek where it empties into the York, Kiskiak stretched around the bluffs overlooking the broad mouth of the stream below.

By the early seventeenth century, Kiskiak—Virginia Algonquian for "Wide land" or "High place"—was home to the weroance Ottahotin and a community that played a significant role in several early colonial-era events.[41] Thirty-seven years before the settlement of James Fort, Spanish Jesuits briefly established a missionary base in the lower Chesapeake.[42] Spanish documentary sources raise the possibility that the settlement was located on the York River in the vicinity of Kiskiak.[43] To date, archaeologists have found no archaeological evidence of the Jesuit mission, which consisted of only a simple hut and perhaps another building that served as a small chapel. Shortly after landing, the Jesuits were attacked and killed by local Natives led by their Virginia Algonquian translator, Paquinquineo.[44]

Prior to this, a young Paquinquineo had been captured by a Spanish ship traveling through the Chesapeake region. Reportedly a member of a chiefly Algonquian lineage and possibly from Kiskiak, Paquinquineo was educated in Mexico, Madrid, and Cuba and christened "Don Luis de Velasco." Drawing in part on colonist Robert Beverley's contention that Opechancanough came to Virginia from the Spanish Indies, some have postulated that Paquinquineo and Opechancanough were, in fact, the same person. Beverley wrote, "This King in Smith's History is call'd Brother to Powhatan, but by the Indians he was not so esteem'd. For they say he was a Prince of a Foreign Nation, and came to them a great Way from the South-West: And by their Accounts, we suppose him to have come from the Spanish Indians, some-where near Mexico."[45] Beverley's passage may be read as indicating that Opechancanough and Wahunsenacawh were in fact linked to one another through a fictive kin relationship. Opechancanough was reportedly 100 years old when he was killed in 1644, which (if accurate) would make him about 63 years old in 1607 and about 16 when initially captured by the Spanish.[46] Despite this intriguing possibility and the rather striking similarity in their names, other scholars have raised doubts that Opechancanough was, in fact Paquinquineo/Don Luis.[47]

Paquinquineo's return to the Chesapeake entailed the best-documented of several sixteenth-century interactions with Europeans that influenced Virginia Algonquians' reception of the colonists from James Fort decades later. When John Smith visited Kiskiak in 1608, the "people so scornefully entertained us, as with what signes of scorne and discontent we could, we departed and returned to our Fort."[48] The residents of Kiskiak subsequently encountered visiting colonists from James Fort on several other occasions and joined a revolt against the colonists in 1622. After violent reprisals by the English and a series of "feed fights," wherein the colonists burned Kiskiak's houses and looted its food stores, the Kiskiak left their town sometime between 1623 and 1627, moving away from Jamestown and north to the Middle Peninsula between the York and Rappahannock Rivers.[49] Kiskiak emerges from these brief references as a prominent Virginia Algonquian town, an important part of the Powhatan chiefdom, and a place of colonial violence.

Building on WMCAR's earlier survey and testing on the NWSY, recent investigations by William and Mary field schools at Kiskiak have begun to trace the detailed history of the settlement. A series of sites located around the embayed portion of Indian Field Creek contain a remarkably intact mix of house patterns, midden deposits, and a ditch enclosure. Such features at Kiskiak are well preserved in large part because the naval base has never been subjected to mechanized plowing or residential development—a rare combination in the Middle Atlantic region. The navy has also taken its role as steward of the cultural resources on the base quite seriously by investing in the identification and protection of cultural resources located on its land.

In several locations along Indian Field Creek, midden deposits extending more than two meters below the surface have collected materials associated with 3000 years of settlement. One of these middens, located on the east bank of Indian Field Creek near its mouth, extends for 50 by 25 meters in plan, filling an area from the current waterline to the edges of the adjacent slope. Excavation of four test units within the midden uncovered a series of stratified cultural deposits. Approximately 60 centimeters below the modern surface, these excavations exposed a charcoal-rich, black, sandy-silt layer densely packed with oyster and clam shell, terrestrial faunal remains, and Native artifacts. Radiocarbon dates indicate that the entirety of the deposits in the midden, from bottom to top, accumulated from 1300 BC through the early seventeenth century. Temporally diagnostic artifacts include quartzite-stemmed broad spears (Savannah River points) recovered from the midden base, and a series of grog-, lithic-, and shell-tempered pottery in the layers above. Seriation of the ceramics reveals the distinctive "battleship-shaped" distribution indicating the presence of relatively undisturbed, stratified deposits.[50]

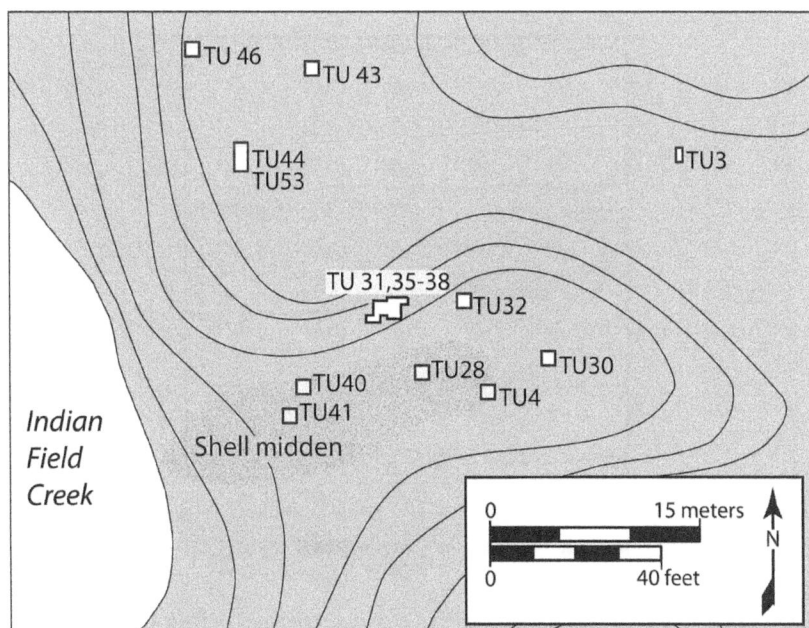

Figure 4.5. Plan of shell-midden excavation area, Kiskiak site.

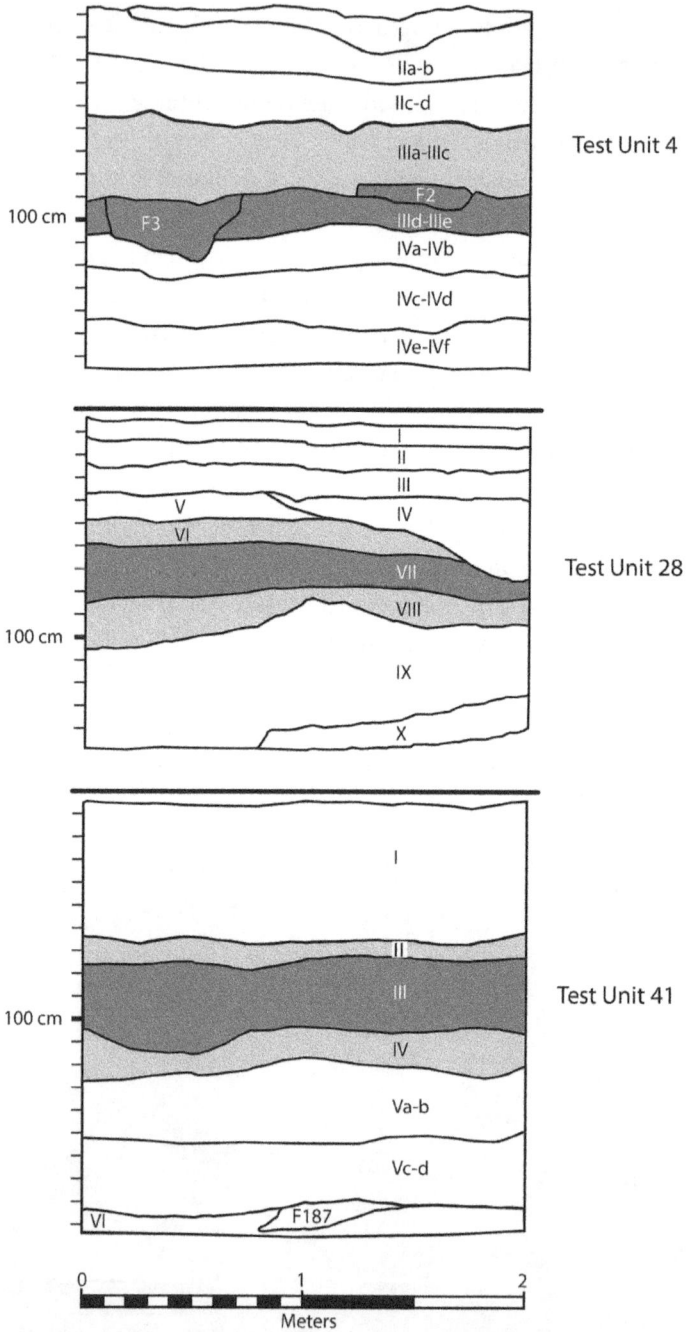

Figure 4.6. Kiskiak site profiles, test units 4, 28, and 41. Dark gray: dense shell with 2YR2/1 black sandy silt. Light gray: moderate shell with 10YR3/1 very dark gray sandy silt.

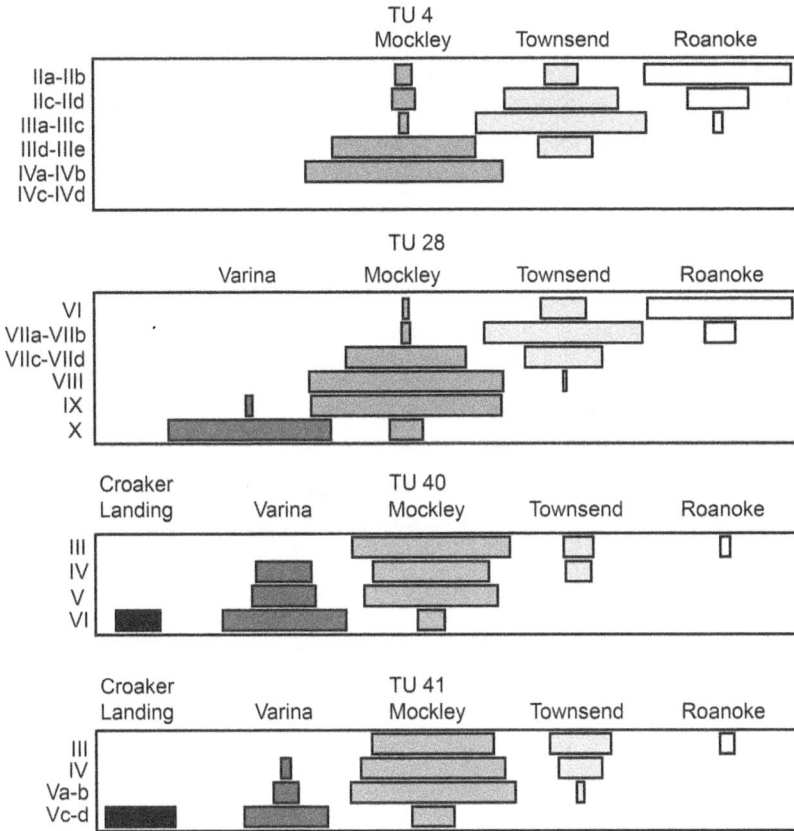

Figure 4.7. Ceramic frequency seriation, Kiskiak site shell-midden units.

Table 4.1. Radiocarbon dates, Kiskiak site

			Calibrated Dates		
Lab Code	Context	Conventional Age (bp)	2-sigma Low	Median Probability	2-sigma High
Beta-302722	TU28 VIa	260 ±30	AD 1520	AD 1650	AD 1950
Beta-163920	TU4 IIIa	340 ±60	AD 1450	AD 1560	AD 1650
Beta-302723	TU28 VIId	1330 ±30	AD 650	AD 680	AD 770
Beta-302724	TU28 VIIIb	1350 ±30	AD 640	AD 670	AD 770
Beta-163921	TU4 IIIe	1640 ±50	AD 260	AD 410	AD 540
Beta-163922	TU4 IVd	3120 ±100	1620 BC	1380 BC	1060 BC

With deposition extending from the Late Archaic period through contact, the Kiskiak midden represents a rare example of a deeply stratified site, one of only a handful reported for coastal Virginia.[51] As such, the midden provides a glimpse of settlement history and historical ecology over the long term in one place. Ordering the ceramics from these deposits through the process of seriation allows the deposits from all four midden units to be placed in sequence.[52] The materials deposited in the midden point to changing intensities of settlement as well as shifting activities. Artifact frequencies show a sharp peak in the deposits dating to the centuries of AD 500 to 900. These layers, which actually contain more shell than soil, include the greatest numbers of flaked stone and fire-cracked rock, as well as the highest densities of ceramics.

In an effort to shed light on the historical ecology of the Indian Field Creek vicinity, William and Mary student Jessica Jenkins counted, weighed,

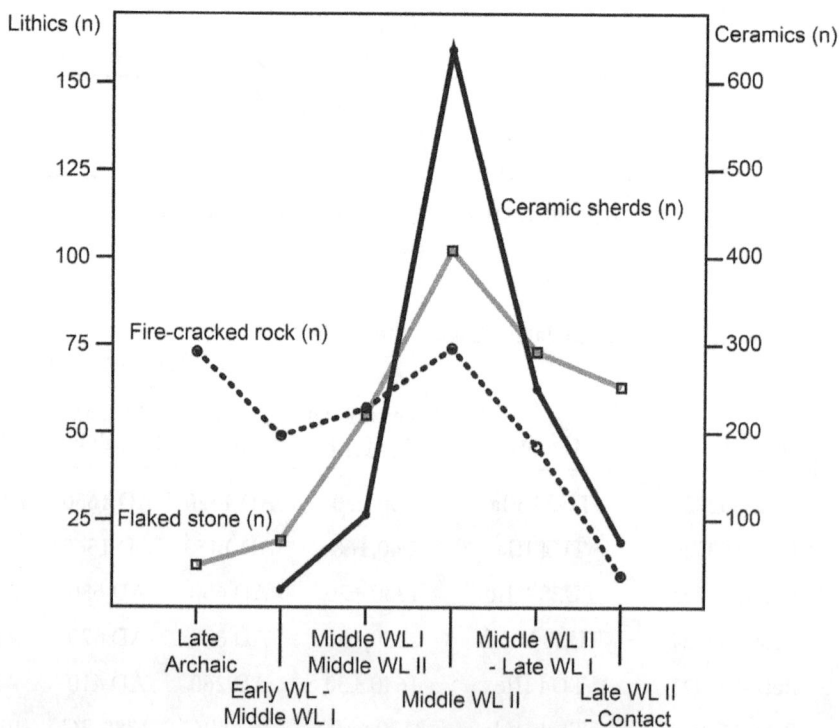

Figure 4.8. Artifact frequencies from shell-midden deposits at the Kiskiak site.

Table 4.2. Distribution of materials in the Kiskiak site midden

Periods	Est. Date Range	Midden Volume (cu m)	Test Unit 4 (stratum)	Test Unit 28 (stratum)	Test Unit 40 (stratum)	Test Unit 41 (stratum)	Ceramics (n)	Fire-Cracked Rock (n)	Flaked Lithics (n)
Late WL II–Contact	AD 1200–1630	2.5	IIa–IId	VI–VIIb	-	-	75	9	63
Middle WL II–Late WL I	AD 900–1200	3.5	IIIa–IIIc	VIIc–VIId	III	III	250	46	73
Middle WL II	AD 500–900	4.7	IIId–IVb	VIII–IX	-	IV	637	74	102
Middle WL I–Middle WL II	AD 100–500	2.0	-	X	IV–V	Va–Vb	106	57	55
Early WL–Middle WL I	1000 BC–AD 100	2.9	-	-	VI	Vc–Vd	20	49	19
Late Archaic	?–1000 BC	0.3	-	-	-	VI	-	73	12

Table 4.3. Faunal remains in the Kiskiak site midden

Periods	Oyster (kg)	Clam (kg)	Test Unit 28 Mean Shell Height (mm)	Test Unit 4 Fauna (NISP)	Faunal Richness (species present)
Late WL II–Contact	189.2	9.9	61.2	7	2
Middle WL II–Late WL I	96.4	5.1	67.1	101	5
Middle WL II	232.0	34.0	55.5	132	11
Middle WL I–Middle WL II	5.1	7.7	53.2	2	1

Note: NISP = Number of individual specimens present.

and measured samples of shell from different strata within the Kiskiak site midden. Much like the patterning in other artifact categories, the amount of shell deposited in the midden peaked during the Middle Woodland II centuries (AD 200–900), declined during the initial Late Woodland centuries (AD 900–1200), and then rose again during the period from AD 1200 through contact. Measurement of the oyster shells' dimensions demonstrated that shell *size* also changed in tandem with the shifts in the *volume* of shell deposited in the midden. Average oyster shell height—the length from hinge to tip—increased during the Late Woodland I centuries (AD 900–1200) and declined thereafter in a statistically significant pattern.[53]

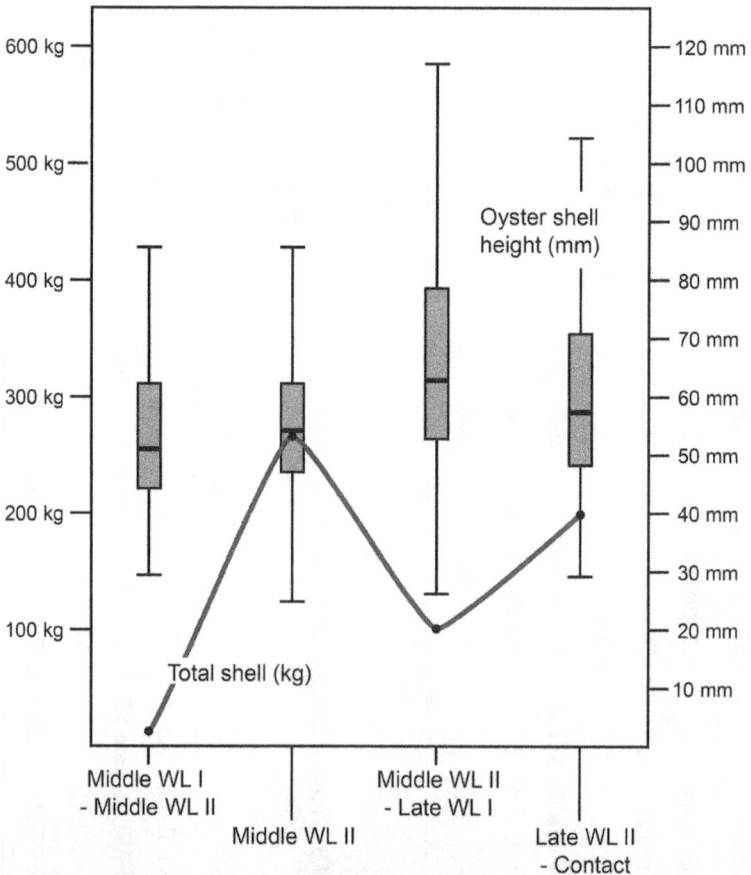

Figure 4.9. Boxplot of oyster shell heights and weights from shell-midden deposits at the Kiskiak site.

The height of oysters gathered for harvest is related, in part, to their maturity at the time of collection.[54] One potential explanation for the changes in shell dimensions is that intensive harvesting of oysters during the centuries between AD 200 and 900, then again during the centuries between AD 1200 and 1600, resulted in the depletion of larger, more mature oysters during these intervals. In the intervening centuries between AD 900 and 1200, when the volume of shell deposited in the midden *declined* substantially, harvested oysters were, on average, significantly *longer*. These centuries saw the introduction of maize-based horticulture in the region and a withdrawal from the intensive use of estuarine base camps, including those along Indian Field Creek. After AD 1200, during the final period represented in the midden, Kiskiak became a regional political center and a sizable town. Survey and excavation data record an increased community population along Indian Field Creek during this period. As the volume of shell *increased* in the midden during these centuries, shell lengths began to *decline* once again.

The amount of shell deposited in the midden and the size of oysters harvested by Kiskiak's residents apparently changed in concert with shifts in subsistence and demography, offering a window into the history of human-environmental relations at this location. The resulting sequence suggests that Kiskiak residents' shellfish harvesting impacted the health of oyster reefs in the area and that this relationship also varied over time in a cyclical manner. It should be emphasized that other factors, including environmental conditions in the estuary, also influenced oyster growth rates, reef conditions, and shell dimensions.[55] Terrestrial fauna in the midden show a similar Middle Woodland II peak in terms of the numbers of individual specimens present and in species diversity, offering support for the inference that Native settlement and subsistence practices played a significant role in the identified pattern.

In addition to the shellfish and terrestrial fauna that Virginia Algonquians deposited at Kiskiak, the historical ecology of Indian Field Creek may be considered in terms of changes in the local vegetation. The pollen that accumulated in the wetlands below the site offers a line of evidence regarding plants growing in the vicinity of the site.[56] An initial analysis of pollen data from the Kiskiak site determined that there is considerable continuity in the species present in the precontact pollen record.[57] With the benefit of the detailed archaeological record along Indian Field Creek resulting from the recent Kiskiak investigations, though, it is also clear that Virginia Algonquian communities did have an impact on the plant species growing along Indian Field Creek. Plant pollen recovered from a core sample taken from the stream bottom, immediately west of the shell midden, traced changes in sedimentation and vegetation from the Late Archaic period through the present day. Inundated, wetland sediments such as these offer ideal conditions for pollen preservation, so WMCAR's recovery of this material provides a powerful line of evidence for considering human–environmental interaction and its impact on the surrounding landscape. The pollen study included a series of radiocarbon dates that place the deposits in sequence.

The previous analysis of this evidence focused on three sharply different patterns in the sediments and pollen assemblages present in the 3.6-meter-long core.[58] Deposits near the base of the core corresponding to the Late Archaic (2500–1200 BC) period included relatively little pollen amidst high concentrations of charcoal and sandy sediments. This portion of the sequence likely represents materials deposited in a backwater slough, a sluggish channel in which water flows slowly through low ground, prior to the expansion of tidal wetlands into Indian Field Creek.[59] During the second phase of the sequence, forests dominated by oak, hickory, and pine stood above tidal wetlands that expanded during the Middle Woodland period through colonial contact. Herbaceous weeds, including ragweed, goosefoot, pigweed, and various grasses, also appear in the pollen assemblages of this interval. Finally, the highest concentrations of charcoal and weedy species mark the third pattern, evident after English colonization of the Chesapeake, at which point oak and hickory decline substantially in frequency.

Starting in the seventeenth century, English colonial planters and American farmers cut down the oak-hickory-pine forests of Tidewater Virginia, initially to plant tobacco and subsequently while developing a more diversified agrarian economy during the eighteenth century.[60] Along Indian Field Creek, as in other parts of the Chesapeake, forest clearing triggered soil erosion and an expansion of weedy species that colonized newly opened forest-edge environments.[61] Historians disagree regarding the extent to which seventeenth- and eighteenth-century economic cycles can be linked to unsustainable agricultural practices and soil exhaustion in the Chesapeake, though the environmental data from Indian Field Creek clearly record a colonial-era landscape quite different than that of preceding centuries.[62]

My reanalysis of the Indian Field Creek pollen data that considers the precolonial sequence in detail provides evidence that Native communities also altered the forest cover along Indian Field Creek well before the seventeenth century. These changes are more subtle and gradual than those apparent during the colonial era, though. The core samples associated with the Middle Woodland I centuries of 500 BC–AD 200 suggest relatively dense forest cover in the area, with high numbers of oak and hickory trees and low values for herbaceous weed species. A Middle Woodland II increase in charcoal fragments and a substantial decline in oak and hickory pollen occurred between AD 200 and 900, at the same time that forager-fishers established larger settlements on the terraces overlooking Indian Field Creek. Based on this evidence, forest management during these centuries may have included selective burning of woodlands and opening of areas for habitation. During the Late Woodland I centuries of AD 900 to 1200, pollen from weedy herbs continued to increase, likely in response to the creation of new forest-edge settings resulting from the introduction of horticulture. Otherwise, pollen and charcoal values during the Late Woodland I centuries returned to levels approximating the Middle Woodland I centuries, suggesting that forager-fisher communities no longer settled the area adjacent to Indian Field Creek as intensively as they had during the previous period. During the Late Woodland II centuries after AD 1200, oak and hickory pollen declined slightly once again, as the presence of charcoal ticked upward. By the Protohistoric and Contact periods (AD 1500–1607), pollen from oak and hickory trees had decreased to its lowest precolonial levels, while weedy species increased to approximately 10 percent of the assemblage for the first time.

The pollen data record a cyclical pattern in the vegetation cover along Indian Field Creek that parallels the oyster shell data and settlement history. The pollen record on the eve of English settlement in the Chesapeake suggests a landscape managed by the burning and clearing of hardwoods that opened the forest canopy. Such practices created edge environments receptive to herbaceous weeds and grasses. Not unlike the "domesticated landscapes" produced by New England Algonquians and by Native people in Amazonia, the Kiskiak site's historical ecology challenges the notion that European colonists stepped into a pristine wilderness in the Chesapeake.[63] Indeed, early colonists, including John Smith and William Strachey, understood that the combination of "old trees on the ground," "clered and

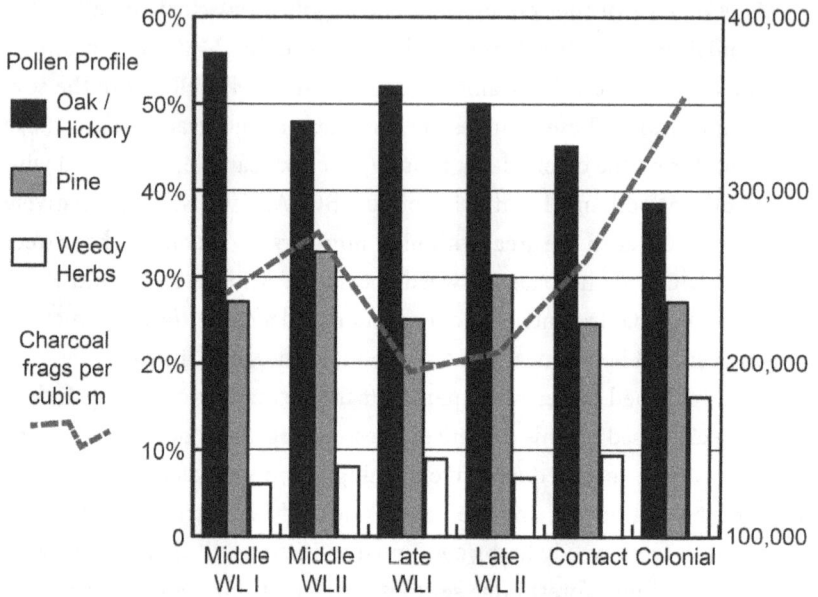

Figure 4.10. Forest cover changes at the Kiskiak site, including pollen profile (solid bars) and charcoal fragments (dashed line). Data from Jones 2005.

opened" land, "little small wood," and forest regrowth that they saw resulted directly from Virginia Algonquians' forest management and horticultural practices.[64] The pollen data, reaching back more than a thousand years prior to Jamestown's settlement, suggest that human–environmental relations varied considerably over time along Indian Field Creek. Kiskiak's landscape circa 1607 was the product of this deep ecological history, particularly the anthropogenic mosaic of cleared ground and forest regrowth that began to take shape four centuries before 1607.

The practices that shaped this environmental history may also be traced through the sequence of features constructed by Virginia Algonquians living along Indian Field Creek. From pits to post stains, the archaeological features associated with different periods of the Kiskiak midden offer a record of daily activities by revealing the types of facilities used in this area of the settlement. The earliest midden features, two basin-shaped pits, date to the Late Archaic or Early Woodland period, based on their stratigraphic positions. A similar pit contained Middle Woodland I (500 BC–AD 200) deposits, including Varina ceramics. Located just north of the midden deposits, feature 156 consisted of a large, scattered hearth with over a hundred fire-cracked rocks, a mix of Mockley and Varina ceramics, and a concentration of burned oyster shell. Middle Woodland II (AD 200–900) deposits are marked by five separate pot drops and two distinct shell lenses. No features linked to the Late Woodland I centuries were present in or around the midden. Features associated with deposits dating from AD 1200 through the early seventeenth century include 29 post stains found above the shell-rich deposit. Immediately north of the midden, a series of similar post stains dating to this interval suggests a structure of some sort adjacent to the midden.

Overall, the sequence of artifacts and features in and around the Kiskiak

Table 4.4. Features in the Kiskiak site midden

Features	Type	Test Unit	Context	Diagnostics	Other Artifacts
[n = 11]	Post molds	28	Stratum IVa (above shell deposit)	Roanoke	-
[n = 18]	Post molds	28	Stratum Vb (above shell-rich deposit)	Roanoke	-
F139	Pot drop	28	Stratum VIIIa	Mockley	-
F140	Pot drop	29	Stratum VIIIa	Mockley	-
F172	Pot drop	40	Stratum IVb	Mockley	-
F171	Pot drop	40	Stratum IVb	Mockley	-
C421	Pot drop	40	Stratum IVa	Mockley	-
F2	Shell lens	4	Stratum IIIc	Mockley	Oyster shell
F3	Shell lens	4	Stratum IIIc	Mockley	Oyster shell
F156	Hearth	43	North of midden	Mockley / Varina	Fire-cracked rock, flaked stone, shell
F180	Shallow pit	41	Stratum Va (below shell-rich deposit)	Varina	Quartzite flakes, fire-cracked rock
F187	Shallow pit	41	Stratum VIII (below shell-rich deposit)	-	Quartzite flakes
F141	Shallow pit	28	Stratum XI (below shell-rich deposit)	-	Quartzite flakes

midden provides evidence that this was a remarkably persistent place of settlement. Placed in the context of the regional settlement patterns and the historical ecological data, the features and stratified deposits index shifting activities along Indian Field Creek. Prior to the first century AD, the low artifact densities and shallow pits point toward small, short-term encampments of mobile foragers, similar to others located across the NWSY during this interval. Feature 156, an oyster-roasting platform associated with both Mockley and Varina ceramics, signals a shift in activities associated with the midden toward more intensive food preparation centered on the processing of shellfish. During the period between AD 500 and 900, the densities of materials recovered from the midden highlight the harvesting, processing, and consumption of large volumes of food. In deposits associated with Mockley ceramics, we see evidence of more intensive oyster and clam harvesting in the overall volume of shell deposited in the midden. Food preparation, likely in areas close to the midden, is apparent in the densities of fire-cracked rocks, the discrete lenses of shell deposits, and the pot drops of mendable Mockley vessels. During the centuries between AD 900 and 1200, the midden area ceased to be a focus of activity.

The final phase of the midden deposits contains evidence of a renewed focus on shellfish harvesting and a prevalence of post stains from building construction. Since the midden area slopes gently down to the west, the evidence of architectural features in this portion of the site was unexpected. The posts may relate to drying racks or hearth hurdles used to elevate shellfish or other foods over a fire. Alternatively, residential architecture or shelters associated with shellfish processing may have been constructed within and adjacent to the midden during its final stages.

Shellfish harvesting, processing, and consumption are clearly central to this narrative of the Kiskiak midden, especially during the Middle Woodland period. Colonists made only a few, brief references to Virginia Algonquians' practices related to shellfish, and these descriptions postdate the earliest shell deposits at Kiskiak by at least a thousand years. Nonetheless, relevant contextual information may be drawn from early colonial imagery and from colonists' records of Native shellfish consumption.[65] Smith obtained oysters from the Kecoughtan during the fall of 1607 when he exchanged hatchets and copper for foodstuffs.[66] The following year Smith returned to Kecoughtan and spent Christmas there. During that visit the Kecoughtan hosted a feast that lasted a week, and Smith listed oysters as the first item on the menu: "Wee were never more merrie, nor fedde on more plenty of good oysters, fish, flesh, wild foule, and good bread."[67] Oysters were clearly an important staple at Kecoughtan, which was located on the lower James River. As with Kiskiak, such a location in the lower portion of the estuary afforded the Kecoughtan ready access to oyster reefs and clam beds.

Some indications of harvesting and processing practices may also be drawn from colonial-era references. One of John White's watercolors depicted North Carolina Algonquians' fishing with spears and a fire in a dugout canoe that they paddled alongside a weir, an enclosure of stakes set in a stream as a fish trap. A passenger in the dugout wields an oyster rake.[68] English colonist William Strachey reported, "The salvages used to boyle oysters and mussells together, and with the broath they made a good spoone meat, thickned with the flower of their wheat."[69] By the early eighteenth century, one account from Maryland notes that "they live much upon oysters getting vast quantities of 'em and so Roast 'em in a fire.[70]

These brief references offer support for several inferences regarding the role of shellfish in the Algonquian Chesapeake. The harvesting and consumption of oysters was a focus of activity during the fall and winter months.[71] Task groups collected oysters using specialized tools as they fished near shore. Communities in the lower estuary prepared considerable quantities of oysters for public feasts. Finally, oysters played a role in diplomatic exchanges and in gift giving.

Forager-Fisher Feasting and Algonquian Social Networks

Where Kiskiak provides a long-term record of an aggregation site on the outer Coastal Plain (i.e., on the lower York, close to the Chesapeake Bay), the Maycock's Point site represents a similar gathering place upstream, in the inner Coastal Plain. Located on the south side of the James River at the mouth of Powell Creek, the site was investigated in 1970 by William and Mary archaeologists and again in 1981–82 by archaeologist Tony Opperman.[72] The analysis of these materials to date has focused on the rich and diverse faunal assemblage and on ceramics recovered from midden deposits. Maycock's Point is west of the brackish water zones that support oyster reefs and clam beds. Instead, midden deposits at Maycock's contain the shells of *Elliptio complanatus*, a freshwater clam that was once abundant in marshes like those on the lower reaches of Powell Creek near its confluence with the James.

The midden deposits at Maycock's Point date to the Middle Woodland period, with radiocarbon assays from AD 200 through 800. Surrounding these deposits are Mockley pot drops, rock clusters of various sizes, post stains, and shallow pits. The site marks a sizable Middle Woodland settlement with substantial houses and large rock-cluster features for food preparation. Maycock's Point's faunal remains (terrestrial and riverine) provide evidence of a series of seasonal, warm-weather occupations during the spring and summer.[73] During the spring, freshwater streams such as Powell Creek next to Maycock's Point experienced runs of anadromous fish, including shad and herring, which could be captured in large quantities using weirs and nets. Maycock's Point evidently represented a substantial seasonal fishing village.

Like other estuarine sites during this period, the middens at Maycock's Point are dominated by Mockley pottery. However, a small number of elaborately incised ceramics have also been recovered from the site. Similar ceramics with complex designs were first identified at the Abbott Farm site near Trenton, New Jersey, and have been labeled Abbott zone-decorated ceramics by archaeologists. The designs on Abbott zone-decorated ceramics include combinations of horizontal and vertical lines incised into the vessel, sometimes in the form of nested triangles, diamonds, or crosshatching in distinct zones below the rim.[74] Abbott zone-decorated ceramics occur as a minority ware on Middle Woodland sites near the Atlantic coast in Virginia through Massachusetts, often in locations of seasonal aggregation where hunter-gatherers fished and harvested shellfish, leaving behind thick midden deposits.[75] In the Chesapeake similar zone-decorated ceramics have been found on five sites in the James and York River drainages, with the largest numbers of these ceramics coming from Maycock's Point.[76] Like Maycock's Point and other locations containing Abbott zone-decorated ceramics, these sites were situated near productive freshwater marshes, wetlands, and riverine settings.

Michael Stewart has offered the most compelling interpretation of Abbott zone-decorated ceramics to date, positing that these vessels were used on special occasions when seasonal fish runs brought together different bands for seasonal aggregations.[77] Such aggregation events centered on fishing, shellfish harvesting, and processing of foodstuffs. The Maycock's Point site, with its decorated ceramics, large hearths, and considerable quantities of food remains in a seasonally occupied settlement, lines up

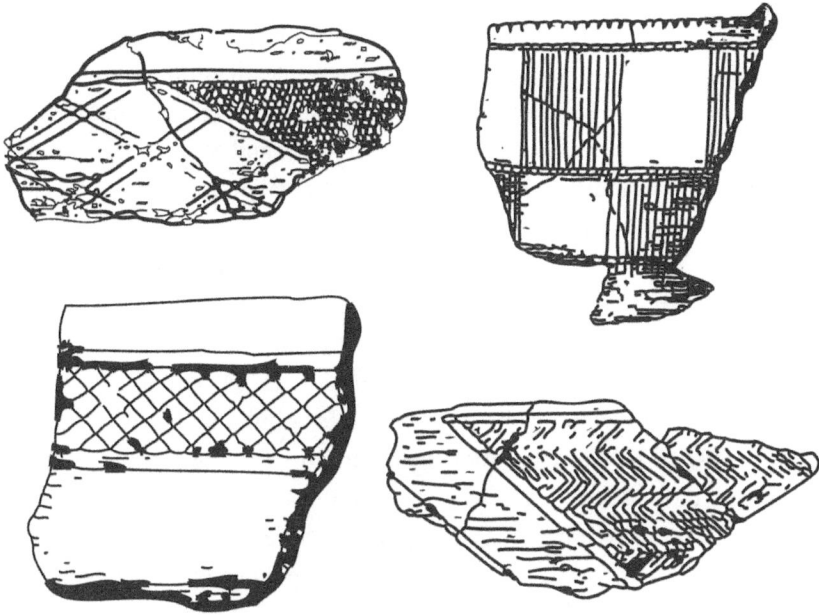

Figure 4.11. Abbott zone-decorated ceramics from Tidewater Virginia. Figure adapted from drawings in Gregory 1983.

well with Stewart's thesis. Extending Stewart's interpretation of zone-decorated ceramics, Jeffrey Hantman and Debra Gold have suggested that such seasonal aggregations at Maycock's Point and similar locations offered opportunities for lineage heads to enhance their influence.[78] Middle Woodland "big men" may have leveraged such gatherings, replete with feasting, gift giving, and new marriage ties, to construct coalitions on a local and a regional scale.

The evidence for a shared ceramic decorative style across a large portion of the coastal Atlantic during the Middle Woodland period raises questions concerning how this style spread so widely. A recent study that has begun to address this question compared ceramics from the Chesapeake and the Delaware Valley.[79] No Abbott zone-decorated ceramics have been recovered in Maryland or Delaware from areas between the Chesapeake and the Delaware Valley, evidence that runs counter to the idea that this pottery moved on a regular basis through weblike trading networks, or "down the line." Using a materials characterization method (laser ablation-inductively coupled plasma mass spectrometry) to determine the elemental composition of the clays within Abbott zone-decorated and Mockley ceramics from the Maycock's Point site, Laura Steadman determined that both wares were, in fact, produced locally in the Chesapeake from the same clays. Ceramics from Abbott Farm, both Mockley and zone-decorated, also had a similar local distribution in the Delaware Valley. Evidently, it was the knowledge of a decorative tradition that moved between the Delaware and the Chesapeake (and quite possibly the potters who had mastered this tradition), rather than the ceramic vessels themselves.

The notion that Abbott zone-decorated ceramics were used in feasting and in gift giving on a local scale relies on an assumed link between decorative embellishment and such practices, a link that is worth exploring. Feasts, understood as ritual events that involve the communal consumption of food and drink, have become the subject of considerable archaeological research in recent decades, with several studies emphasizing the significance of public feasts as socially and politically charged affairs.[80] Researchers have developed functional categories of feasts and criteria for identifying feasting events in the archaeological record.[81] These include evidence of unusual food preparation facilities, exotic foods and beverages, special consumption spaces, and special vessels distinct from those used to serve quotidian meals or for routine food preparation. Archaeologists typically rely on a suite of such evidence to make the case that large-scale, public feasting occurred in the Native North American past, including the quantity and variety of food remains, places and occasions marked for special events, and unusual ratios of serving vessels to cooking vessels.

As noted above, the Middle Woodland shell middens in the James and York River drainages offer evidence along these lines. At Maycock's Point, for example, a concentrated season of fishing and shellfish harvesting produced large amounts of food remains along with architectural structures, large rock-cluster features, and decorated ceramics, all of which appear infrequently in the Middle Woodland archaeological record. Additional evidence may be drawn from the shapes and sizes of the ceramic vessels recovered from the Maycock's Point site. One method of estimating vessel shapes and sizes from individual sherds involves measuring their curvature in plan and in profile.[82] The curvature of sherds in plan (i.e., viewed from above) offers evidence of a pot's diameter. Profile curvature provides a means of determining whether vessel forms more closely approximated the straight cylinder of a jar or the curvilinear dimensions of a rounded bowl.

The figure below depicts measurements from a sample of Mockley (n = 20) and Abbott zone-decorated (n = 20) rims recovered from Middle Woodland deposits at the Maycock's Point site. As indicated in the figure, differences in vessel dimensions between the two ware types are apparent. Where Mockley ceramics commonly have rims ranging from 15 to 30 cm in

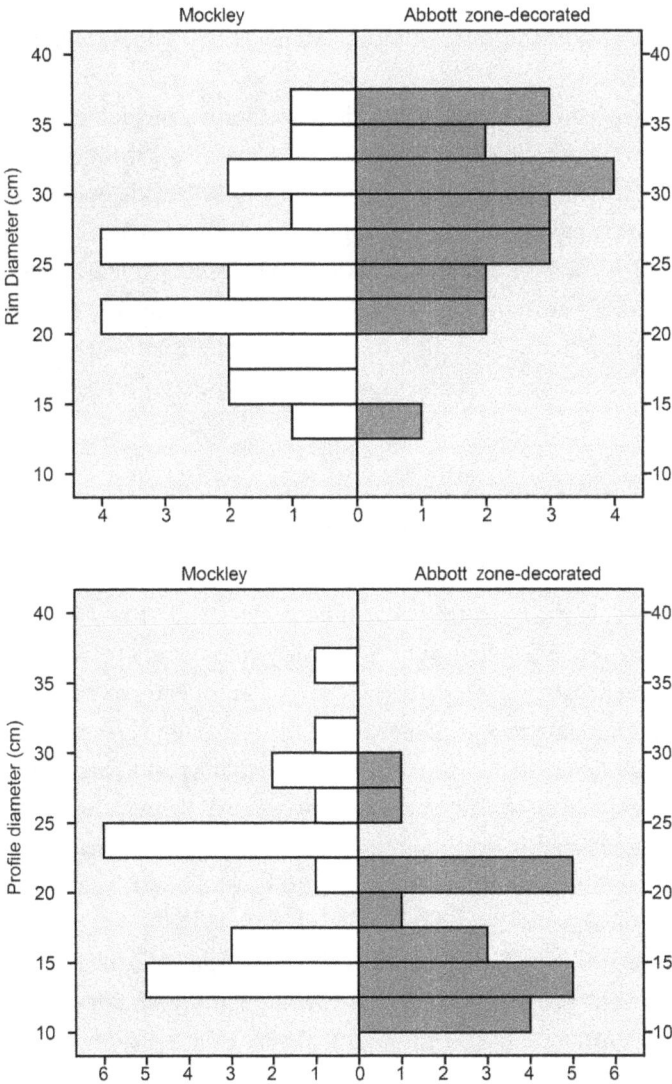

Figure 4.12. Histograms of rim diameters (*top*) and profile diameters (*bottom*) of Mockley and Abbott zone-decorated ceramics from the Maycock's Point site.

diameter, Abbott zone-decorated rim openings peak at slightly larger sizes just over 30 cm in diameter. Profile curvature measurements differed as well. The Abbott zone-decorated profiles peaked at the lower range of values, suggesting more sharply curving vessels. Several Mockley sherds also fell into the lower end of the profile curvature values, though once again the Mockley sherds displayed a wider range of measurements, including a second peak at about 23 cm. While subtle, these differences in sherd measurements point toward contrasts in Mockley and Abbott zone-decorated vessel forms.[83]

Mockley vessels had a wider array of sizes and forms, including those that approximate cylindrical jars and relatively shallow bowls while Abbott zone-decorated vessels were typically shallow bowls with wide openings. This pattern offers some support for the notion that Abbott zone-decorated ceramics were used at Maycock's Point as serving vessels while Mockley pots fulfilled a wider array of purposes as a quotidian ware. The shapes of Abbott zone-decorated vessels from Maycock's Point are consistent with the hypothesis that the ware represented a special type used in seasonal feasting.

Population Movements and Language Shifts

The geographic region in which similar zone-decorated ceramics were produced—near the Atlantic coast from Virginia to Massachusetts—covers a wide swath of the area inhabited during the early colonial era by Eastern Algonquian speech communities. At the time of European contact, the Eastern Algonquian subgroup consisted of at least 17 languages spoken from coastal Canada to the North Carolina Outer Banks and within adjacent inland areas. Given this distribution, the seasonal aggregations and feasting events associated with Abbott zone-decorated ceramics may have included Algonquian-speaking communities in coastal areas from New England to the Chesapeake.[84]

Such evidence of widely shared practices along the Atlantic coast has led scholars to seek evidence for the arrival of Algonquian speech communities in the Middle Atlantic region through a history of population movements and language shifts (i.e., the adoption of a new language) within already resident communities.[85] Researchers have attempted to link the linguistic and archaeological evidence associated with this process, leading some to the view that the introduction of shell-tempered Mockley ceramics and related changes in subsistence, settlement, and community organization signaled the earliest arrival of Algonquian speakers, including those who would become the Powhatan.[86]

Such arguments may be placed in the context of a greater openness among archaeologists in recent years to consider population movement as critical to understanding precontact North America.[87] After a period of skepticism toward the notion that migration offers a compelling explanation of important developments in the precontact record, population movements have been reintroduced in archaeological explanations in a number of regions.[88] This effort has been bolstered in part by a greater willingness to consider Native communities' oral traditions that emphasize migrations from distant homelands.[89] In the Chesapeake, for example, the Nanticoke recounted stories during the colonial era of deep genealogical ties with the Lenape to the north and of migration to the Eastern Shore of the Chesapeake Bay.[90] The Conoy, in turn, reported that they arrived in the Potomac valley from the Eastern Shore after migrating across the bay 13 generations before 1638.[91]

A starting point for considering the deep histories of Algonquian speech communities in the Chesapeake is Leonard Bloomfield's comparison of Algonquian languages that led to his construction of Proto-Algonquian.[92] A proto-language is a hypothetical or reconstructed language from which a number of documented languages are believed to have descended. Building on this research, Frank Siebert postulated a Proto-Algonquian homeland in the Great Lakes region.[93] He identified terms for a set of animals common to several Algonquian languages, including seal, caribou, bison, and lake trout, all of which lived in this area. Ives Goddard later identified patterns in Algonquian vocabulary, phonology, and grammar pointing to a west-to-east "cline" (or graduated change), with the greatest time depth in the Algonquian languages to the west and the shallowest in the languages to the east.[94]

Linguists divide the resulting Algonquian languages into three separate groups: Plains Algonquian, Central Algonquian, and Eastern Algonquian. The Algonquian languages spoken in coastal Virginia and North Carolina represent the southeastern edges of the Eastern Algonquian group. During the early seventeenth century, Eastern Algonquian dialects stretched from the North Carolina Outer Banks to the Canadian Maritimes. The linguistic evidence suggests that Eastern Algonquian languages documented at contact were separated for a considerable time from the languages spoken in the Great Lakes region and on the Plains.[95] Based on patterning in vocabulary and grammar, Eastern Algonquian languages likely underwent a period of common development apart from the Algonquian dialects spoken to the west. According to Frank Siebert's model, an "Archaic Coastal" variant of Eastern Algonquian was ancestral to several Algonquian languages spoken along the eastern seaboard from the Chesapeake to New England, including Virginia Algonquian as well as Wampanoag, Narragansett, and Montauk.[96] The linguistic continuity of these languages was evidently interrupted by the arrival of an intrusive group of Eastern Algonquian speakers in the Middle Atlantic whose languages differed from the Archaic Coastal variant. The descendants of this intrusive Algonquian group included the Mahican on the Hudson and the Lenape of the Delaware River Valley. In this way, the linguistic evidence points toward a complicated and extended process of Algonquian language spread and population movement centuries before the colonial era. The movements of at least some of these Algonquian-speaking groups brought them into areas already occupied by established societies.

Drawing from these linguistic foundations, several researchers have tried with some success to link archaeological evidence to the spread of Algonquian speech communities from a Great Lakes homeland to the Atlantic seaboard and, eventually, into the Chesapeake.[97] Three efforts to corroborate the linguistic and archaeological evidence have yielded similar results, with each study citing the Middle Woodland period as the most likely interval when Algonquian speech communities first arrived in the Chesapeake. Al Luckenbach and his colleagues, for example, estimate that the Eastern Algonquian languages separated circa AD 200 based on a glottochronological comparison of seven of these languages.[98] Glottochronology is a method used to estimate the date of divergence for distinct, but related, languages based on the degree to which their basic vocabularies differ.[99] Applying methods similar to those used to identify a Proto-Algonquian homeland, Luckenbach and his colleagues found linguistic evidence for a Proto–*Eastern* Algonquian homeland within a large area that included central New York, northern New England, and the Canadian Maritimes.[100] Out of this northerly homeland, the authors postulate, Eastern Algonquian-speaking populations migrated through a process of "adaptive radiation" that brought coastal-oriented groups southward along the Atlantic seaboard's estuarine and riverine settings.[101] Luckenbach and his colleagues suggest possible links between the expansion of Algonquian speech communities and a series of archaeological phases. These end with the makers of Mockley ceramics and Fox Creek projectile points, fishing-oriented communities that made the passage from the Eastern Shore into coastal Virginia and North Carolina.

Stuart Fiedel has offered a similar model of Algonquian expansion, though he arrives at a somewhat later range of dates for the separation of Eastern Algonquian languages. Fiedel's glottochronological calculations indicate that Eastern Algonquian languages spread along the Atlantic coast sometime between AD 200 and 900.[102] Based in part on the existence of Proto-Algonquian terms for ceramic pots, smoking pipes, bow and arrow, and earthworks—innovations that appear relatively late in the archaeological record—Fiedel has concluded that Algonquian speakers arrived in the Chesapeake during the latter half of the Middle Woodland period.[103] Revisiting these issues, J. Peter Denny has recently proposed links between Algonquian population movements and a range of archaeological phases in the Great Lakes, New England, and Middle Atlantic.[104] He concludes by noting that the most compelling evidence for Algonquian speech communities in the Chesapeake comes in the form of the cultural continuity apparent in the region from the initial appearance of Mockley-producing fishing communities through the Powhatan-affiliated towns of the early colonial era.

These archaeological studies reach similar conclusions, supporting a general model of Eastern Algonquian language spread in the Chesapeake between AD 200 and 900. Linguistic studies suggest that Eastern Algonquian speech communities had a complicated history of movement along the Atlantic seaboard during this interval. Even with this convergence of views regarding the early history of Algonquian speech communities in the Chesapeake, such efforts to link historical linguistics and archaeological evidence are greeted with skepticism in some quarters.[105] Critics point out that the method used to estimate the divergence of Eastern Algonquian languages, glottochronology, has been challenged by linguists who identify problems with the method's basic assumptions.[106] Those who still regard glottochronology as a useful heuristic often consider the method most effective when limited to a period of 500 to 2,500 years of linguistic history.[107]

Luckenbach and his colleagues' assessment of Eastern Algonquian languages estimate a period of divergence lasting approximately 2,200 years, fitting within this range.[108]

Even as the outlines of early Algonquian landscapes in the Chesapeake come into view, questions remain concerning the related historical processes. Archaeological patterns that appear to confirm the proposed historical linguistic sequence, including changes in material traditions, settlement patterns, and subsistence orientations, may come about through a number of historical or adaptive processes. How much of the spread of Eastern Algonquian languages was the product of migrations or of language shifts within indigenous communities also remains unclear. So does the size and nature of population movements: did small family groups simply expand their settlement rounds a short distance into new areas, or did entire communities establish base camps that anchored settlement rounds in new locations? Studies of similar language dispersals in other parts of the world have concluded that they resulted not only from migrations of specific groups (i.e., "demic diffusion") but also through intermarriage and language shifts driven by the expansion of trade networks, ceremonial regimes, and new subsistence modes.[109]

The historical and adaptive processes behind the spread of Algonquian languages across a vast area in North America likely involved any one of these processes at different points in time and geography. The spread of Algonquian speech communities clearly deserves more study, including localized analyses keyed to well-dated archaeological assemblages and specific historical models. No doubt the relevant developments varied considerably in areas as different as the Canadian Shield and the Atlantic Coastal Plain.

Nonetheless, the Middle Woodland evidence of estuarine-oriented subsistence practices alongside shell-tempered pottery in the coastal Middle Atlantic offers some indications of how Algonquian speech communities likely spread into the Chesapeake, starting circa AD 200. Rather than just being simple markers of identity, shell-tempered Mockley ceramics signaled the introduction of loosely bounded learning networks and social interaction across a range of communities in the region, likely including those with distinct linguistic traditions. Abbott zone-decorated ceramics point toward a material tradition shared even more widely, across a broad portion of the coastal Atlantic. These developments are recorded within places of forager-fisher aggregation along Indian Field Creek and at Maycock's Point. Other places in the Chesapeake, such as the Lake Powell sites introduced at the beginning of this chapter, document smaller gatherings that brought different communities of practice into contact. Such gatherings of diverse peoples heralded the introduction of a new mode of dwelling in the Chesapeake at the historical roots of the Algonquian landscape of Tsenacomacoh.

Chapter 5

The Coarse-Pounded Corn People

On a bright winter afternoon in 2004, my colleague Danielle Moretti-Langholtz and I crossed the Chickahominy River and drove anxiously from Williamsburg toward the Chickahominy Tribal Center. We were late for a meeting with the Chickahominy tribal chief Stephen Adkins and assistant chief Wayne Adkins to discuss the Chickahominy River Survey. Conducted by William and Mary archaeologists during the late 1960s and early 1970s, the survey identified over a hundred Native sites along the banks and bluffs of the Chickahominy River. More than simply an effort to find archaeological sites along the river, the project sought to identify and excavate prominent towns of the Chickahominy Indians dating to the early colonial era. At a time when almost no research was aimed at Native archaeology in the Chesapeake, William and Mary professors Norm Barka and Ben McCary conducted an ambitious, comparative study of settlements across the 87-mile-long (140 km) river.[1] Perhaps most remarkable was their decision to move beyond a single-site focus and toward a regional perspective on the Chickahominy past. Even with support from the National Science Foundation, though, professors Barka and McCary struggled to bring the project to completion with a report of its results or an interpretation of their significance.

As I drove west, Danielle worried that we might collide with one of the deer wandering across Lott Cary road in the setting sun. My anxiety centered on the reception the tribal leaders were likely to give us. Chief Adkins had been tight-lipped on the phone, but we gathered that he knew little about the survey. Conducted at a time when archaeological ethics prioritized protection of scholars' intellectual property above all else, the survey did not include consultation with communities descended from those studied by the researchers. Like many projects of its day, the Chickahominy River Survey lacked an effort to reach the public at all. Its goals centered on using the *Map of Virginia* and the Zuñiga Chart to locate the sites of early-seventeenth-century Chickahominy towns. Of particular interest to the researchers were the human remains uncovered at several sites. The archaeologists disinterred more than a hundred individuals over the course of the survey, most from ossuaries—collective burial pits containing bundles of disarticulated human remains. Along with our departmental colleague, bioarchaeologist Michael Blakey, Danielle and I sought to bring the Chickahominy River Survey results to light, starting by informing the descendant community of the collection.

The survey represented both considerable research potential and an ethical dilemma. While the legal status of the human remains in the collection remained somewhat murky, archaeological ethics and the field's best practices had changed dramatically in the years since the survey commenced. As a tribe formally acknowledged by the Commonwealth of Virginia but not by the federal government, the Chickahominy lack formal "standing" as American Indians under the National Historic Preservation Act and the Native American Graves Protection and Repatriation Act. During the colonial and postcolonial eras, the Chickahominy and other American Indians in the Chesapeake experienced a history of violent removal from ancestral towns, coordinated resistance to English encroachment, community fragmentation, racial segregation, tribal reconfiguration, and public reemergence.[2] The seventeenth-century history of *English* colonization, though, meant that the tribes in the region never signed a treaty with the United States government recognizing their status as American Indians.

The Chickahominy tribal leaders listened carefully as Danielle and I described the survey. We suggested that, though the artifacts and burials had gone unstudied for decades, there was still considerable potential to learn from the past by inventorying the collection and by analyzing the materials. We added that the right way to do so—in fact the only way to do so in keeping with the practices of twenty-first-century archaeology—would be to study the collection with the consent of the tribe and in partnership with tribal members. Chief Adkins spoke first and thanked us for coming to him with information about the collection. He conveyed a deep concern for ancestors stored so quietly at the college for so long. Assistant Chief Wayne Adkins, an engineer by training, followed with detailed questions regarding the best methods to study the collection and the potential significance of any resulting research. The two men promised to consult with the Chickahominy Tribal Council regarding next steps.

The tribal council did consent to the study, requesting a visit with their ancestors for a ceremony before any work began. While some council members clearly felt uneasy with the proposition that the human remains would be disturbed by an inventory, all felt obligated to listen to what their ancestors might have to tell them about the past. Wayne Adkins agreed to serve as a tribal liaison and an advisor on our research protocols.

The resulting partnership has yielded substantial results.[3] While the Chickahominy River Survey was initially keyed to *English* colonial maps representing Chickahominy towns circa AD 1607, the archaeological evidence records a deeper history of a *Native* landscape from the early centuries AD through the seventeenth century. The Chickahominy River is the most extensive stream on the James-York peninsula, and the Chickahominy were among the most powerful and populous Algonquian-speaking groups in the Chesapeake. In fact, most of the deposits, features, and artifacts from the survey date to the Middle Woodland (500 BC–AD 900) and Late Woodland (AD 900–1500) centuries, prior to the colonial era. The most noteworthy result of the survey is thus its documentation of a series of Native settlements during a period when mobile forager-fishers became town-based horticulturalists. During these centuries social networks coalesced across the region at different scales, eventually giving rise to the Powhatan chiefdom and the Chickahominy, two of the most formidable Algonquian polities in the early colonial Chesapeake.

As a regional study keyed to settlements along an entire drainage, the Chickahominy River Survey produced evidence of spatial practices on a riverine scale, including stratified deposits, collective burial grounds, residential towns, a palisaded compound, and a site with several massive pits containing the remains of large-scale meals. The bone chemistry of the human skeletal remains chronicles a shift from the estuarine-oriented subsistence of forager-fishers to maize-based horticulture, a historical process that reshaped the ways people moved across and dwelled within this riverine landscape. The documentary evidence of the Chickahominy Indians with which to compare these results is limited, since most colonial chroniclers focused their gaze on Wahunsenacawh and the Powhatan chiefdom. Still, there are hints in the early records that the Chickahominy, with 16 towns governed by a council of eight "great men," retained forms of Virginia Algonquian social organization and political mobilization distinct from those of the Powhatan chiefdom.[4] Even as they emphasized their distinctiveness and independence in their encounters with English colonists, though, the Chickahominy shared in subsistence practices, settlement forms, trading networks, and political alliances across the broader Virginia Algonquian world. In fact, the cultural practices of the "Coarse-Pounded Corn People"—particularly their material culture and mortuary regime—circulated widely beyond the river drainage.

Chickahominy Coalescence

How, then, did the Chickahominy come to be such a prominent, independent polity alongside the powerful, expansionary Powhatan chiefdom? In short, what led to the coalescence and persistence of the Chickahominy? The following chapter develops the thesis that Native residents in the drainage came together as the Chickahominy through a historical process of placemaking that created and sustained social relationships between residents in the drainage. The archaeological record indicates that this process began centuries prior to Jamestown's settlement, leaving its mark on the riverine landscape in a meshwork of connected places.

Such arguments may be understood in terms of archaeologists' growing interest in the emergence of new social identities, sometimes framed in terms of "ethnogenesis."[5] Ethnogenesis, the "birthing of new cultural identities," involves the emergence of new social collectives or ethnic identities through community coalescence.[6] In an early definition of ethnic identity, Max Weber emphasized notions of group affinity based on beliefs of shared ancestry drawn from "similarities of physical type or of customs or both" or "of memories of colonization and migration."[7] For a group to have an ethnic identity, this belief in group affinity must "be important for the propagation of group formation."[8] Much early academic treatment of ethnic identities emphasized a notion of ethnicity as a primordial set of traits attached to each nation.[9]

In contrast, more recent scholarly approaches to social identities start with skepticism toward such narratives of primordial essences.[10] Instead, social affiliations are understood as multiple, fluid, and contested.[11] Notions of group affiliation in the precolonial era likely hinged on factors quite different than those contributing to modern notions of ethnicity. Rather than assuming that a social identity exists as a fixed essence of an isolated, unchanging, and homogeneous "people," recent studies often emphasize dynamic processes of interaction—exchange, intermarriage, diaspora, and language shift—that introduce new social links and shared cultural practices.[12] In these approaches, social affiliations emerge as instrumental cultural tools that people create and alter through histories of group interaction.[13]

Drawing from such "instrumental" and "interactionist" approaches, a series of studies have explored the construction of new social collectives as a response to the violent disruption wrought by European colonial encroachment and the cultural nationalism of the postcolonial era.[14] Building on William Sturtevant's classic study of the Seminole tribe and its coalescence out of refugee Creek communities, scholars have traced histories shaped by creolization, transculturation, and hybridity that introduced new groups during the colonial era.[15] European colonial expansion unleashed a history of disease, demographic collapse, forced relocation, enslavement, ethnic soldiering, and genocide in the "shatter zone" of American frontier settings.[16] At times these processes prompted the creation of new groups, understood variously as tribes, confederacies, maroons, or ethnicities, which struggled to create enduring communities in places of radical and violent change.[17]

Such histories, informed by documentary sources from colonial archives, offer rich accounts of the ways social identities were created, contextualized, and manipulated. Colonial-era sources likewise document the salience of the Chickahominy in the colonial Chesapeake, though the accounts suggest that the Chickahominy coalesced as a network of politically and militarily unified towns *before* Europeans settled in the region. Colonial expansion, violent conflict, and a Chickahominy role as ethnic soldiers did indeed have an impact on the Chesapeake. It was initially the Powhatan chiefdom, though, that represented the imperial threat. Documentary references from Jamestown colonists point toward the existence of a potent Chickahominy political organization during the sixteenth century, when residents in the drainage resisted Wahunsenacawh's expansionary strategies.

Even earlier than this, communities on the Chickahominy developed creative responses to the economic and ecological niches available to them in the drainage by incorporating new cultural practices between AD 500 and 1300. Evidence discussed in detail below indicates that residents of the Chickahominy drainage began to bury their dead in ossuaries circa AD 500, centuries before communities across the coastal Chesapeake participated in similar collective burial rituals. The residents of settlements along the Chickahominy adopted other practices, including those linked to shell-tempered pottery, maize-based horticulture, and dispersed town settlements, which also spread widely across the Virginia Algonquian world. During the centuries after adopting ossuary burial, the residents of the Chickahominy River valley constructed places for multicommunity gatherings upstream of and downstream from the horticultural towns in the central portion of the drainage. This riverine landscape included burial grounds in the drainage's marshy interior. The lower portion of the river valley was marked by a fortified compound and a gathering place for large feasts. The social relationships formed within these prominent places shaped Chickahominy coalescence in the years prior to Jamestown.

The Chickahominy during the Early Colonial Era

By the early colonial era, the "Coarse-pounded Corn People" distinguished themselves from the Virginia Algonquian communities within the Powhatan chiefdom as a people ruled by priests, and not by chiefs or weroances. William Strachey wrote that the Chickahominy were a

> Warlick and free people, albeit that pay certayne dutyes to Powhatan, and for Copper wil be waged to serve and help him in his warrs, yet they will not admitt of any werowances from him to governe over them, but suffer themselves to be regulated and guided by their priests, with the assistance of their elders, whome they call Cawcawwasoughs, and they may make 300 men.[18]

The Chickahominy emerge from such colonial references as both independent from and enmeshed within the political and economic structures of the Powhatan chiefdom. Periodically allying themselves as ethnic soldiers for the Powhatan, the Chickahominy played a role common in other "tribal zones" at the violent edges of empires.[19] At times European colonial expansion triggered intensive indigenous warfare, though for the Chicka-hominy it was an expanding Powhatan chiefdom that brought Chickahom-iny warriors to the field during the century prior to English colonization.

Unlike other Algonquian groups led by a weroance and under Wahun-senacawh's authority by 1607, governance within Chickahominy communi-ties involved priests, and a council of elders and headmen referred to as manguy or mangoap, literally "great men."[20] This arrangement may repre-sent the survival of an older form of Algonquian social organization that preceded the appearance of chiefly structures and the rise of Wahunsena-cawh's paramountcy in Tidewater Virginia. Buck Woodard and Danielle Moretti-Langholtz have evaluated the evidence of Chickahominy social organization and structures of decision making to reach this conclusion.[21] Pointing to the record of 16 towns represented by eight manguy, Woodard and Moretti-Langholtz suggested that a system of eight clans and two moi-eties framed social relations among the Chickahominy.

The Zuñiga Chart depicts the Chickahominy drainage with 16 towns lining the floodplain terraces, neck lands, and islands elevated above the drainage's extensive wetland marshes. The Zuñiga Chart hints at the dis-persed nature of Chickahominy settlements by depicting dots, presumably houses, scattered along the river in clusters near the named towns. Smith visited Chickahominy settlements on several occasions to explore the re-gion and to trade for corn. He offered brief descriptions of Manosquosick (maan-uh-SKWOH-sihk) and Moysonec (MOI-suh-nehk), large towns in the central portion of the drainage, whose residents traded extensively with the English.[22] Manosquosick was reportedly situated a quarter mile from the river on an elevated terrace. The town included 30 to 40 houses over-looking a floodplain with several freshwater springs. An adjacent marsh measuring about five miles in diameter attracted fish and migratory birds in numbers that impressed Smith. Further upstream, Moysonec stretched across a neck of land formed by a meander in the river with a four-mile circumference. Houses and residential spaces in this central portion of the drainage were not limited to the concentrated areas of settlement that comprised named towns but were also scattered along elevated terraces near the river. Below these terraces, the Chickahominy raised maize with squash and beans in garden plots along the floodplain.

Even as the Chickahominy shared cultural practices with the broader world of Virginia Algonquians, their independence from the Powhatan

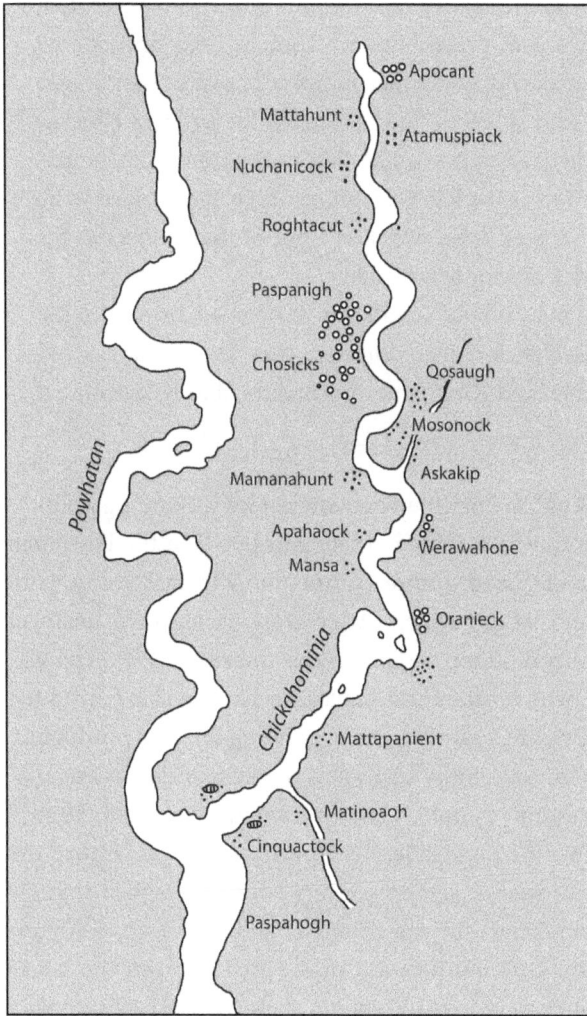

Figure 5.1. Zuñiga Chart's depiction of the Chickahominy drainage. Adapted from Brown 1890:184.

chiefdom was pivotal in their recorded history. The Chickahominy remained separate from the Powhatan chiefdom despite their home near
the center of the Powhatan domain on the York and James Rivers. Chickahominy political autonomy did not last, however. Wahunsenacawh and the
English made peace following the marriage of Powhatan's daughter Pocahontas to colonist John Rolfe in 1614. As Smith reported, the Chickahominy followed suit the same year, signing a treaty with Thomas Dale.

These people, so soone as they heard of our peace with Powhatan, sent two messengers with presents to Sir Thomas Dale, and offered him their service, excusing all former injuries, hereafter they would ever be King James his subjects, and relinquish the name of Chickahamania, to be called Tassautessus, as they call us, and Sir Thomas Dale there Governour, as the Kings Deputie; onely they desired to be governed by their owne Lawes, which is eight of their Elders as his substitutes. This offer he kindly accepted. . . .

The eight chiefe men should see all this performed, or receive the punishment themselves: for their diligence they should have a red coat, a copper chaine, and King James his picture, and be accounted his Noblemen.[23]

The arrival of the English amplified and altered long-standing political dynamics in the region, which included tensions between the Powhatan chiefdom, with its centralized authority, and the Chickahominy, with their leadership council of great men. After Wahunsenacawh's death in 1618, the Chickahominy fell increasingly under the sway of Opechancanough, Wahunsenacawh's brother and successor. During this period the rising population of English colonists and expanding tobacco production led to the seizure of Chickahominy lands and the violent deaths and displacement of Chickahominy people.[24] The Chickahominy joined the 1622 and 1644 revolts against the English led by Opechancanough. In 1646 the Powhatan leader Necotowance signed a treaty with the English that established separate homelands for the colonists and for Virginia Algonquians, pushing Native communities out of the area between the James and the York. The Chickahominy subsequently moved to the Pamunkey Neck between the Mattaponi and Pamunkey Rivers, allying with the Pamunkey.

The next 150 years of Chickahominy history are poorly documented, with the Chickahominy and other Virginia Indian communities disappearing into the rural countryside in areas beyond the reach of colonists and settlers.[25] During the nineteenth century, families who retained a connection to the Chickahominy past began to return to their ancestral lands along the river.[26] Their descendants remain in the region today, particularly on the west side of the Chickahominy River in Charles City County, where the Chickahominy Tribe has over 750 members, and in New Kent County, where the Eastern Division of the Chickahominy Tribe has about 130 members.

Changing Settlement Forms on the Chickahominy: Moysonec

After identifying 104 Native sites along the river, the archaeologists with the Chickahominy River Survey focused their excavations on seven locations. These sites produced over a hundred pit features, 33 radiocarbon dates, and seven ossuary burial grounds.[27] The Moysonec site and the related Moysonec Field F site had the widest date range of any settlement in the drainage, and together they help frame key changes in the Chickahominy cultural landscape. Likely part of a single, dispersed settlement, the two sites match the location of the Chickahominy town with the same name described in Smith's accounts. Circa 1607 Moysonec was part of a core area of Chickahominy residential towns near the center of the drainage, and the area saw a long sequence of settlement stretching back to at least 500 BC. Stratified deposits at the site begin during the centuries from 500 BC to AD 200 and contain relatively few artifacts and no pit features. When shell-tempered, Mockley ceramics first appear at the site circa AD 200, they occur in small numbers amidst larger frequencies of pebble- and crushed-lithic-tempered pottery. Also dating to this interval were several hearth features lined with fire-cracked rocks and filled with burned oyster shells. The roasted oysters were probably brought to the site from downstream. Though tidal, the Chickahominy River contains relatively low salinity levels—well below the threshold that supports oysters.

These developments along the Chickahominy River parallel those seen at the Kiskiak site, which we have interpreted as evidence of distinct forager-fisher communities coming into contact. As discussed in chapter 4, the presence of pottery from multiple ceramic traditions in the same deposits may represent the continued existence of distinct communities of practice in the area, with the artifact patterning a by-product of intercommunity gatherings, trading, and intermarriage.

A sharply different pattern appears at Moysonec between AD 1300 and 1600 in deposits that represent the first well-defined middens at the site. These deposits contain dense charcoal concentrations and considerably more features and artifacts than were present in the deeper levels, pointing toward the establishment of a larger and more permanent settlement.

Table 5.1. Radiocarbon dates, Chickahominy River survey

Site	Lab Code	Context	Conventional Age (bp)	Calibrated Dates		
				2-sigma Low	Median Probability	2-sigma High
Moysonec Field F	Beta-203621	Feature 22	1480 ±60	AD 430	AD 580	AD 660
	GX-4173	Feature 30	915 ±130	AD 780	AD 1110	AD 1380
	Beta-203619	Feature 6	520 ±60	AD 1300	AD 1410	AD 1470
Wilcox Neck	Beta-284952	Ossuary 1A	1540 ±40	AD 430	AD 510	AD 600
	Beta-287736	Ossuary 1B	1530 ±40	AD 430	AD 530	AD 610
	Beta-284953	Ossuary 2A	1440 ±40	AD 550	AD 610	AD 660
	Beta-287737	Ossuary 2B	590 ±40	AD 1300	AD 1350	AD 1420
Clark's Old Neck	Beta-287741	Burial 3	1330 ±40	AD 650	AD 690	AD 770
	Beta-203622	Feature 18E2	1020 ±40	AD 900	AD 1010	AD 1150
	Beta-203615	Feature 67D2	930 ±40	AD 1020	AD 1100	AD 1210
	Beta-203614	Feature 25J2	890 ±40	AD 1040	AD 1140	AD 1220
	GX-1761	Feature 18C2	840 ±110	AD 990	AD 1170	AD 1390
	GX-1765/1766	Feature 67A2	740 ±70	AD 1160	AD 1260	AD 1400
	Beta-289592	Burial 2	690 ±30	AD 1270	AD 1290	AD 1390

Site	Lab number	Context	Radiocarbon age			
Edgehill	GX-1537	Feature 9N3	1120 ±110	AD 670	AD 900	AD 1150
	Beta-284947	Ossuary 4A	1030 ±40	AD 900	AD 1000	AD 1150
	Beta-284951	Ossuary 5A	980 ±40	AD 990	AD 1080	AD 1160
	Beta-203623	Feature 9U3	860 ±40	AD 1040	AD 1180	AD 1260
	Beta-287733	Ossuary 3B	550 ±40	AD 1300	AD 1390	AD 1480
	GX-1536	Feature 6C3	475 ±55	AD 1320	AD 1450	AD 1620
	Beta-284949	Ossuary 2A	350 ±40	AD 1460	AD 1550	AD 1640
	Beta-284948	Ossuary 1A	290 ±40	AD 1480	AD 1570	AD 1800
Cypress Banks	GX-1532	Feature 23W3	1090 ±140	AD 670	AD 930	AD 1210
	GX-1534	Feature 19H3	890 ±105	AD 900	AD 1130	AD 1290
Moysonec	Beta-203620	Feature 1	310 ±60	AD 1450	AD 1570	AD 1800
Buck Farm	GX-1759	Trench 8B1	695 ±105	AD 1050	AD 1300	AD 1440
	GX-1758	Trench 8A4	690 ±90	AD 1170	AD 1300	AD 1420
	GX-1756	Trench 6R2	550 ±85	AD 1270	AD 1380	AD 1620
	Beta-203616	Trench 7N5	390 ±40	AD 1440	AD 1500	AD 1630
	Beta-287738	Burial 10	390 ±40	AD 1440	AD 1500	AD 1630
	GX-1757	Feature 6T3	360 ±90	AD 1410	AD 1550	AD 1950
	GX-2262	Trench 8B3	265 ±80	AD 1450	AD 1640	AD 1950
	Beta-249895	Pig burial	110 ±40	AD 1680	AD 1830	AD 1950

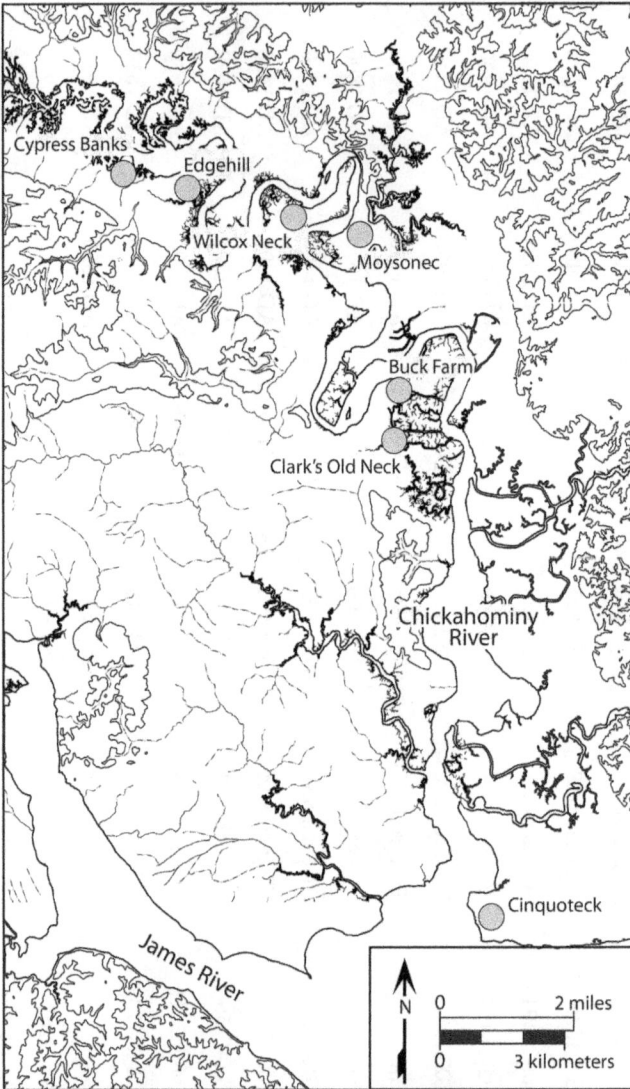

Figure 5.2. Chickahominy River drainage. Adapted from USGS 7.5-minute series quadrangles.

The deposits occur in concentrated pockets across the site, corresponding to scattered houses and related sheet middens. These domestic spaces record the establishment of a dispersed town along the banks of the Chickahominy River. Such a pattern continued into the early seventeenth century, when John Smith described the location.

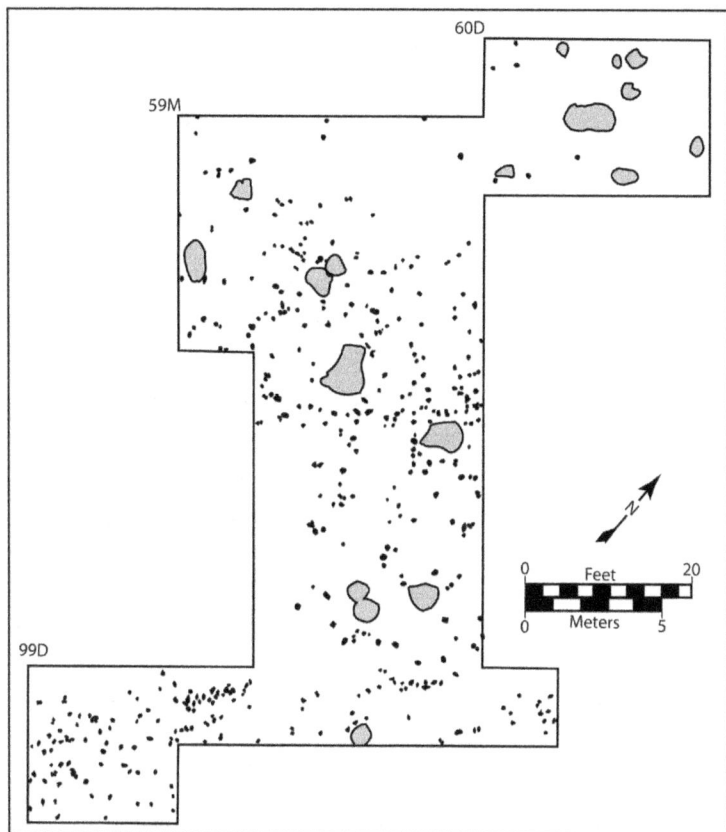

Figure 5.3. Excavation block at the Moysonec Field F site, with post-mold stains (black) and pit features (gray). A structure footprint is suggested by the elliptical post-mold pattern near the center of the block.

Communal Burial Practices on the Chickahominy: Wilcox Neck and Edgehill

The Chickahominy River Survey uncovered human skeletal remains within the Wilcox Neck, Edgehill, and Clark's Old Neck sites.[28] These sites included seven communal ossuaries and a burial containing two individuals who died several centuries apart. The two ossuaries at the Wilcox Neck site have produced some of the earliest dates for collective mortuary practices in the Chesapeake region. Ossuaries are shallow burial pits that hold the remains of multiple individuals, from as few as four to over 600. The remains in Chesapeake ossuaries are often disarticulated bundles of bone that result from a two-stage ritual process. Similar "secondary" burial practices were adopted widely across the Chesapeake after AD 1200 in the form of ossuaries in the coastal region and burial mounds in the interior.[29] A number of researchers have considered the ossuaries and mound burial practices of Native societies in the Chesapeake, illuminating demographic patterns, dietary practices, health trends, and the symbolic and political dimensions of mortuary rituals.[30]

Ossuary burial in the coastal Chesapeake generally incorporated deposits of human remains after an initial preparation of the deceased. Few if any objects accompanied ossuary burial features in the region. Ossuaries in the Chesapeake generally went unnoticed or unmentioned in the early colonial documentary record. Colonist Henry Spelman's brief reference to mortuary practices indicates that the Patawomeck placed the bodies of the deceased three to four yards above the ground on scaffolds, wrapped in a mat.[31] During the initial mortuary ceremony, relatives assembled and threw shell beads. A feast, singing, and dancing followed. Once the bodies decomposed, families collected the bones, wrapped them in mats, and hung them within houses.

With only limited references to burial practices in the colonial-era accounts from the Chesapeake, scholars have turned instead to descriptions of the Huron Feast of the Dead, events that are well documented in the *Jesuit Relations*.[32] The classic description of this ceremony comes from Father Jean de Brébeuf and dates to 1636.[33] The Huron, Iroquoian-speakers living near Lake Ontario, held periodic Feasts of the Dead, when families disinterred the remains of relatives and carried them to a collective burial ground. After they were removed from their initial burial location, bones were cleaned, wrapped in a robe, and brought to the place of the feast. The ceremony that followed gathered residents from several settlements and centered on feasting and gift giving. The bone bundles, accompanied by offerings, were initially suspended on scaffolds above a large pit before they were buried. Neighboring Algonquian speakers in the same region performed similar feasts of the dead, including seventeenth-century events sponsored by the Nipissing and by the Ottawa.[34] The Nipissing event incorporated families from several communities, including both Algonquian and Iroquoian speakers. The Ottawa event concluded with the ritual sacrifice of dogs. Both ceremonies involved feasting, gift giving, and the renewal of alliances among neighboring communities.

At the Wilcox Neck site on the Chickahominy River, the skeletal remains within Ossuary 1 were arranged in a roughly circular shape measuring approximately eight feet (2.4 meters) in diameter. The feature contained at least 29 individuals, the largest number of human remains from any burial feature identified on the Chickahominy. Most of the skeletal remains were arranged in a series of tight concentrations or bundles of human bone clustered around a large and intense fire marked by a charcoal-rich stain and fire-cracked rock at the feature's center. A few of the bone bundles included partially articulated remains, though the majority of bone elements were disarticulated. Most of the bundles included the remains of two or three individuals. Heavy charcoal flecking was scattered beneath the remains closest to the center of the ossuary, and bones located near the heat source

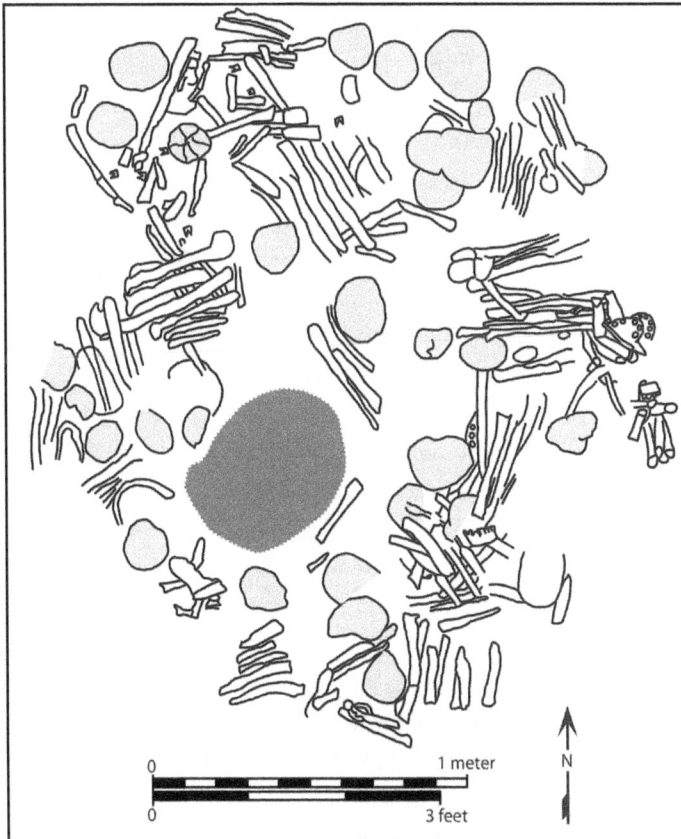

Figure 5.4. Ossuary 1, Wilcox Neck site.

were charred black. Along the eastern periphery of the pit, burned bone fragments represent the remains of at least one cremation.

The spatial arrangement of Ossuary 1 suggests that the final step in the mortuary process was centered on a large fire, around which ritual participants placed bundled remains. The consistent practice of bundling the remains and arranging them with reference to the large fire feature suggests that the ossuary was probably used only once. Ossuary 1 included the remains of individuals from both sexes and all age categories.

Located 160 feet (50 meters) east of Ossuary 1, Ossuary 2 measured 10 feet (3 meters) in diameter and contained the remains of at least 16 individuals. A discrete concentration of charcoal in the southern area of the ossuary records the presence of a fire feature similar to the one identified within Ossuary 1. As with Ossuary 1, it appears that Ossuary 2 was open to all segments of society.

Radiocarbon dates from Wilcox Neck indicate that ossuaries were in use along the Chickahominy River from at least the sixth and seventh centuries AD.[35] Ceramics recovered from the feature fill included both shell-tempered Mockley ceramics and sand- and lithic-tempered Varina ceramics. These are some of the earliest dates for ossuary burial in the Chesapeake and across the broader Middle Atlantic region. Similar ossuaries at the Edgehill site a short distance upstream on the Chickahominy produced radiocarbon dates from the tenth through the seventeenth century AD, indicating that collective burial practices represented an enduring tradition on the Chickahominy. Ceramics associated with these later sites included only the shell-tempered Mockley and Townsend wares.

The ossuaries at Wilcox Neck document collective burial practices that began during the same century, when shell-tempered Mockley ceramics became more prevalent than sand- and lithic-tempered Varina pottery in the Chickahominy drainage. Residents of the Chickahominy drainage began burying their dead in ossuaries at the same time that new social networks, marked by the Mockley ceramic tradition, appeared in the archaeological record. Potters in the Chickahominy and across much of the broader Chesapeake began to participate in a more uniform ceramic tradition and, quite likely, a more open and fluid community of practice. After AD 500, potters across the coastal Chesapeake and in parts of the Delaware Valley and Albemarle Sound regions also began to produce shell-tempered pottery (i.e., Mockley ware) with uniform cordage patterns (S-twists) as

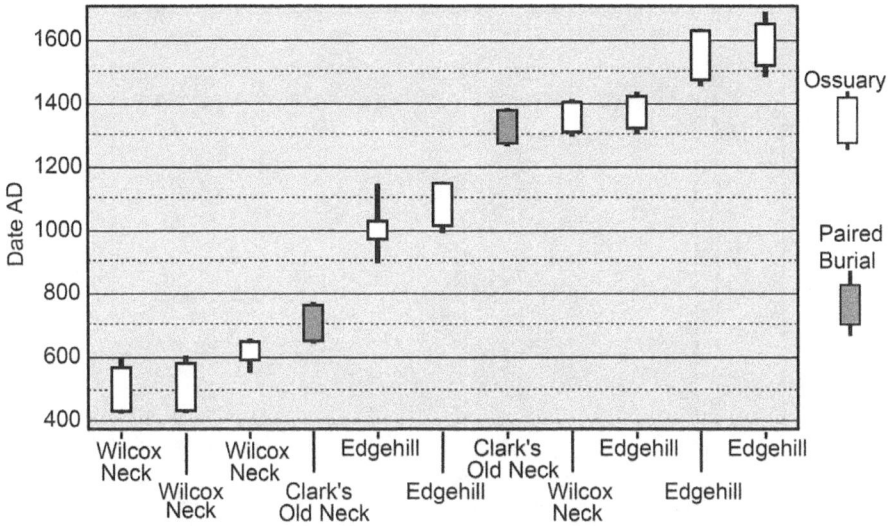

Figure 5.5. Calibrated radiocarbon dates from ossuaries and paired burials on the Chickahominy River, one-sigma range (box) and two-sigma range (lines).

lithic- and sand-tempered ceramics receded from view across much of the region. The gatherings for ossuary burial at Wilcox Neck coincided with the beginnings of this development.

Located approximately two miles (3.2 kilometers) upstream from Wilcox Neck, the Edgehill site included at least 78 individuals buried in five small ossuaries similar to those uncovered at Wilcox Neck. The Edgehill site traces the continuity of secondary burial practices on the Chickahaminy through the early colonial era. The ossuaries at Edgehill contained from 8 to 28 individuals and returned radiocarbon dates from AD 1000 through 1600. Each of the ossuaries was constructed by digging an elliptical pit measuring 2–3 meters in length and 1–2 meters in width, with the long axis oriented northwest to southeast. Two of the five ossuary pits (Ossuary 1 and Ossuary 2) included evidence of a central fire prepared before the remains were placed in the pit. The pit orientations and shapes were similar to ossuaries excavated at other sites across the Chesapeake region. The number of individuals interred within the Chickahominy ossuaries was similar to those from other drainages, with the notable exception of ossuaries along the Potomac River.[36] Like those uncovered at the Wilcox Neck site, the Edgehill ossuaries appear to represent ceremonial events that took

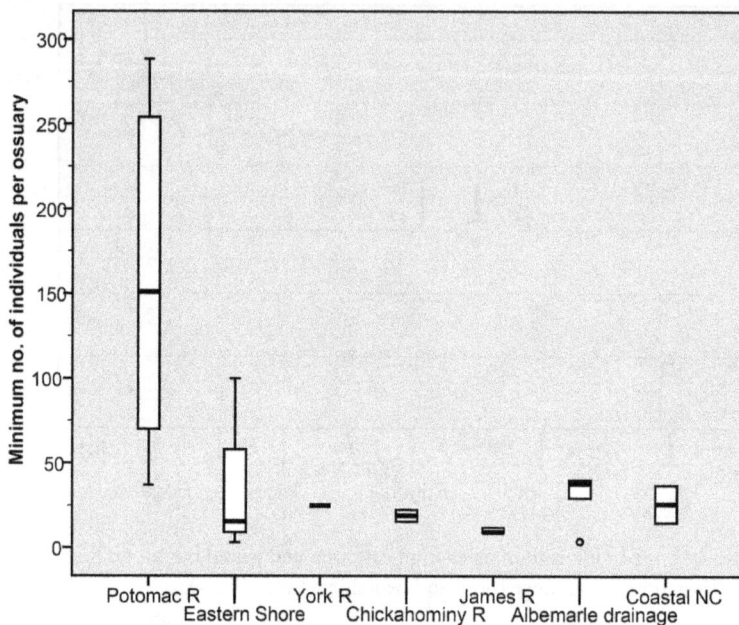

Figure 5.6. Boxplot of minimum number of individuals interred within ossuaries in coastal Maryland, Virginia, and North Carolina. Data from Blick 2000, Curry 1999, and Gallivan et al. 2009.

place over a short period of time. Most of the remains were not articulated prior to burial. Within three of the ossuaries, the crania were arranged in a circular pattern along the edges of the pit.

With the exception of Ossuary 5, no objects were associated with the human remains at Edgehill. Scattered across Ossuary 5 were five shell beads made from columella, the central axis of large univalves. A concentration of faunal remains within this ossuary included deer, catfish, raccoon, and turtle shell. The cluster of animal bones within this feature may represent the vestiges of a meal that was part of the mortuary ceremony. The disarticulated remains of a dog were also buried immediately adjacent to Ossuary 5, suggesting a close association with the ossuary interment.

The Edgehill ossuaries provide evidence of mortuary practices during a period when Algonquian communities in the Chesapeake began to establish large, permanent towns in the central portion of the drainage. Like the earlier Wilcox Neck ossuaries, these burial grounds were located in the western interior of the Chickahominy drainage. Each of the ossuaries contained skeletal remains of both sexes. With the exception of infants, whose remains typically do not preserve well in the archaeological record, all age classes are present in the Edgehill ossuaries. The Edgehill ossuaries represent the final step in a multistage mortuary process that was apparently open to all sectors of the community. Similar to other ossuaries in the region, the Edgehill features were likely the focus of periodic ceremonies that incorporated the remains of those who had died since an earlier ceremony. One of the ossuaries at the Edgehill site includes evidence that feasting and the separate burial of a dog's remains played a role in the mortuary ceremony there.

As communal burial features spanning the stretch of time between AD 500 and 1600, the ossuaries at Wilcox Neck and Edgehill provide evidence of remarkable continuity in mortuary ceremony along the Chickahominy River. Ossuaries along the Chickahominy record the interment of ancestors in much the same way over many generations. Rather than serving as prominent territorial markers or celebrations of renowned individuals, the ossuaries speak to persistent ritual practices and enduring connections to place.

The ossuary inventories also provide evidence of changes in the social

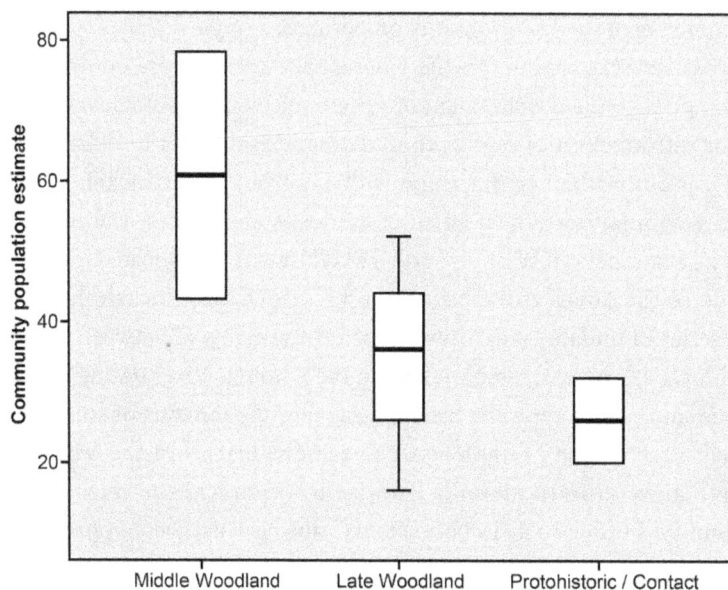

Figure 5.7. Estimated population of community contributing to ossuaries on the Chickahominy River.

scale of mortuary ceremonies held in the Chickahominy drainage. As demonstrated in a study of Potomac River ossuaries, the population from which different ossuaries drew deceased individuals may be inferred through the calculation of a mortality rate and the length of time represented by each ossuary.[37] Ethnohistorical references to the Feast of the Dead in the Great Lakes region suggest intervals of eight to twelve years between secondary interment events.[38] Applying an estimated ten-year interval between ceremonies to the Chickahominy ossuaries results in population estimates ranging from 60 early in the sequence to less than half that value by the colonial era.

The overall pattern suggests that the size of the groups contributing to the ossuaries at Wilcox Neck and Edgehill was relatively small and declined through time. While other archaeological data sets from the region record rising population levels across the region, particularly between AD 1300 and 1600, it appears that mortuary rituals associated with ossuaries on the Chickahominy incorporated a limited scope of individuals. This scope evidently narrowed further from the eleventh through the seventeenth century. During a period when populations rose in the Chickahominy drainage and community sizes increased, the bioarchaeological evidence suggests, mortuary rituals drew from an increasingly limited social sphere on the Chickahominy. The numbers point toward a shift from multicommunal rituals to those centered on a single community or, perhaps, a single lineage.

Since ossuary excavations in the Chesapeake region were commonly conducted prior to the development of systematic bioarchaeological methods or the introduction of radiocarbon dating, it is difficult to determine with any certainty whether this trend is distinctive to the Chickahominy drainage. A similar pattern of small ossuaries is apparent at the nearby Quiyoughcohannock (KWEE-aw-cuh-HAHN-awk) site located on the south side of the James and close to the mouth of the Chickahominy.[39] There, a series of undated ossuaries contain the remains of between 4 and 20 individuals. In contrast, ossuaries along the Potomac River dating to the Late Woodland period typically brought together the remains of 50 to 250 individuals and, in one example, over 600 individuals.[40] In the Virginia Piedmont, above-ground mounds likewise incorporated the remains of several hundred individuals in "bone beds" during what were apparently large-scale, multicommunity events.[41]

With their inclusivity and uniform treatment of the dead, these ossuary and mound burials seem to signal decidedly egalitarian values compared to other forms of burial. Yet such large, public gatherings that included feasting, gift giving, and elaborate ceremonial performances also provided opportunities for the expression of a complicated range of cultural principles. As Christine Jirikowic has suggested in her assessment of ossuary burial practices on the Potomac, ceremonial performances there that gathered hundreds of participants may have expressed themes of collective unity and continuity between generations.[42] Such themes may, in fact, illustrate how large, collective mortuary rituals expressed a supposedly natural order maintained by weroances, priests, or other sacred practitioners. In a similar way, the Piedmont burial mounds of the Monacan involved the uniform treatment of large numbers of the dead that may have conveyed core principles of the social order. In Jeffrey Hantman's interpretations of the Monacan evidence, social power was manifested in the historical associations between ancestors and territory invoked by the continuous accumulation of burial mounds.[43] The coastal Potomac and the Virginia Piedmont both witnessed the development of centralized, hierarchical chiefdoms by the early colonial era. On the Chickahominy, ossuary-based mortuary ceremonies involved the interment of relatively few ancestors and, apparently, a range of people that became more tightly constricted over time. Exactly how these practices related to cultural values and structures of authority important to communities on the Chickahominy is not entirely clear. It is, however, striking that ossuaries along the Chickahominy—an area that rebuffed chiefly leadership—were smaller in scale than those in adjacent regions.

With the earliest of them dating to the Middle Woodland period, ossuary-centered practices also have a longer history on the Chickahominy than in other parts of the Chesapeake. Against a backdrop of interaction between foragers and fishers from distinct communities of practice, Native communities living along the Chickahominy began burying ancestors in ossuaries circa AD 500. These practices marked persistent places of gathering and of collective burial in the drainage interior that were revisited for centuries to come.

Feasting at the Clark's Old Neck Site

Located on a neck of land that overlooks a "sunken marsh" in the lower portion of the Chickahominy drainage, the Clark's Old Neck site was dominated by seven remarkably large pit features containing dense concentrations of decorated pottery, fire-cracked rocks, and charred animal bone.[44] With one notable exception, these features returned calibrated radiocarbon dates between AD 1100 and 1300. Two human burials and five dog burials were also recovered from these large pits. An unusual location in several respects, Clark's Old Neck includes only one architectural structure and none of the sheet-midden deposits common to residential towns in the central portion of the drainage. Instead, the site appears in the archaeological record as a place of periodic, short-term gatherings for large, public meals.

The largest of the seven pits at Clark's Old Neck, feature 67A2, measured 17.8 feet (5.4 m) in diameter and contained over five cubic meters of fill, a space large enough to hold the entire field crew of students excavating at the site in 1969. Excavators uncovered the disarticulated bones of a dog near the top of the pit, and three underlying charcoal-rich lenses contained dense concentrations of fire-cracked rock and animal bone. Pit feature 18C2 consisted of a similar series of charcoal-rich lenses full of charred faunal remains, predominantly deer and fish bones, including an Atlantic sturgeon plate. Atlantic sturgeons are anadromous fish that migrate up the Chesapeake Bay's tributaries to spawn during the spring. Mature Atlantic sturgeons are typically eight feet (2.4 m) long and weigh over 300 pounds (140 kg). Feature 18C2 records a series of at least four large-scale food preparation events, judging from the lenses of charcoal-rich soil and the faunal remains.

After its final use, feature 18C2 was capped with a rich deposit of ceramic and lithic artifacts as well as a dog burial. The top deposit contained the majority of the feature's artifacts, including smoking-pipe fragments and 775 large ceramic sherds. Much of the pottery from this feature and from the other large pits at Clark's Old Neck was decorated with incised lines, cord-wrapped dowels, and punctation. The frequent use of decoration distinguished the ceramics at Clark's Old Neck from most sites in the Chickahominy drainage. The decoration included a set of incised and punctated decorations added to a band of 8 to 12 incised lines that run parallel to the vessel mouth. Elements of this decorative tradition, including the banded decoration zones and dense, crosshatched lines, resemble designs on Abbott zone-decorated ceramics dating to earlier centuries. The decorated ce-

Table 5.2. Summary of large pit features, Clark's Old Neck site

Feature	Max. Diameter (m)	Max. Depth (m)	Est. Volume (cu m)	Human Burials	Dog Burials	Charcoal Lenses	Shell-Tempered Ceramics	Projectile Points	Pipe Fragments
67D2	4.3	1.7	4.3	-	-	3	441	-	3
25J2	3.2	1.1	2.5	-	-	2	1219	36	2
18C2	3.0	0.9	1.9	-	1	4	775	6	4
67A2	5.4	1.3	5.5	-	1	3	596	28	3
60R2/3	3.4	1.3	3.0	2	2	2	283	3	2
F1	3.1	1.0	2.4	-	1	3	Unscreened	Unscreened	Unscreened
60K2	3.9	0.9	3.1	-	-	1	Unscreened	Unscreened	Unscreened

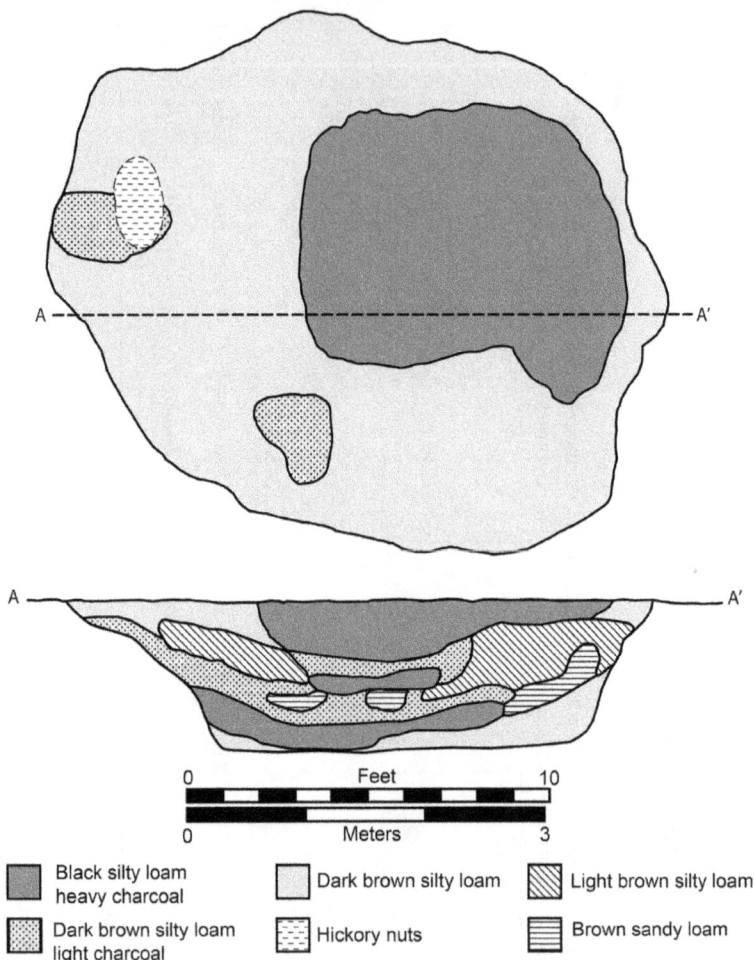

Figure 5.8. Clark's Old Neck, feature 67A2 plan and profile.

ramics at the Clark's Old Neck site appear to be part of a stylistic tradition shared broadly across the Middle Atlantic.[45]

One of the other large pits at the Clark's Old Neck Site, feature 60R2/3, contained two human burials placed near the top of the feature alongside two dog burials. A male aged 48 to 60 years when he died was buried in a flexed position. This articulated burial shows signs of advanced age, including osteoarthritis in the lower spine and tooth loss. Another individual interred in the feature was a slightly built female in her mid-twenties. A

Figure 5.9. Incised and punctate decorations from Clark's Old Neck site ceramics. Adapted from Ogborne 2004.

disarticulated, secondary bundle burial, the remains of this young woman were placed just above the flexed legs of the older male. The young woman was in good health at the time of her death. Her teeth did not exhibit hypoplasias (lines indicative of nutritional deficiencies during childhood) or carious lesions (i.e., cavities). The most significant bioarchaeological patterns related to this individual were all postmortem. The bones were worn smooth, displaying a polish that may have resulted from frequent handling. Red staining from hematite (a reddish mineral consisting of ferric oxide) was present on bone surfaces, especially the manubrium (the upper part of the sternum). Black stains and white calcination were also present on several bones, likely from exposure to heat and smoke. The polish, red staining, and calcination of these remains were introduced following death and after the elements had been disarticulated.

The female bundle burial produced a calibrated radiocarbon date circa

AD 700, while the male produced a calibrated date of circa AD 1300. This remarkably wide range of dates from human remains associated with the same burial context bears explanation. One possibility is that the burials record two distinct occupations of the settlement during the Middle and Late Woodland periods. This seems unlikely, though, since few of the ceramics and none of the other radiocarbon assays from the site date to the Middle Woodland centuries. Moreover, the young female with the *earlier* radiocarbon date was placed *above* the legs of the older male, seemingly with care taken not to disturb those remains. The stratigraphic sequence suggests either that the two burials were interred together or that the young woman was added later. The burials in 60R2/3 may reflect the long-term curation and reburial of human remains in the Chickahominy drainage. Indeed, written accounts from Henry Spelman, referenced above, allude to such practices among the Patawomeck.

This large pit and the others at the Clark's Old Neck site required a substantial commitment of time and labor to build. All of the pits contained charred animal bone, decorated pottery, and smoking pipes deposited in charcoal-rich lenses along with fire-cracked rocks. Dogs were buried at the top of four of the large pits. One of the pits contained the remains of a man and a young woman who died generations apart, apparently highlighting a historical association between individuals from the Middle and Late Woodland periods. These large pit features were evidently used to prepare meals that brought substantial numbers of people to Clark's Old Neck.

The large pits were clustered around a set of post stains that trace the footprint of a structure. North of this building, a ditch just over 1 meter wide extends across the site for a distance of at least 15 meters. The site's spatial organization apparently included a single structure surrounded by massive food-preparation facilities positioned near a linear ditch feature. The Clark's Old Neck site appears to be a carefully arranged space and a place of periodic gathering from AD 1100 to 1300. Such events likely played a role in the transformation of the Chickahominy landscape from the mobile hunter-foragers to the dispersed farmsteads of the Late Woodland period.

A Palisaded Compound in the Lower Drainage: Buck Farm

Excavations at the Buck Farm site uncovered a palisaded settlement measuring approximately 80 by 60 feet (25 by 18 meters) surrounded by two concentric ditch features. The Chickahominy River Survey archaeologists excavated both of the ditches and the entire space they surrounded, a relatively small area of approximately 2,000 square feet (186 square meters). Radiocarbon dates from the ditches indicate that the palisade was in use between AD 1300 and 1600. Evidence that a fire destroyed the palisade appears in the form of charcoal lenses and burned logs in the ditches dating to the late sixteenth century. A human burial within the palisaded area held the remains of a male aged 30 to 45 years. A series of 11 animal burials—the remains of dogs, pigs, and a bird—were also present within the palisaded area.

Archaeologists have identified several other palisaded sites in the Virginia coastal plain, though the Buck Farm site stands apart for its small size, animal burials, and light artifact density. The best documented of these palisaded settlements—the Potomac Creek site in the Potomac River drainage, and the Great Neck site near the mouth of the James—were both contemporaneous with the Buck Farm site. The diameter of the Potomac Creek site was approximately 280 feet (85 meters), surrounded by a palisade fortified with bastions that enclosed an area of over 61,000 square feet (5,750 square meters). Applying the ratio of 20 square meters per person, a figure used to estimate the populations at palisaded towns in the Northeast, produces an estimated Potomac Creek population of 250 to 300 residents.[46] Using the same ratio at the Buck Farm site produces an estimate of fewer than 10 residents.

The Buck Farm site represented a settlement that differed in important ways from the large, fortified community at Potomac Creek. Where other palisaded settlements at the Potomac Creek and Great Neck sites had sizable residential communities, the Buck Farm palisade surrounded a relatively small area, apparently with few residents. Drawing from these patterns and from references in colonial accounts, Christopher Shephard has suggested that the palisaded Buck Farm site was either a weroance's compound or a *quioccosan* (kwee-AW-kuh-sihn)—a temple tended by a priest.[47] Only a few details of Virginia Algonquian priests' compounds are offered in the documentary accounts, though it is clear that quioccosans were physically separated from residential communities due to the dangerous power of priests. Colonial author Robert Beverley reported of Virginia Algonquians, "They never fail to secure within their palisade all their religious relics and the remains of their princes."[48] Ditch enclosures throughout the Eastern Woodlands sometimes served as barriers to restrict the movement of spirits or to protect enclosed areas from unwanted supernatural influences.[49] Similar practices may have also played a role in the construction of the Buck Farm site.

Horticultural Practices and Corn Consumption on the Chickahominy

During the early days of the Jamestown colony, the Chickahominy provided an extraordinary amount of maize to John Smith as he traveled through their towns and traded with them.[50] More broadly, colonial-era accounts and imagery from the Chesapeake often emphasize the productivity of horticultural practices among the Algonquian societies living in the coastal region.[51] Maize appears often in the feasts that greeted European colonists' arrival in a village, and the maize-based map of Tsenacomacoh described by Smith during the divination ceremony points toward its semiotic importance to Virginia Algonquians. Keying off of such documentary references, researchers have suggested that maize-based horticulture played a fundamental role in precontact transitions to settled town life and in the emergence of hierarchical polities in the Chesapeake.[52] Despite the frequent reference to horticulture in colonial-era sources, archaeological evidence of domesticated plants—especially maize, beans, and squash but also the starchy and oily seed crops of the Eastern Agricultural Complex—has been limited in the Chesapeake. Archaeologists in the region have analyzed botanical materials from a range of sites, generally finding only few plant comestibles—wild or domesticated.

In an effort to pull together all of the existing macrobotanical data from across the Chesapeake, a project archaeobotanist Justine McKnight and I have labeled the Chesapeake Archaeobotanical Database, we have concluded that understanding the archaeobotanical patterning related to maize and other domesticates requires the analysis of large, radiocarbon-dated samples from multiple sites.[53] We have assembled a suite of radiocarbon dates of domesticated plants in the region in an effort to trace their arrival and spread in the region. The results suggest that maize first arrived in the Chesapeake during the Late Woodland period, initially appearing in areas west of the Blue Ridge before being carried east to the Piedmont and arriving in the Coastal Plain circa AD 1100. Beans appear in the archaeological record somewhat later, circa AD 1450. Even after their initial appearance in the coastal Chesapeake, the numbers of domesticates recovered from archaeological sites in the region are usually quite modest. The contrast between maize's prominence in the documentary record and its scarcity in the macrobotanical record raises questions concerning the history of horticultural practices in the region.

While macrobotanical evidence of charred plant remains in the archaeological record offers an important line of evidence of subsistence practices, it is also a source with limitations in the Chesapeake. Preservation of plant remains, even charred samples from feature contexts, is generally poor in the temperate Chesapeake. Algonquian groups in the Chesapeake stored corn in above-ground cribs or in large baskets rather than in pits below ground, a practice that decreases the likelihood of archaeological discovery.[54] Additionally, trash-disposal practices within dispersed, riverine towns often resulted in thin, scattered sheet middens buried under fluvial deposits or disturbed by plowing. Until recently, archaeologists' efforts to recover plant remains in the region were limited to small soil samples and phase-based dating, rather than using radiocarbon assays to directly date plant remains.

Archaeologists have responded to such limitations by combining several analytical methods, including those focused on microbotanical evidence and bioarchaeological analysis.[55] Stable isotope analysis of skeletal remains offers one of these methods for identifying trends in diet prior to the colonial era. Chemical elements from the foods people consume are deposited in bones and teeth, leaving behind a signature of dietary practices.[56] The ratios of carbon and nitrogen isotopes present in human bone chemistry are particularly useful in detecting the types of plants and animal proteins consumed by a person.[57] In the Eastern Woodlands, carbon isotope ratios from human bones provide a proxy measure of the relative importance of local plants versus maize in a person's diet. Maize is a tropical domesticate with a different isotopic signature than the region's native vegetation. Carbon isotope ratios generally rise within skeletal populations as maize consumption increases, while the nitrogen isotopic ratio provides an indicator for the source of animal protein in diet. This value is relatively high for those consuming marine, estuarine, and riverine species, and relatively low for those whose diets center on terrestrial animals, including deer.

In coastal areas like the Chesapeake, though, the relationship between

Table 5.3. Directly dated cultigens from Coastal Plain and Piedmont sites in Virginia and Maryland

Lab Code	Site	Radiocarbon Age (bp)	Cal. 2-sigma Low	Cal. Med. Prob.	Cal. 2-sigma High	Source
ZEA MAYS (CORN)						
Beta-216846	Maycock's Point (44PG40)	930 ±40	1020	1100	1210	McKnight and Gallivan 2008
Beta-216847	Maycock's Point (44PG40)	910 ±40	1030	1120	1210	McKnight and Gallivan 2008
Beta-227090	Great Neck (44VB7)	910 ±40	1030	1120	1210	McKnight and Gallivan 2008
Beta-226807	Point of Fork (44FV19)	870 ±40	1040	1170	1260	McKnight and Gallivan 2008
Beta-230508	Werowocomoco (44GL32)	840 ±40	1050	1200	1270	McKnight and Gallivan 2008
Beta-211100	Werowocomoco (44GL32)	770 ±50	1160	1250	1380	Gallivan et al. 2005
Beta-226805	Partridge Creek (44AH193)	720 ±40	1220	1280	1390	McKnight and Gallivan 2008
Beta-230509	Werowocomoco (44GL32)	650 ±40	1280	1350	1400	McKnight and Gallivan 2008
Beta-275419	Claggett Retreat (18FR25)	650 ±40	1280	1350	1400	McKnight 2010a
Beta-239507	Werowocomoco (44GL32)	630 ±40	1290	1350	1400	McKnight and Gallivan 2008
Beta-211101	Werowocomoco (44GL32)	610 ±40	1290	1350	1410	Gallivan et al. 2005
Beta-159908	Fisher (44LD4)	590 ±40	1300	1350	1420	McKnight 2001

Beta-211102	Werowocomoco (44GL32)	570 ±40	1300	1350	1430	Gallivan et al. 2005
Beta-242478	Hughes (18MO1)	490 ±40	1320	1430	1470	McKnight 2010b
Beta-237910	Reedy Creek (44HA22)	480 ±40	1330	1430	1480	McKnight and Gallivan 2008
Beta-323136	Kiskiak (44YO2)	450 ±30	1420	1440	1480	This study
Beta-230507	Werowocomoco (44GL32)	430 ±40	1410	1460	1620	McKnight and Gallivan 2008
Beta-259068	Cumberland 18CV171	390 ±40	1440	1500	1630	McKnight 2009a
Beta-259071	18ST570	370 ±40	1450	1530	1640	McKnight 2009b
Beta-226809	Potomac Creek (44ST2)	350 ±40	1460	1550	1640	McKnight and Gallivan 2008
Beta-177247	Buggs Island (44MC491)	350 ±40	1460	1550	1640	Abbott et al. 2003
Beta-302722	Kiskiak (44YO2)	260 ±30	1520	1650	1950	This study
PHASEOLUS VULGARIS (BEAN)						
Beta-259069	Rosenstock (18FR18)	590 ±40	1300	1350	1420	McKnight 2009c
Beta-230506	Werowocomoco (44GL32)	440 ±40	1410	1450	1620	McKnight and Gallivan 2008

isotopic values present in bone chemistry and subsistence practices is, unfortunately, not quite this straightforward. Carbon isotope ratios are influenced not only by the plant foods consumed but also by the animal foods in a diet. A diet rich in fish and shellfish also results in high isotopic carbon ratios. Carbon isotope ratios for people eating lots of fish and shellfish may, in fact, mimic those of maize eaters, complicating the effort to trace the history of maize in bone chemistry. One way that researchers have separated the impact of fish from corn in the diets of coastal peoples involves jointly considering trends in carbon and nitrogen isotopes.[58] By comparing both sets of values and their patterns over time, researchers can disentangle the relative importance of fish and maize in coastal settings. In other words, nitrogen isotopic ratios provide a separate line of evidence for determining whether high carbon isotopic ratios are likely the result of the consumption of maize or of fish. A high nitrogen value points toward heavy marine fish and shellfish consumption, a diet that would push carbon values toward levels associated with corn consumption even when maize actually plays only a small role in the diet.

After the Chickahominy Tribal Council requested that we study the evidence of Chickahominy subsistence practices in greater detail, we selected a sample of teeth from the survey collection for a stable isotope analysis.[59] In an effort to identify detailed trends in the data rather than phase-based averages, the study included direct radiocarbon dates on human bone in addition to the stable isotope analysis. Stable nitrogen isotope ratios for skeletal remains along the Chickahominy River declined between AD 600 and the 1500s, falling below 12.0 during the eleventh century AD. Nitrogen isotope ratios above 12.0 typically result from diets high in fish (marine or riverine) and shellfish.[60] Not surprisingly, the earliest samples, dating to the Middle Woodland centuries, when fishing represented a central focus of lifeways across the region, produced the highest nitrogen isotopic ratios. Fish and shellfish no doubt continued to play a role in Native subsistence along the Chickahominy throughout the Late Woodland centuries based on the faunal remains recovered from sites dating to this period. Even so, the evidence suggests that the relative importance of terrestrial herbivores, including deer, increased during these centuries.

Figure 5.10 records changing carbon isotope ratios over time, pointing toward values that initially decreased from the sixth through the twelfth centuries AD, then subsequently increased for the next four centuries.

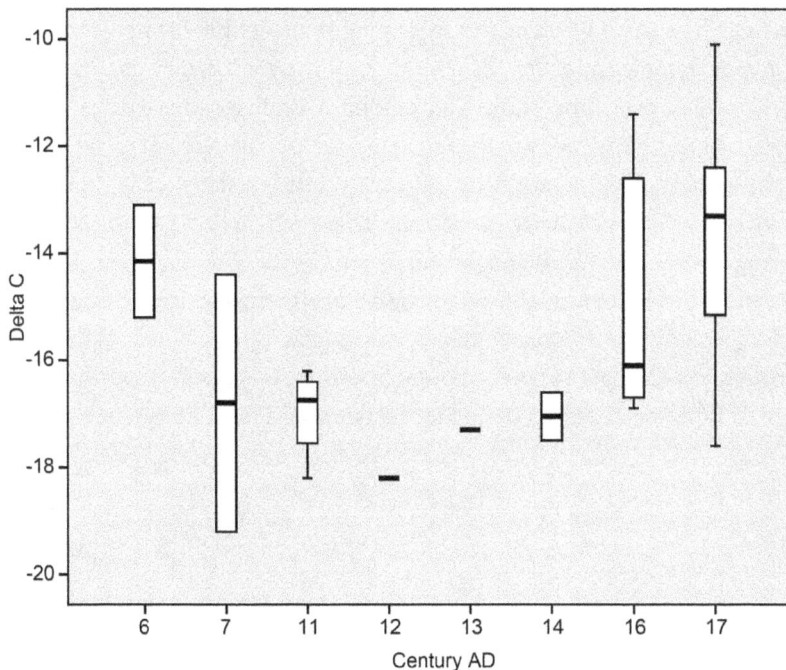

Figure 5.10. Boxplot of carbon isotope ratios over time from the Chickahominy drainage. Delta C values above -14.4 typically reflect a diet high in C4 plants (i.e., maize) or marine fish and shellfish.

Based on the nitrogen isotopic ratios for these skeletal remains and the radiocarbon dates for maize in the region, the relatively high values recorded in the earliest samples are likely the product of diets centered on fish and shellfish rather than maize. The Late Woodland data, beginning during the twelfth century shortly after maize appears in the region, point toward a pattern of modest, though generally increasing, maize consumption. Beginning during the sixteenth century, the bone chemistry of some individuals living on the Chickahominy River contained carbon isotope values that topped the -14.4 value, a threshold indicating that maize likely constituted more than 50 percent of the diet. The timing of this increased consumption of maize during the sixteenth century, *prior to* Jamestown's settlement, suggests that it was likely *not* the product of a sustained European colonial presence.

Figure 5.11 offers a model of stable isotope values for various diets involving indigenous plants, maize, marine and estuarine protein, and terrestrial herbivores. The values offer a heuristic guide to stable isotope values by diet.[61] The small black circles in this figure depict the mean carbon and nitrogen isotopic ratios for the Chickahominy data. Dietary changes were fairly modest over time in the Chickahominy drainage, departing in small though detectible ways from the estuarine-focused patterns of those buried in the earliest ossuaries at Wilcox Neck. A subtle but statistically significant change is apparent as diet shifted from a heavy reliance on fish and shellfish during the Middle Woodland period toward a Late Woodland diet that incorporated more mammal protein, native plants, and maize. The data also reflect a significantly greater reliance on maize during the Protohistoric through the Contact period. The stable carbon isotope values from individuals buried at Edgehill dating to the 1500s and from individuals buried

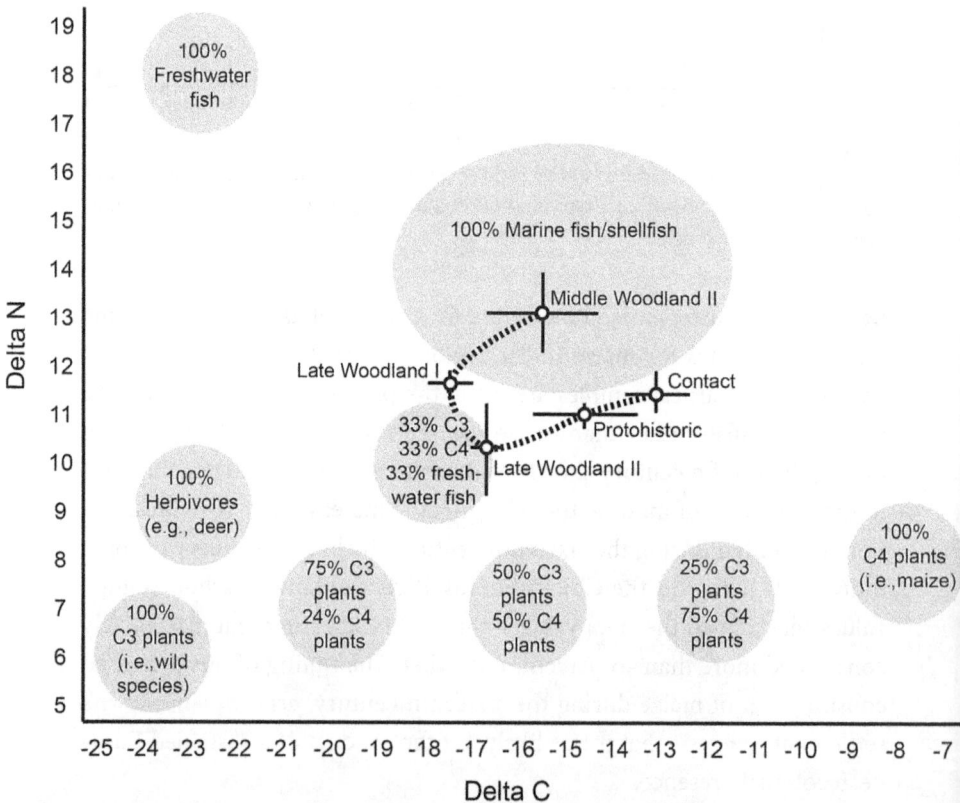

Figure 5.11. Comparison of Chickahominy stable isotope analysis results with values for various diets (gray circles). Mean stable isotopic values (small black circles) with standard errors of the mean (black lines) come from the Chickahominy River sample.

at Cinquoteck in the early 1600s also show a wide range of carbon isotopic values. These values point toward differences in the importance of maize in the diets of different people living along the Chickahominy River during these centuries.

In sum, the stable isotope analysis and radiocarbon dating of Chickahominy remains record a general decrease over time in the importance of estuarine resources in favor of terrestrial fauna. A gradual increase in the importance of maize is evident during the Late Woodland period, which corroborates the results of other studies, including macrobotanical analysis and studies of dentition.[62] A sharp rise in maize consumption occurred during the late sixteenth and early seventeenth centuries. The data from these last two centuries also point toward greater dietary variability and, quite possibly, differential access to maize.

A Meshwork of Places and Practices

The Chickahominy River Survey documents anchor points for a historical narrative that includes communal burial grounds used initially by forager-fishers and later by horticulturalists, a location of feasting that gathered many participants, several dispersed residential towns, and a palisaded compound. A limited number of deposits along the Chickahominy date to the Middle Woodland period, but those that do document the introduction of shell-tempered Mockley ceramics as a minority ware in the same contexts as the sand- and lithic-tempered ceramics, which have a long history in the area. This pattern points toward trade and interaction between different forager-fisher communities of practice. No sizable Mockley base camps appear among the excavated sites, suggesting that such locations occurred elsewhere along the James and York Rivers. Circa AD 500, Native communities in the Chickahominy drainage began to celebrate mortuary rituals around collective burial grounds. The earliest of these ossuaries were in use centuries before similar practices are documented elsewhere in the region.

Corn began to play a role in subsistence practices circa AD 1100, though large riverine towns did not appear along the Chickahominy until AD 1300, subsequent to maize's initial introduction. The richest archaeological evidence from the Chickahominy River Survey dates to the centuries after AD 1300. Measures of feature volume, ceramic density, and lithic diversity show a marked increase within these contexts, which contain shell-tempered, fabric-impressed ceramics. During the fourteenth century AD, residents of the drainage established dispersed settlements along the Chickahominy's floodplain terraces, with houses surrounded by sheet middens, particularly in the central portions of the drainage later known as Moysonec. The stable isotope data, macrobotanical evidence, and patterning in dental caries indicate that these towns raised maize in floodplain gardens along the river. In the interior portions of the drainage, Native communities continued to bury their dead in ossuaries as they had for centuries. Downstream, a palisaded enclosure and a location of periodic feasting marked the edges of what would be the Chickahominy world.

As the Chickahominy were reportedly "regulated and guided by their priests," their coalescence as a unified group in all likelihood centered on ceremonial events and ritualized places. In the results of the Chickahominy River Survey, we see the development of a cultural landscape that by AD 1300 included residential communities as well as persistent places of social gathering, feasting, and ceremony. In short, the evidence highlights a meshwork of places and practices through which the Algonquian residents of the river drainage gathered and interacted with one another. The archaeological record does not offer a clear indication of the events or ideas through which the residents of the river drainage became the "Coarsepounded Corn People," though it does provide some indications of how this historical process unfolded over time. The archaeological evidence suggests that a Chickahominy coalescence occurred after AD 1300, channeled by social gatherings within the drainage and by interactions with surrounding groups. The locations identified by the survey record a history of placemaking that left its mark on the landscape, ultimately channeling the response of the Chickahominy to the rise of Wahunsenacawh and to the arrival of the Jamestown colonists.

Chapter 6

The Place of the Antler Wearers

An icy fog hung over Purtan Bay, veiling the river and coating the pines on shore when the Native delegations reached Werowocomoco. Visiting the location for the first time, they came from Mattaponi, Nansemond, Pamunkey, Rappahannock, Chickahominy, and Upper Mattaponi. It was February 2003, and an archaeological survey of the area had uncovered evidence that the terrace overlooking Purtan Bay held the remains of a Native town. We had invited the chiefs of the local tribes, descendants of the Virginia Algonquians who constructed the town and dwelled there for centuries, to see the site and to discuss the possibility of collaborative research.

The survey, conducted by my colleagues David Brown and Thane Harpole in consultation with Randy Turner, provided further evidence that the site was indeed Werowocomoco, the Powhatan political center.[1] Responding to the public's fascination with Pocahontas, John Smith, and the story of his rescue at Werowocomoco, scholars had long sought to pin down the site's whereabouts. Beginning in the nineteenth century, historians and archaeologists compared colonial-era maps with early descriptions of the town to conclude that Werowocomoco was most likely situated along Purtan, a broad bay on the northeast bank of the York River.[2] In the 1970s, testing by archaeologist Daniel Mouer uncovered Native artifacts that further narrowed the focus to the central riverine terrace between Leigh and Bland creeks.

The terrace matches key details in the colonial descriptions of the town. Early references describe Werowocomoco as 12 to 16 miles from James Fort beside a broad, shallow bay fed by three creeks.[3] Lynn Ripley, who owns the property with her husband, Bob, had collected artifacts from plow-disturbed areas and from the eroding bluff along the riverfront. These included Native ceramics, projectile points, glass beads, and copper sheeting associated with a Late Woodland through Contact-period settlement. While much of the archaeological research in the Chesapeake has been aimed at documenting English colonial settlement and early American life within plantations, Lynn's collection brought to light a Virginia Algonquian settlement with a much deeper history.

The six Virginia tribes who visited the site on that winter afternoon agreed to help us develop an archaeological investigation centered on partnerships with Native communities.[4] The tribes formed a Virginia Indian Advisory Board to the project, with representatives who have since met with the Werowocomoco Research Group and the Ripleys as we developed our research design, funding options, and reporting protocols. The resulting collaboration brought together Virginia tribes, scholars, and the property owners for a long-term study of the site.

"What I'd really like to learn about," Rappahannock chief Anne Richardson let us know during our initial meeting, "are the Native people who lived at this site *before* Jamestown. . . . There's a lot of talk about Jamestown these days, but I'd prefer to hear more about Indian towns like this one before all of that." Jeff Brown, the Pamunkey representative, urged us to consider Werowocomoco as something more than simply a wild place in the backwoods beyond James Fort's palisade. Other Native leaders asked us to address the question of why Wahunsenacawh moved to Werowocomoco, when he was from the town of Powhatan to the west, on the James River. Rather than provide us with their own answers to such questions, they advised us to look beyond the English narratives and toward the precolonial history in order to understand Werowocomoco's significance.

In the years since we began working with Virginia's tribal communities at Werowocomoco, our collaborative efforts have evolved from outreach to Native leaders to training a handful of American Indian archaeologists to working for the tribes on their own cultural resource management and museum programs. The decision by leaders of Virginia tribes to engage with the research at Werowocomoco represented a step toward archaeological practice oriented more closely to Native-driven questions and concerns. A move toward more inclusive approaches to archaeological research has been developing in North America for at least three decades and has influenced projects in the Chesapeake and the Middle Atlantic well before the Werowocomoco research began. Archaeologists and descendant communities have worked together to create various forms of community-oriented, collaborative, and civically engaged archaeology.[5] These efforts were prompted in part by federal legislation, including the Native American Graves Protection and Repatriation Act of 1990, and by descendant communities' growing insistence that archaeology respond to their own ways of understanding the past. Archaeologists and museum curators have also begun to develop new practices in response to difficult questions regarding who "owns" the past. Locally and across the globe, conflicts over whether objects and human remains should be understood as either the common heritage of mankind or the cultural property of a specific community are now open to debate.

Drawing from these conversations, various forms of "Indigenous archaeology" have emerged in recent years that involve the active participation of Native peoples. In George Nicholas' widely cited definition, Indigenous archaeology involves efforts to "(1) make archaeology more representative of, responsible to, and relevant for Indigenous communities; (2) redress real and perceived inequalities in the practice of archaeology; (3) inform and broaden the understanding and interpretation of the archaeological record through the incorporation of Aboriginal worldviews, histories, and science."[6] Such approaches are diverse and still developing, with emphasis placed variously on critiques of colonial historiography, cultural revitalization in contemporary communities, indigenous modes of interpretation, political activism in support of Native sovereignty, and alternative approaches to cultural resource management.[7]

Such priorities have, to date, had a modest impact in the Chesapeake. Outside the limited academic research oriented toward Native pasts, archaeological practice here is dominated by compliance-oriented cultural resource management (CRM). A tight regulatory framework of federal laws and state government implementation, CRM provides only limited openings for consultation or for innovative forms of collaboration. These openings may widen, though, as Native communities achieve recognition, including federal acknowledgment. Six of the eleven tribes recognized by the Commonwealth of Virginia—the Chickahominy, Eastern Chickahominy, Monacan, Nansemond, Upper Mattaponi, and Rappahannock—have sought federal acknowledgment through an act of Congress. The Pamunkey Tribe won federal acknowledgment in 2015 through a process administered by the Bureau of Indian Affairs. The Pamunkey have also established a heritage program centered on their tribal museum. The tribe has recently developed an exhibit exploring Pamunkey sovereignty through the history of diplomatic negotiations with English colonists and the Virginia Commonwealth. The museum is currently directed by tribal member Ashley Spivey, a PhD student who has contributed to the Werowocomoco research since 2005. After acquiring archaeological fieldwork experience at Werowocomoco, Pamunkey tribal representative Jeff Brown became a professional archaeologist, working in CRM, in public archaeology, and as a member of PBS' Time Team America. While our efforts to date have been modest in scope, by creating spaces for members of the Virginia Indian community the Werowocomoco Research Group has encouraged research that combines indigenous values with an academic research agenda.[8]

The resulting research at Werowocomoco has focused on tracing the site's deep history and on its changing place within Virginia Algonquian landscapes of the past and present, themes of shared interest to our partners in the Native community and to the members of the Werowocomoco Research Group. The site has produced evidence of brief occupations stretching back to the Early Archaic period (8000–6000 BC), though it was not until the Late Woodland period (AD 900–1500) that a large town was constructed along Purtan Bay. Circa AD 1200 residents cleared forests in the area, planted gardens, erected houses along the riverfront, and created a small trench enclosure in the interior of the site. During the fourteenth century AD, residents excavated a much larger earthwork enclosure, surrounding the earlier one. Separated from residential spaces along Purtan Bay, these trenches surrounded an area containing non-local ceramics, smoking-pipe fragments, and several architectural structures. The largest of these structures dates to the early seventeenth century and contained pieces of copper traded from James Fort. The location, layout, and materials associated with this building suggest that it was in all likelihood Wahunsenacawh's residence.

This archaeological sequence suggests that the settlement represented a prominent Native town with a history of monumental landscape features from the thirteenth century through the early seventeenth century. A biography of place highlights Werowocomoco's history as a ritualized location that played a role in the Virginia Algonquian "spatial imaginary," the meaningful dimension of social space.[9] This chapter discusses Werowocomoco's location, its archaeological record, and related documentary evidence, before turning to its significance as "Place of the antler wearers."

Werowocomoco's Location

While the archaeological record of the terrace along Purtan Bay clearly demonstrates that the area holds the remains of a large Native town, confirming the site's identity as Werowocomoco has required a careful consideration of colonial-era maps and other early documentary sources. Recounting his second visit to Werowocomoco in the *True Relation*, John Smith describes the geographic setting of Wahunsenacawh's town, noting, "The Bay where he dwelleth hath in it 3 Cricks, and a mile and a halfe from the chanel all os [i.e., ooze]. Being conducted to the towne, I found myself mistaken in the creeke, for they al there were within lesse then a mile."[10] Smith's written accounts initially placed Werowocomoco 12 miles from James Fort, though in the text of his *Map of Virginia* published later, he lengthened this distance to 14 miles. Colonist William Strachey described the distance between James Fort and Werowocomoco as "some 15 or 16 myles."[11]

The riverine terrace adjacent to Purtan Bay corresponds well with these descriptions and with Werowocomoco's location on several colonial-era maps. The York River in this area, 15 miles (24 km) north of James Fort, is remarkably straight and wide. The terrace overlooking Purtan Bay is just over a mile from the York River channel. Fed by Purtan, Leigh, and Bland Creeks, Purtan Bay is bounded by the extensive wetlands of Purtan Island upstream and by Barren Point downstream. Measuring just under a mile (1.3 km) across, Purtan Bay ranges from two to six feet (0.6–1.8 m) in depth and exposes mudflats near shore at low tide—that is, Smith's ooze. The site itself spreads across a relatively flat, 50-acre (20 ha) terrace that rises 10 to 20 feet (3–6 m) above mean sea level. The terrace forms a neck of land bounded by Leigh Creek, Purtan Bay, and Bland Creek. Freshwater springs flow into Leigh and Bland Creeks in the site interior, to the east where the peninsula narrows. Sixteen hundred feet (500 m) east of the bay, the land rises again to form a second terrace, 20 to 30 feet (6–9 m) above mean sea level, which forms the site's western border.

Primary cartographic sources for Werowocomoco's location include Robert Tindall's 1608 *Draught of Virginia*, the 1611 Zuñiga Chart, and John

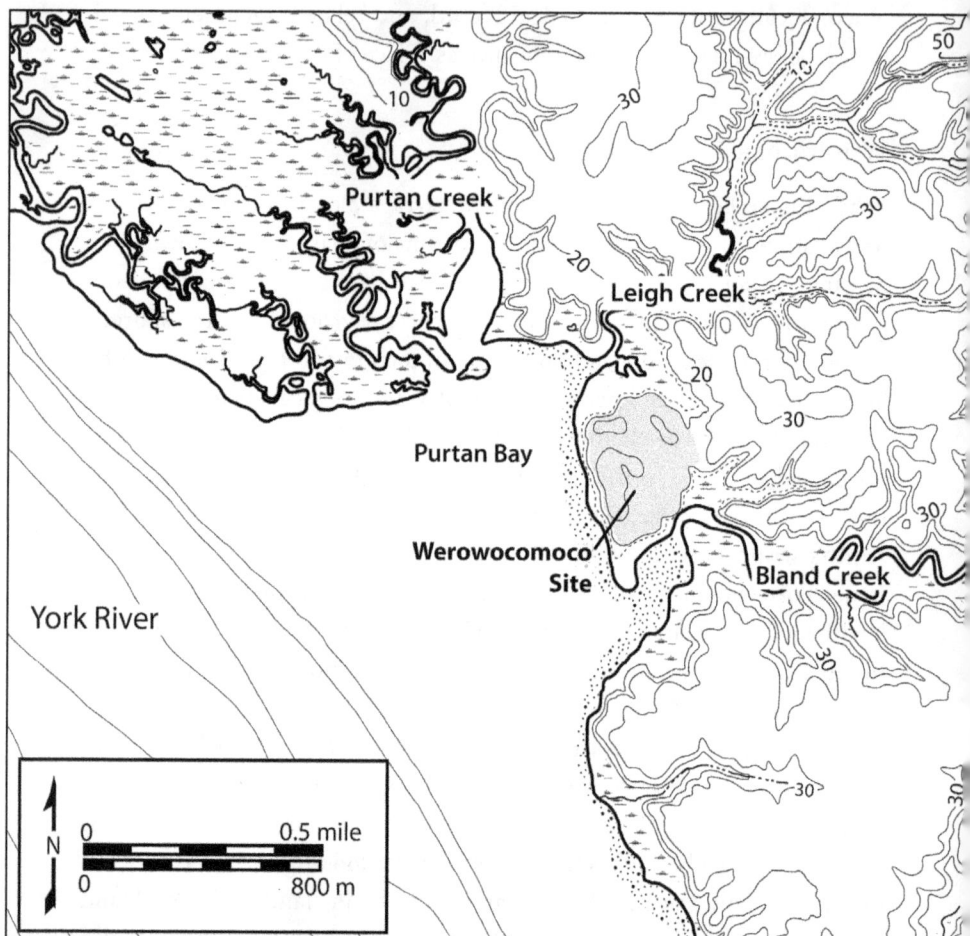

Figure 6.1. Werowocomoco site vicinity, adapted from USGS 7.5-minute series Clay Bank quadrangle.

Smith's 1612 *Map of Virginia*. Tindall's *Draught* represents the oldest surviving chart prepared by a colonist at James Fort.[12] One of the original colonists, Tindall accompanied Captain Christopher Newport to the towns of Powhatan and Werowocomoco.[13] Like the Zuñiga Chart, Tindall's *Draught* emphasizes shoreline details critical for riverine navigation. Tindall's chart depicts "King James his River" from its mouth to the town of "Poetan" (Powhatan). "Prince Henneri his River" (i.e., the York) extends from its mouth to a location west of the Pamunkey-Mattaponi confluence. The town of "Pamonke" (i.e., Pamunkey) appears west of this confluence in the vicinity of the contemporary Pamunkey Reservation. Downstream from

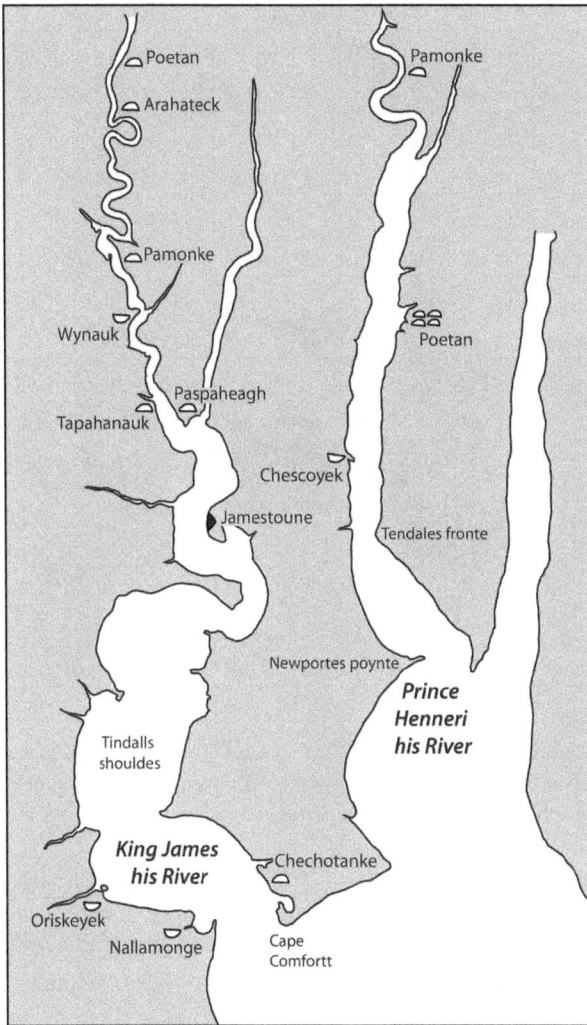

Figure 6.2. Inset from Robert Tindall's *Draught of Virginia*.
Adapted from Brown 1890:151.

the Pamunkey–Mattaponi confluence, Tindall portrayed a second town labeled "Poetan," a settlement marked by four houses that most likely represents Powhatan's residence at Werowocomoco. The shoreline mapped at this settlement traces a bay fed by three streams that enter in the vicinity of the town. The only other York River settlement illustrated on the chart is "Chescoyek" (i.e., Kiskiak). Consistent with other early maps, Kiskiak is placed on the southwest side of the York, just upstream from its mouth.

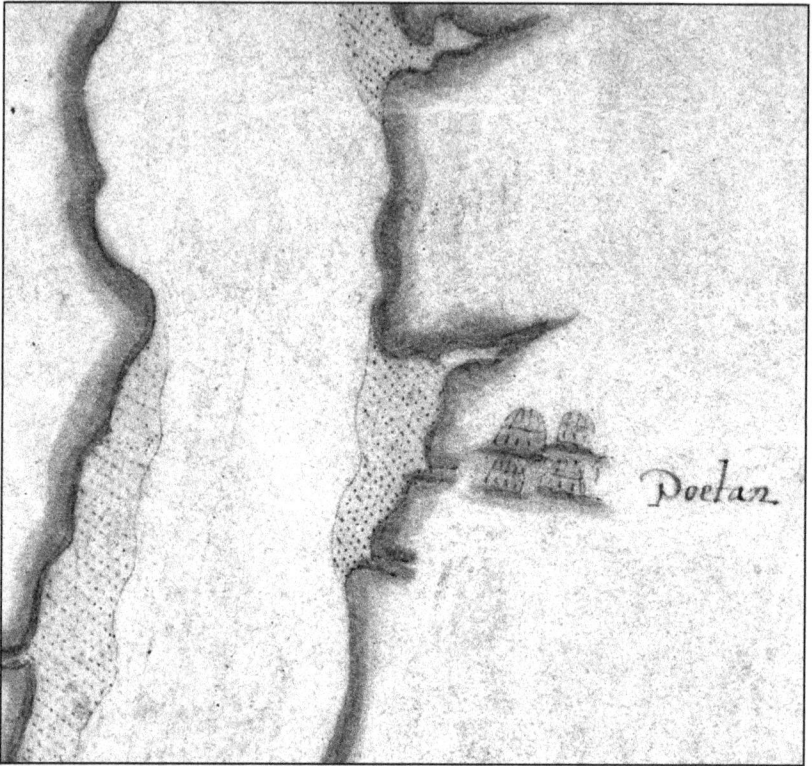

Figure 6.3. Inset from Robert Tindall's *Draught of Virginia*. Photograph of original map from the British Museum collection, courtesy of Jamestown Rediscovery.

Below Kiskiak, the chart depicts "Tendales fronte," a narrowing of the York River originally named for the cartographer and now known as Gloucester Point.

Using the scale provided on Tindall's *Draught*, the distance from the Pamunkey–Mattaponi confluence to Poetan is approximately 11 miles, the distance from Poetan to Chescoyak is 10 miles, and the distance from Poetan to Tindall's Point is 15 miles. These correspond closely with the distances from Purtan Bay as measured on a modern map of the York: Purtan is approximately 11 miles below West Point, 11 miles above the Kiskiak site, and 14 miles upriver from Gloucester Point. Tindall's depiction of the York River Poetan also matches the shoreline at Purtan Bay. Given these congruencies, it is not surprising that scholarship has maintained over a century that Purtan Bay represents the most likely location of Werowocomoco.[14]

Establishing a Horticultural Town, circa AD 1200

Werowocomoco's archaeological record documents a dynamic history of placemaking and remaking critical to its significance as the Powhatan center place. The earliest evidence from Werowocomoco comes in the form of projectile points dating to the Archaic through Early Woodland periods that appear sporadically along Purtan Bay and the two creeks bordering the site. These materials suggest a series of short-term encampments at the location prior to AD 400. Our excavations have identified no features or intact midden deposits from these early occupations.

Small concentrations of burnt oyster shells associated with Mockley ceramics (tempered with shell and cord-marked or net-impressed) began to occur in several discrete areas overlooking Leigh and Bland Creeks circa AD 400. Along Purtan Bay, a series of stratified deposits beneath the plow zone contained artifacts dating from the Middle and Late Woodland periods. The deepest of these deposits contained a series of shallow pits with oyster shell fragments and Mockley ceramics. These features returned calibrated radiocarbon dates ranging from AD 400 to 700

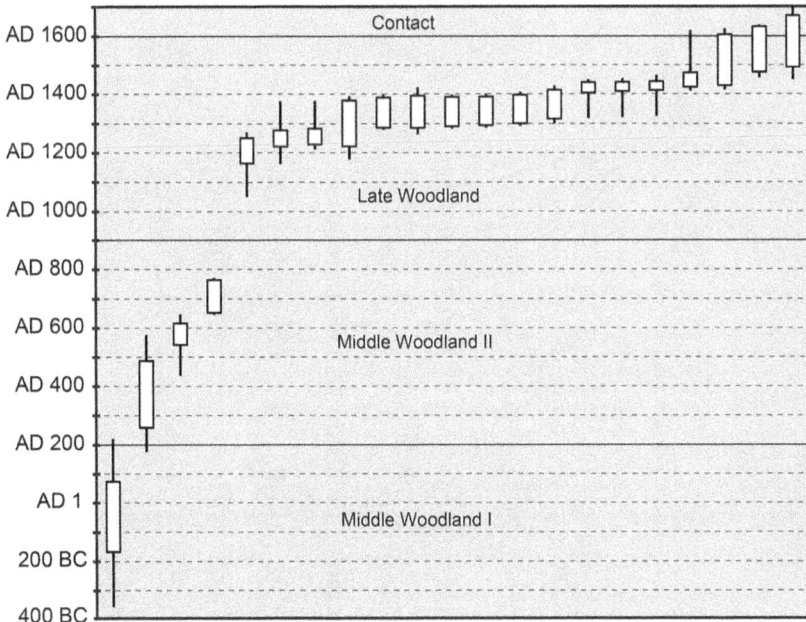

Figure 6.4. Calibrated radiocarbon dates for Werowocomoco site features. One-sigma range (box) and two-sigma range (lines) displayed.

Table 6.1. Radiocarbon dates, Werowocomoco site

Lab Code	Context	Context Note	Conventional Age (bp)	Calibrated Dates		
				2-sigma Low	Median Probability	2-sigma High
Beta-207437	TU403 IIIB	Riverfront midden base	2020 ±100	360 BC	40 BC	AD 220
Beta-207436	TU347 IIA	Riverfront midden	1660 ±80	AD 220	AD 395	AD 570
Beta-208956	F608	Small, shell-filled pit	1490 ±40	AD 440	AD 580	AD 490
Beta-207435	F606	Riverfront midden	1330 ±40	AD 650	AD 690	AD 770
*Beta-230508	F552	Trench F552	840 ±40	AD 1050	AD 1200	AD 1270
Beta-206166	TU402 IIA	Riverfront midden	750 ±40	AD 1200	AD 1260	AD 1380
Beta-198729	F428	Midden-filled pit	730 ±60	AD 1200	AD 1300	AD 1390
*Beta-230509	F552	Trench F552	650 ±40	AD 1280	AD 1340	AD 1400
Beta-208957	TU500 IIIA	Riverfront midden	640 ±70	AD 1260	AD 1340	AD 1420
*Beta-262464	F959	Post, east of trenches	640 ±40	AD 1280	AD 1350	AD 1400
*Beta-239507	F161	Base of trench F161	630 ±40	AD 1280	AD 1350	AD 1400

*Beta-186840	F182	Feature within trench F162	500 ±40	AD 1320	AD 1420	AD 1450
Beta-211101	TU500 IIIA	Riverfront midden	610 ±40	AD 1290	AD 1350	AD 1410
Beta-211102	TU500 IIIC	Riverfront midden	570 ±40	AD 1300	AD 1350	AD 1370
Beta-198730	F184	Pit within house pattern	510 ±40	AD 1400	AD 1430	AD 1450
*Beta-186839	F65	Feature within trench F161	490 ±40	AD 1320	AD 1430	AD 1470
Beta-230506	F428	Midden-filled pit	440 ±40	AD 1420	AD 1460	AD 1490
Beta-230507	F428	Midden-filled pit	430 ±40	AD 1420	AD 1520	AD 1610
*Beta-208955	F587	Post within large structure	350 ±40	AD 1460	AD 1550	AD 1640
*Beta-198731	F161	Deposits at top of trench F161	340 ±40	AD 1460	AD 1560	AD 1640
Beta-207438	TU500 IIA	Riverfront midden, top	270 ±70	AD 1450	AD 1620	AD 1950

*Contexts associated with trenches.

Table 6.2. Summary of Werowocomoco site archaeological patterns

Dates	Evidence	Location
8000 BC–AD 400	Projectile points and a light deposit of lithic-tempered ceramics	Riverfront
AD 400–700	Shallow pits with burned oyster shell and Mockley ceramics	Riverfront
AD 800–1200	Light density of Townsend ceramics, few features	Riverfront
AD 1200–1350	Small trench feature (F.552) associated with Townsend ceramics	Interior
Circa AD–200	Earliest maize cupule in trench Feature 552	Interior
AD 1200–1500	Rising densities of edge species, domesticates, and artifacts	Riverfront / interior
AD 1350–1650	Two large, parallel trench features (F.161 and F.162) constructed/filled	Interior
Circa AD 400	Residential structure (7m by 4m), associated with Townsend ceramics	Riverfront
Circa AD 1450	Earliest bean in midden-filled pit, associated with Townsend ceramics	Riverfront
AD 1500–1600s	Declining densities of edge species, domesticates, and artifacts	Riverfront / interior
Circa AD 1550	Structure (22m by 6m), associated with Townsend/Roanoke ceramics	Interior
AD 1607–1609	Copper sheeting acquired from James Fort	Interior

Above the riverfront deposits associated with Mockley ceramics, a charcoal-rich horizon contained higher densities of shell-tempered, fabric-impressed pottery from the Townsend series mixed with shell-tempered, Roanoke simple-stamped ceramics closer to the surface. These deposits returned radiocarbon dates with median calibrated probabilities from AD 1200 through 1600, bracketing the most intensive period of settlement at the site.

The intact deposits at the Werowocomoco site document two distinct phases of settlement along Purtan Bay. The first of these, the Mockley phase, records small, seasonal encampments of forager-fishers. Oyster processing occurred during this phase of settlement, though the resulting artifact densities and midden accumulations were quite limited compared to contemporaneous settlements downstream at the Kiskiak site. Purtan Bay is near the upstream limits of the salinity levels that support oyster reefs in the York. Above the Mockley horizon, the stratified deposits at Werowocomoco record a four-century hiatus in settlement activity along Purtan Bay. In fact, across the entire Werowocomoco site, only a small number of contexts date to the interval between AD 800 and 1200.

The second phase of settlement reflected in the stratified deposits, the Werowocomoco phase, stretches from AD 1200 through the early seventeenth century and includes evidence of extensive changes in the local landscape. A significant increase in settlement activity during the thirteenth century is apparent in the radiocarbon dates, artifact densities, and archaeobotanical assemblage. Plant remains recovered from the site highlight increases in the amount of wood charcoal, edge species, and maize fragments present between AD 1200 and 1500. These patterns point toward a substantial reconfiguration of the environmental setting as residents cleared the hardwood trees along Purtan Bay and spread across the terrace in a dispersed horticultural community. In these cleared settings, conifers and weedy plants colonized the soils beneath an open canopy. The earliest maize at the site dates to the early thirteenth century AD, reflecting the establishment of a horticultural settlement. Additional radiocarbon dates on maize and beans record the continuation of horticultural practices at the site through the early seventeenth century.

Earthwork Construction, AD 1200–1350

Beginning at the same time that Virginia Algonquians established a horticultural town lining Purtan Bay, residents constructed a series of trenches within the site's eastern interior. The earliest of these was a trench feature located approximately 270 meters east of the riverfront. The first of several linear earthworks constructed at Werowocomoco, feature 552 measured approximately 1.5 meters across and 1 meter in depth, with a basin-shaped profile. Oriented roughly north–south, the trench stretches across an expanse of approximately 80 meters before turning eastward at both ends. Feature 552 continues for roughly 15 meters to the east before being erased by plow disturbance in this portion of the site. The feature contained char-coal-rich deposits at the base and a light density of Townsend ceramics and lithic artifacts throughout.

Two additional trench features located 20 meters west of feature 552 produced later calibrated radiocarbon dates ranging from AD 1350 to 1600. Approximately 1 to 1.5 meters across and 0.5 to 1 meter in depth below the plow zone, features 161 and 162 run parallel, separated by a distance of just over 1 meter. The trenches, which also contained a light density of ceramics and lithic artifacts, maintain similar dimensions while extending approxi-mately 210 meters north to south. The two features turn gently to the east

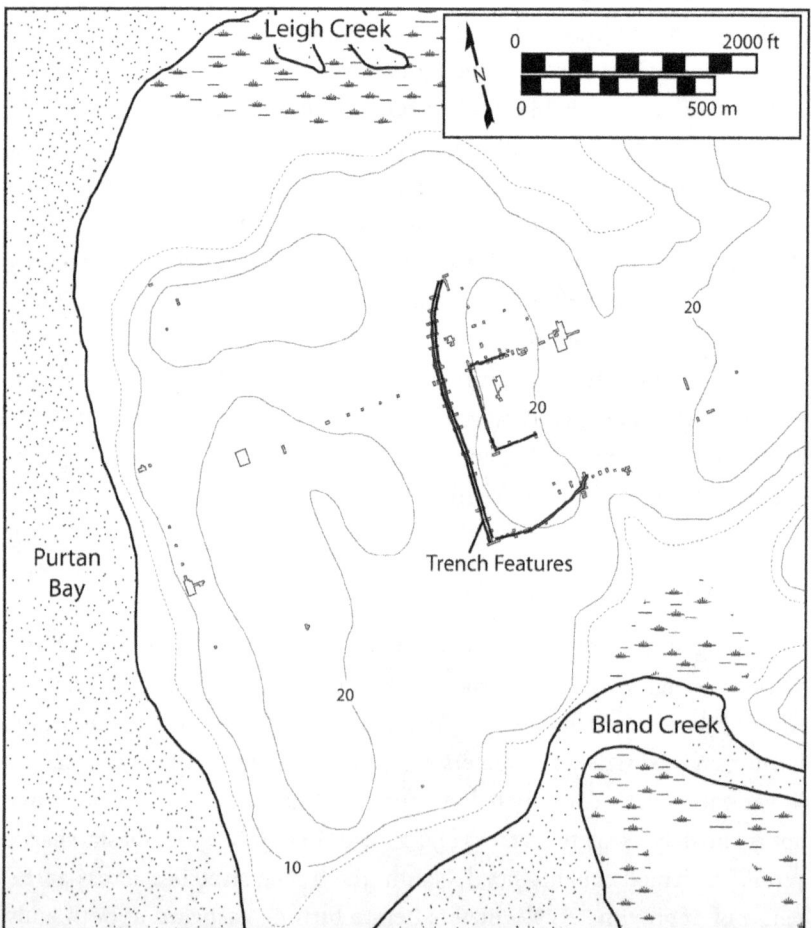

Figure 6.5. Werowocomoco site plan.

Figure 6.6. Werowocomoco site features 161 and 162. Photograph by Thane Harpole.

on the north side and sharply to the east on the south side. A narrow (40 cm) gap in the trenches appears near the center of the site, pointing toward a likely entryway in the trenches.

The radiocarbon assays suggest the initial construction of a relatively small set of trenches—possibly an enclosure—circa AD 1200. These early trench features predate the larger pair of trenches constructed at about AD 1350. Radiocarbon dates from the interior trench (feature 552) indicate that the feature filled during the period from AD 1200 to 1350. The outer trenches filled between AD 1350 and the early seventeenth century.

In concert with this radiometric record, the soil profiles of the trenches at the Werowocomoco site offer evidence of how these features were excavated and filled. The earliest trench—feature 552—included a series of thin (1–4 cm deep) lenses at the bottom of a basin-shaped profile. These deposits were well sorted, meaning that the sediment sizes were all fairly

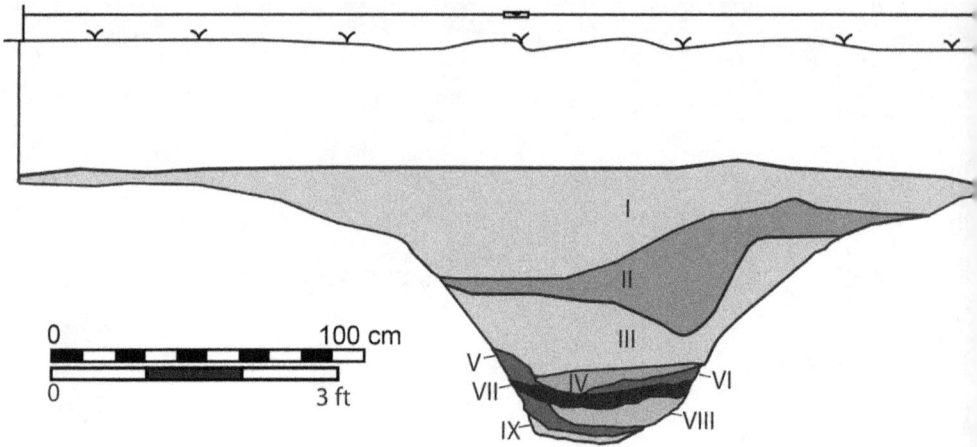

Figure 6.7. Feature 552 profile.

similar. Composed of fine-grained sands and silts overlying the feature's clay base, these thin lenses record the repeated deposition of surface wash that flowed into the trenches after they were opened. No artifacts were recovered from these deposits.

Three more-substantial strata (15–25 cm deep) above the sandy lenses in the trench feature consisted of an organic-rich, dark brown, sandy loam with heavy charcoal flecking. Made up of poorly sorted soils and sediments, these deposits contained a mix of clays, silts, and sands. All of the artifacts included in the feature were recovered from these deposits. A radiocarbon assay from the top of these layers returned a median calibrated date of AD 1350. This date is similar to a cluster of five other radiocarbon dates across the site, including the earliest results for the larger trench features. Soil profiles from these (longer and later) features include a series of relatively shallow lenses similar to those identified at the base of feature 552. The stratified deposits in features 161 and 162 included well-sorted sands and silts with associated radiocarbon dates from the fourteenth through the sixteenth century AD.

Taken as a whole, the radiocarbon dates and geoarchaeological evidence from the trenches at Werowocomoco suggest a sequence of construction events circa AD 1200 and 1350. A small set of trenches opened circa AD 1200 initially received light deposits of waterborne sediment. Circa AD 1350, feature 552 filled rapidly with organic- and artifact-rich soils from a living surface. At approximately the same time, residential spaces at the site expanded, and a much larger set of trenches—features 161 and 162—was constructed.

Trench construction at Werowocomoco likely involved simple tools, including digging sticks, bone or stone hoes, and baskets used to move excavated soil. The radiocarbon assays clustering around AD 1350 and the trench profiles suggest that a coordinated labor force filled the earliest trench features in a relatively short burst of effort during the fourteenth century AD. At approximately the same time, Native laborers constructed a complicated array of longer trenches at the site. The construction sequence suggests that the settlement's residents may have deliberately refilled the smaller trench feature at the same time that they opened the larger trenches.

While we have not exposed these features in their entirety, there are some indications that the feature 161 and 162 trenches match the D-shaped pattern found on the earliest known depiction of Werowocomoco—the Zuñiga Chart discussed in chapter 2. Our excavations on the north side of these features did not proceed into a densely forested area. Soil deflation and erosion have impacted the southern portion of the features. Here, feature 161 was difficult to identify, and the remnants of feature 162 were narrow and shallow. Still, the straight-sided trenches on the river-side to the west and the curving pattern to the east together suggest a D-shaped configuration similar to the one depicted on the Zuñiga Chart. Recall that the Zuñiga Chart, dating to 1608, records John Smith's passage through Tsenacomacoh during the earliest days of the James Fort colony. Another seventeenth-century map, the *Dartmouth Map of Virginia*, depicts a similar double D-shaped pattern at Werowocomoco.[15] These early colonial-era maps may, in fact, depict the layout of the two large trench features that were still in evidence at Werowocomoco in 1607.

Chiefly Architecture at Werowocomoco, circa AD 1560

East of the three trench features and 400 meters from the riverfront, our excavations uncovered post-mold stains from a large Native structure dating to the latter half of the sixteenth century. The highest density of Native post molds appeared in excavation units located along the eastern edge of the site, highlighting an area with repeated construction and reconstruc-

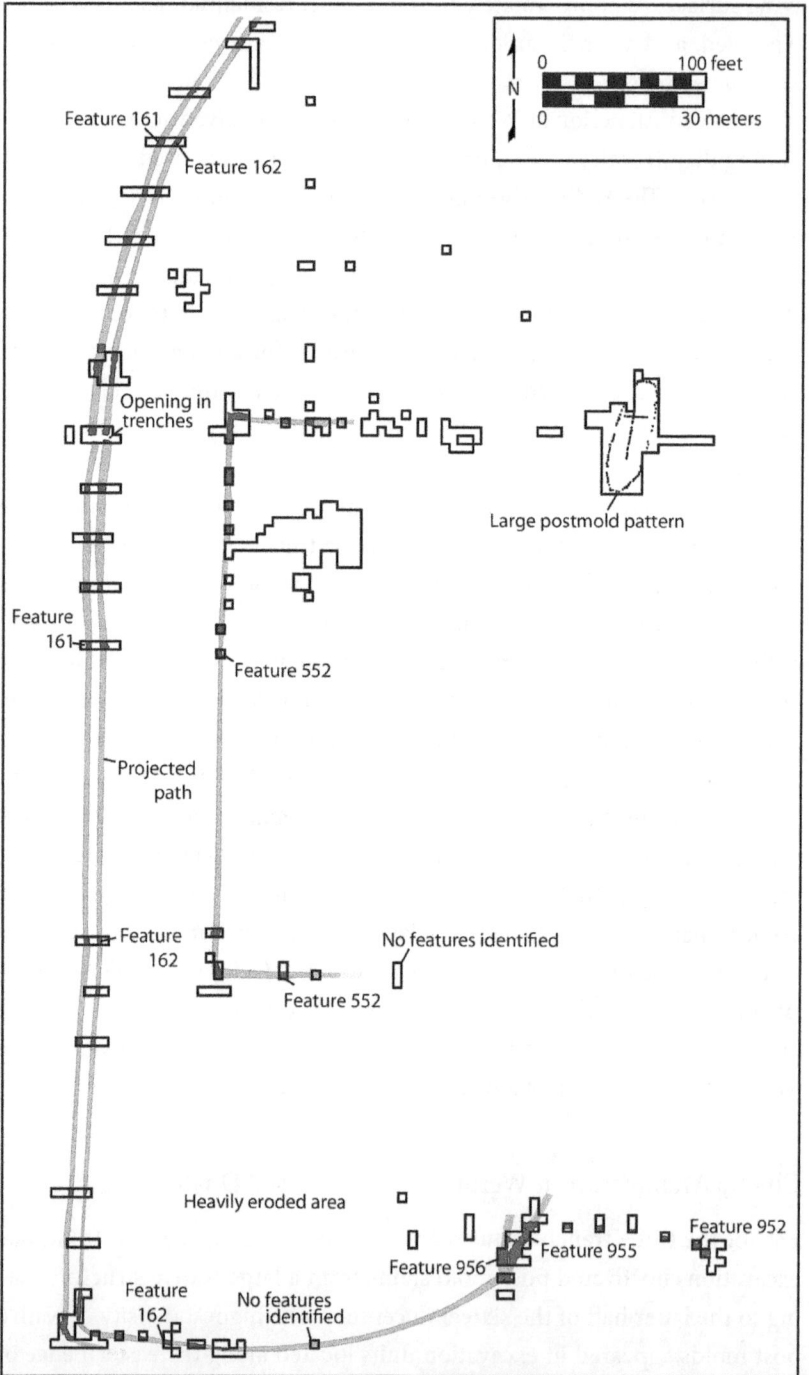

Figure 6.8. Werowocomoco site interior showing trench features.

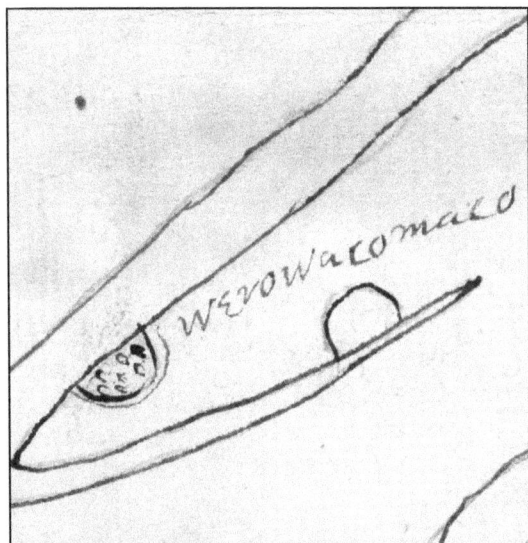

Figure 6.9. Inset from the *Dartmouth Map of Virginia*.
Harry Ransom Center, University of Texas at Austin.

tion of substantial architecture. Wood charcoal recovered from one post mold returned a radiocarbon date with a calibrated range centered in the latter half of the sixteenth century, suggesting that the building was probably in use during the years when Wahunsenacawh was in residence at Werowocomoco.

Twenty pieces of sheet copper matching the chemical signature of metal traded from James Fort were collected by property owner Lynn Ripley from the area around this structure prior to our excavations.[16] Since then our excavations have recovered an additional 12 pieces of copper with similar appearance and chemical composition. All but one of these artifacts were located within the enclosure formed by trench features 161 and 162, pointing toward a close association between trade copper and the site interior. The copper sheeting had been cut into rough squares ranging 3–7 cm across, and some had been rolled into tubular beads.

Identifying the size and shape of the post mold pattern associated with these materials proved challenging due to plow disturbance of the shallow post mold stains. The abundance of small stains in this area further complicated the effort. Nonetheless, the excavators noted a clear line of post molds running north/northeast to south/southwest, and a second line roughly

Figure 6.10. Jamestown trade copper recovered from the Werowocomoco site.

perpendicular to this one near the center of the block. Arcing lines near the northern and southern edges of the block were also apparent during the excavations. The figure below combines these lines in an interpretation of a possible structural pattern measuring approximately 22 by 6 meters. With an area of over 100 square meters, this structure represents one of the largest Native house patterns identified in the Chesapeake.[17]

Several lines of evidence support the inference that this post-mold pattern does indeed represent the footprint of a large Native structure, possibly one associated with Wahunsenacawh. First, the elliptical shape of the pattern matches most other Native structures identified in Tidewater Virginia. Second, while the structure at Werowocomoco appears remarkably long and wide, a handful of other unusually large structures in the region have similar widths and center support posts.[18] Third, the modest counts

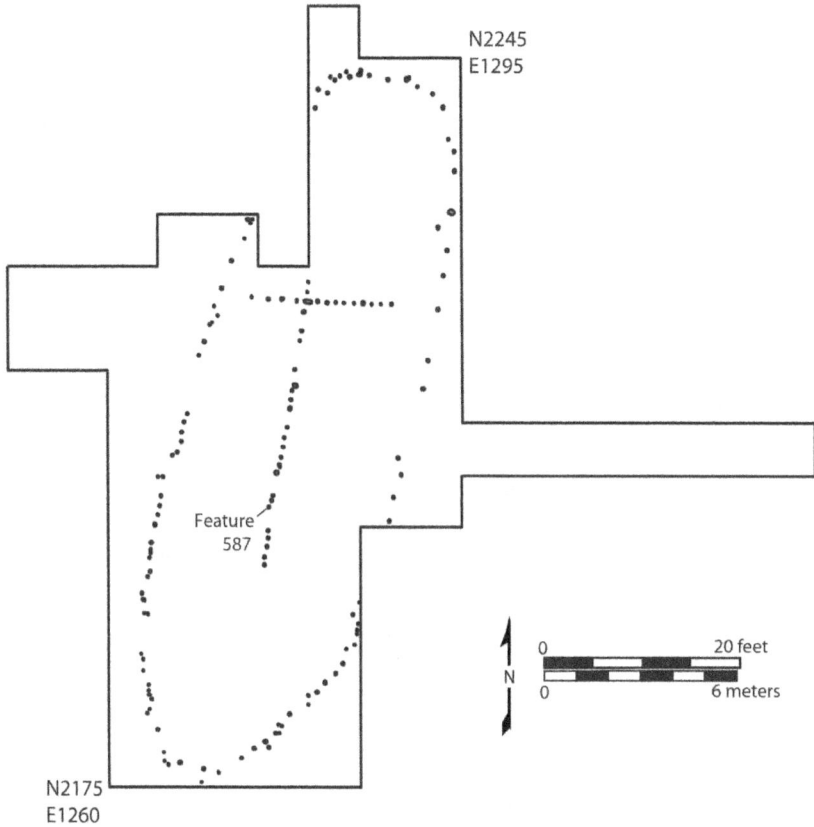

Figure 6.11. Large house pattern, possibly Wahunsenacawh's residence, identified at the Werowocomoco site.

of Native artifacts recovered from the area around the house—with the exception of fire-cracked rock—accord well with relatively clean domestic space marked by a series of hearths.

English colonists' references to chiefly architecture also call to mind elements of the identified post-mold pattern. In his *Relation of Virginia*, Henry Spelman wrote:

> Their buildings are made like an oven with a little hole to come in at, but more spacious within, having a hole in the midst of the house for smoke to go out at. The king's houses are both broader and longer than the rest, having many dark windings and turnings before any come where the king is.[19]

John Smith's *A True Relation* offers a similar account of Wahunsenacawh's houses:

> By this, the great King hath foure or five houses, each containing fourscore or an hundred foote in length, pleasantly seated upon an high sandy hill.[20]

Of the archaeologically identified examples in the Tidewater region, only the 72-foot-long structure identified at Werowocomoco comes close to Smith's estimate that Wahunsenacawh's houses measured 100 feet or more in length. The structure appears to have a screen in the northern end and a center line of support posts, creating internal divisions that echo Spelman's account of a chief's house.

Smith also offers indications of Werowocomoco's layout in one of his written accounts that point toward the significance of the excavated structure. He describes Wahunsenacawh's house as located "thirtie score" from the waterside:

> The next day coming a shore in like order, the King having kindly entertained us with a breakfast, questioned us in this manner: Why we came armed in that sort, seeing hee was our friend, and had neither bowes nor arrowes; what did wee doubt? I told him it was the custome of our Country, not doubting of his kindnes any waies. Wherewith, though hee seemed satisfied, yet Captaie Nuport caused all our men to retire to the water side, which was some thirtie score from thence.[21]

Whether Smith's reference to thirty score (i.e., 600) alludes to a distance of 600 feet (about 200 meters), 600 paces (about 400 meters), or 600 yards (about 550 meters) is left unclear in the text.[22] The implication, though, is that Wahunsenacawh met the colonists in a structure located far enough from the riverfront to prompt Smith to remark on its location. Measured on a straight line, the large structure at Werowocomoco is 350 to 450 meters from Purtan Bay, depending upon where the colonists put ashore. This is an unusually long distance between houses in a Virginia Algonquian town, and one that approximates the distance reported by Smith as measured in paces. Due to riverfront erosion at the site in recent years, this expanse would have been somewhat greater during the early seventeenth century. Though it is not clear exactly where Smith's party landed, his reference to the long stretch between Wahunsenacawh's residence and the waterside accords well with the location of the large post-mold pattern in the site interior.

Finally, the association of the large structure at Werowocomoco with the copper from James Fort, along with the late-sixteenth-century radiocarbon assay, offers chronological evidence that the building in the site's interior was likely Wahunsenacawh's. Wahunsenacawh effectively monopolized the flow of copper from the colonists during James Fort's early days.[23]

Inscribing Deep Time at Werowocomoco

Reaching well beyond the brief period of colonial interactions at the site, Werowocomoco's material, architectural, and historical records trace a 400-year biography of place. The evidence documents the formation of a dispersed horticultural town, the opening of monumental trench features, and the construction of a large building in the site interior, inscribing the settlement with a unique landscape that changed considerably from AD 1200 through the early colonial era. Critical events in this placemaking and remaking process occurred circa AD 1200, 1350, and 1560. The record prior to AD 1200 suggests that forager-fishers made periodic use of the terrace overlooking Purtan Bay without constructing a substantial settlement. Circa AD 1200, trench construction began in the interior at the same time that residential architecture, scattered sheet middens, and Townsend ceramics appeared along the riverfront. The earliest maize we recovered at the site dates to the early thirteenth century AD, pointing to the establishment of a horticultural settlement at that time. During the thirteenth century, residents established a dispersed town at the location, likely during a brief stretch of time that saw the construction of a small trench enclosure in the interior and the rapid expansion of residential spaces along the riverfront. Starting in the fourteenth century AD, the town's residents excavated two parallel trenches in an apparent D-shaped pattern that extended over 200 meters.

The botanical evidence from Werowocomoco records the deforestation of large areas within the site and the introduction of maize, starting in the thirteenth century AD. A subsequent decline in the abundance of plant remains during the sixteenth and early seventeenth centuries, including domesticates and edge species, complicates our understanding of Werowocomoco. Like the botanical evidence, the radiocarbon dates and artifact densities point to a decline in Werowocomoco's population during the sixteenth century, the period of Wahunsenacawh's residence.

The Werowocomoco site contains some of the best-documented archaeobotanical evidence of subsistence practices from a Native site in the Chesapeake region. The available evidence, though, does not record large volumes of maize production or increased horticultural production during the sixteenth century or the early colonial era. There are no indications in Werowocomoco's archaeobotanical record of expanded horticulture production or of greater maize consumption during the period when Wahunsenacawh was in residence. This evidence runs counter to the notion that Wahunsenacawh adopted a strategy of "staple finance" designed to enhance his political status through greater control of food production.[24] In fact, Werowocomoco appears to have seen *less* horticultural activity and *fewer* residents during the sixteenth and early seventeenth centuries than during the previous three centuries. As corroborated by John Smith's warrior counts for Virginia Algonquian towns, Werowocomoco housed a relatively small number of residents during the early colonial era.

The trench features in the site interior inscribed Werowocomoco with a distinctive spatial configuration that remained in use from AD 1200 through the early colonial era when Wahunsenacawh was in residence. This area of the site contained significantly lower artifact densities than the residential areas lining the riverfront. Limited evidence of regional interaction during the precolonial era does appear, though, in the form of an increased diversity of pottery types after AD 1200. The area within the trenches contains not only the Townsend pottery common across the site but also Roanoke simple-stamped pottery (common to the south side of the York River) in significant numbers. Other ceramic types, including Gaston simple-stamped pottery (n = 6) from the west and Potomac Creek pottery (n = 2) from the north were present in small numbers in this area of the site. These materials appeared in association with modest numbers of smoking-pipe fragments (n = 19), which were all but absent from the residential areas lining the riverfront. Evidence of colonial-era trade at the site is more pronounced. By the early seventeenth century, sheet copper from James Fort was concentrated in the spaces surrounding a large structure. So, while trade in highly valued copper clearly played a prominent role within early colonial Werowocomoco, the evidence for precolonial trade at the site is limited. In fact, a chiefly strategy of "wealth finance" centered on controlling exchanges of highly valued materials appears quite late in Werowocomoco's archaeological record, during the period when the Powhatan chiefdom coalesced around Werowocomoco.[25]

While no site in the Chesapeake has earthworks matching the scale of Werowocomoco's trenches, similar features have been identified within several prominent settlements in the region.[26] At the Kiskiak site, located downstream and on the opposite side of the York River, excavations uncovered a curvilinear trench on the bluff overlooking the York River.[27] Measuring 80 cm wide and 20–30 cm deep, feature 7 extends for at least 40 meters north–south, curving westward, away from the riverfront. Artifacts from Kiskiak's trench feature include Townsend fabric-impressed and Roanoke simple-stamped ceramics, as well as a high density of oyster shell, clam shell, and animal bone. A radiocarbon date obtained from maize recovered within a hearth adjacent to the curvilinear trench returned a date in the fifteenth century AD.[28] As detailed in chapter 4, Kiskiak was a prominent center with the Powhatan chiefdom during the early colonial era and home to a weroance tributary to Wahunsenacawh.

As discussed in chapter 5, trench features appear on the Chickahominy River at the Wilcox Neck site and the Buck Farm site. The Clark's Old Neck site, evidently a place of regular public feasting from AD 1100 to 1300, includes a linear trench that extends at least 15 meters across the site. The Buck Farm site is surrounded by two concentric trench features constructed and filled between AD 1300 and 1600. The outer trench at the Buck Farm site held a palisade that encircled a space containing several animal burials. Buck Farm remains enigmatic, though there are some indications in its size and layout that the location may have represented a chiefly compound or a quioccosan.

To the north on the Potomac River, the Potomac Creek site and the Moyaone site were each enclosed by trench features associated with robust palisades surrounding densely occupied settlements.[29] These trenches and similar features at palisaded sites in the Potomac River piedmont evidently served as borrow pits for soil banked against a stockade wall for support.[30] The Potomac Creek site began as a heavily fortified town with a large residential population circa AD 1300. During the seventeenth century the location lacked a resident population but continued to serve as a burial ground for the Patawomeck, with ossuaries in use through the early colonial period.[31]

Trenches clearly played a role marking prominent places and segregating ritualized spaces in the Chesapeake, especially during the period from AD 1200 through the early colonial era. Several of the locations with trenches also featured palisades, especially in the Potomac River valley. In at least some circumstances, trench and palisade enclosures appear to have defined ceremonial spaces surrounding burial grounds and animal sacrifices, including those at the Buck Farm site on the Chickahominy River and at the late-stage Potomac Creek site. Other trenches, including those identified at the Werowocomoco site, do not appear in tandem with palisades. The trenches at the Wilcox Neck site did not hold palisade posts but did mark spaces associated with feasting, human interments, and dog burials. The trenches at the Kiskiak site were linked to a political center and the residence of a prominent weroance. In short, trenches in the Virginia Algonquian world marked places of feasting, burial, political power, priestly authority, and protected space.

Early Colonial Encounters at Werowocomoco

Werowocomoco's landscape history provides a basis for reconsidering the early colonial encounters documented by colonists who visited the town. Seven such encounters at Werowocomoco were recorded by colonists from James Fort. The earliest, and best known, event at the town of Werowocomoco occurred in December of 1607, when Smith was captured, brought to the town, and released after a period of captivity lasting roughly four weeks.[32] Nearly half of the original colonists were dead by this time as a result of starvation, disease, and hostilities with the Powhatan chiefdom. Wahunsenacawh carefully followed the colony's struggles to acquire food, sending gifts of maize, deer, and other provisions at strategic moments that saved at least some of the colonists from starvation. He received copper objects, glass beads, and iron hatchets in return.

When the captive Smith arrived at Werowocomoco, he wrote that he was met by 200 "courtiers" who studied him closely.[33] Later Smith numbered the "able" male population of Werowocomoco at 40, a relatively small number compared with several other towns Smith visited.[34] Smith was eventually brought to Wahunsenacawh's house, where he met the Mamanatowick and his impressive retinue. In his original account Smith describes events at Werowocomoco as including feasting and long speeches spoken by Wahunsenacawh and by Smith.[35] When Wahunsenacawh inquired as to why the colonists had come, Smith feigned that they had been driven by Spanish enemies, bad weather, and damaged vessels to the area. His recent exploration, Smith explained, was aimed at discovering a passage to the west and at avenging the death of one of the colonists at the hands of the Monacans. Wahunsenacawh insisted that Smith and the English leave James Fort and move their settlement to Capahosic, a small settlement downstream of Werowocomoco. Wahunsenacawh would see to it that the colonists were fed and protected if they followed these instructions and provided Wahunsenacawh with hatchets and copper. Smith was then released and escorted back to James Fort.

In a later version of these events published in 1624, Smith added an account of a threatened execution and rescue by Pocahontas. Considering the amount of attention that has been paid this event, it is remarkable how little Smith wrote about it. Smith refers to himself in the third person:

> Having feasted him after their best barbarous manner they could, a long consultation was held, but the conclusion was, two great stones were brought before Powhatan: then as many as could layd hands on him, dragged him to them, and thereon laid his head, and being ready with their clubs, to beate out his braines, Pocahontas the Kings dearest daughter, when no intreaty could prevaile, got his head in her armes, and laid her owne upon his to save him from death: whereat the Emperour was contented he should live to make him hatchets, and her bells, beads, and copper.[36]

In this version of the captivity narrative, Smith reported that two days later he experienced a final ceremony before being released. Smith was taken to a large structure in the woods and placed before a fire. Wahunsenacawh appeared from behind a mat in the structure with a large group of men, all of whom were painted black. The paramount chief instructed Smith to obtain two cannons and a grindstone at James Fort in compensation for the town of Capahosic. Wahunsenacawh declared to Smith that he would "for ever esteeme him as his sonne Nantaquod."[37] Smith departed for James Fort soon thereafter.

In February 1608 the colonists received word from Wahunsenacawh that he wanted to meet Smith's "father" Christopher Newport, setting the stage for the second documented encounter at Werowocomoco.[38] Upon arriving at Wahunsenacawh's house, Smith gave Wahunsenacawh a suit of red cloth, a white greyhound, and a hat. Three of Wahunsenacawh's "nobles" accepted the gifts with speeches of alliance and friendship. On their third day at Werowocomoco, Newport began to trade with Wahunsenacawh, seeking food in return for hatchets and copper pots. Objecting to the idea of haggling, Wahunsenacawh demanded that Newport lay out all of the items the English brought for trade. Wahunsenacawh would choose what he wanted and reciprocate as he saw fit. Newport went along with this arrangement and received four bushels of corn from Wahunsenacawh. Annoyed at Newport's perceived ineptitude at negotiating with Wahunsenacawh, Smith then pulled out some blue glass beads. Wahunsenacawh demanded that Smith offer the beads in trade. When Smith agreed to relinquish the blue beads, he reportedly obtained 200 to 300 bushels of corn in return.

In the following days the colonists discussed with Wahunsenacawh a possible joint attack on the Monacans, plans never set in motion. They also received a series of insistent invitations from Opechancanough to pay him a visit. Eventually Newport acquiesced and the colonists traveled up the river to visit Wahunsenacawh's brother at Pamunkey. After several days of feasting and trading with Opechancanough, the colonists traveled back down the river, briefly stopped at Werowocomoco, before returning to James Fort.

Later, in the fall of 1608, Smith had become president of the colony, and Newport had returned to Virginia with a second relief supply. Newport brought more colonists, including eight "Dutch-men and Poles," who would come to play a role at Werowocomoco.[39] Newport also carried instructions from the Virginia Company to crown Wahunsenacawh as a vassal to King James. Smith traveled to Werowocomoco, his third trip there, to invite Wahunsenacawh to James Fort for the coronation.[40] While waiting to meet Wahunsenacawh, Smith experienced a ceremony he labeled a "Virginia Maskarado." Smith was brought to a field and placed before a fire when a group of Virginia Algonquian women ran from the forest and began to dance and sing. They were clothed with leaves and adorned with white, red, and black paint. The group's leader wore deer antlers on her head while others carried bows and arrows, clubs, and swords. After an hour of the performance, the women returned to the woods. The next day, Wahunsenacawh arrived. Smith offered him presents and assistance in attacking the Monacans. When Smith invited him to come to James Fort for the coronation, Wahunsenacawh angrily refused both the invitation and the offer of assistance, insisting that he could avenge the injuries caused by the Monacans on his own. Wahunsenacawh instructed Newport to travel to Werowocomoco in eight days for the ceremony. Smith returned to James Fort with the message.

The fourth recorded event at Werowocomoco centered on Wahunsenacawh's coronation, a ceremony Smith dismisses in a single paragraph.[41] Christopher Newport presented gifts to Powhatan, including a pitcher, a basin, a bed, and a red cloak. Powhatan did not comply with the English efforts to crown him:

> But a foule trouble there was to make him kneele to receive his Crowne, he neither knowing the majesty nor meaning of a Crowne, nor bending of the knee, endured so many perswasions, examples, and instructions, as tyred them all; at last by leaning hard on his shoulders, he a little stooped, and three having the crowne in their hands put it on his head, when by the warning of a Pistoll the Boats were prepared with such a volley of shot, that the King start up in a horrible feare, till he saw all was well.[42]

Powhatan then reciprocated by offering Newport his shoes and a mantle (Powhatan's Mantle, perhaps?). Wahunsenacawh also provided seven or eight bushels of corn and admonished the colonists not to pursue their plans to travel west to Monacan territory.

The fifth recorded encounter at Werowocomoco occurred late in December 1608 through January 1609, following a period when Wahunsenacawh had reportedly commanded his people to cease trading with the colonists and allow them to starve.[43] In a situation of growing desperation, Smith led a party to the town of Nansemond and obtained a large quantity of corn by firing muskets, burning a house, and threatening to put the entire settlement to the torch. Seeking to repeat this tactic, Smith planned a return to Werowocomoco in order to capture Wahunsenacawh and all of his provisions. Wahunsenacawh provided an opening for this when he sent word to James Fort that he would provision the settlement if the colonists constructed an English-style house for him at Werowocomoco and sent a grindstone, swords, guns, a rooster, a hen, copper, and beads. The colonists agreed to the requested gifts, minus the swords and guns. Smith sent three

"Dutchmen," recently arrived lumber mill men, and two Englishmen to build the house.[44]

In December 1608, a year after his captivity within Werowocomoco, Smith returned there by river. Upon his arrival, Wahunsenacawh brusquely asked when the colonists planned to leave. When Smith reminded him of his offer of provisions, Wahunsenacawh repeated his demand for guns and swords, adding sardonically that corn was more valuable than these items, since corn could be eaten. Smith responded that he had no swords or guns to spare but had sacrificed to have his men build Wahunsenacawh a house and expected friendship in return. Wahunsenacawh raised his own doubts about the purpose of their settlement:

> Some doubt I have of your comming hither, that makes me not so kindly seek to relieve you as I would: for many doe informe me, your comming hither is not for trade, but to invade my people, and possesse my Country, who dare not come to bring you Corne, seeing you thus armed with your men. To free us of this feare, leave aboord your weapons, for here they are needlesse, we being all friends, and for ever Powhatans.[45]

Wahunsenacawh then provided corn to the colonists in return for a copper kettle. At the conclusion of this, the sixth close encounter at Werowocomoco, Wahunsenacawh discussed war and peace with the colonists, urging that they choose the latter.

Upon Smith's departure from Werowocomoco, Wahunsenacawh sent two of the Dutchmen at Werowocomoco to James Fort to collect weapons.[46] The Dutchmen claimed, falsely, that Smith had requested the arms. The following day, six or seven additional colonists decided to abandon the "misery" of James Fort for Werowocomoco, stealing swords and firearms as gifts for Wahunsenacawh. In the meantime, Smith and his party sailed upstream from Werowocomoco to obtain corn from Opechancanough at Pamunkey. The colonists later headed back downstream, stopping once again at Werowocomoco. After sending men ashore to reconnoiter the town, Smith learned that Wahunsenacawh had vacated his new house and left the town. After this, the seventh and final recorded event at Werowocomoco, the colonists returned to James Fort with the supplies they had obtained on the trip. Subsequently, Wahunsenacawh moved his residence westward to Orapax on the upper reaches of the Chickahominy River.

Werowocomoco as a Space of Colonial Entanglements

The documented history at Werowocomoco indicates that Wahunsena-cawh orchestrated the colonists' exposure to Powhatan ritual, exchange, and the built environment such that Werowocomoco emerges from the documents as a space of colonial entanglements. Smith and a number of other colonists lived for a time at Werowocomoco between AD 1607 and 1609. The Dutch craftsmen obtained weapons at Wahunsenacawh's behest, and other colonists slipped away to Werowocomoco after stealing arms as gifts for the paramount chief. While the English focused their diplomatic efforts on Wahunsenacawh, Opechancanough repeatedly sought to establish his own, separate alliance with the colonists. Read carefully, this history runs counter to the notion that the early-seventeenth-century history of the Chesapeake entailed a simple, dichotomous "contact" of English colonizer and Powhatan Native, each conceived as bounded, unified entities existing independent of each other and of particular events in the seventeenth-century Chesapeake.[47] An alternative conception of Werowocomoco emphasizes the town as a space of struggle and negotiation that created and sustained new political strategies amidst the rapidly shifting relations of colonialism.

The most prominent events involving such an intertwined colonial relationship occurred when Wahunsenacawh transformed Smith into a Powhatan weroance and when the colonists struggled to crown Powhatan as a vassal to King James. Powhatan's efforts to remake Smith may or may not have involved his daughter Pocahontas. For over a century, scholars have debated whether or not Pocahontas truly did "rescue" Smith during the 1607 winter, while more recently researchers have focused on the significance of the overall captivity narrative to Powhatan culture and history. From the mid-nineteenth century, historians have suggested that Smith invented or exaggerated Pocahontas' role in the captivity narrative to enhance his importance and to enliven the story.[48] Other scholars have pointed out that notions of romantic involvement between Pocahontas and Smith may be overblown, given Pocahontas' young age. For example, Helen Rountree and Camilla Townsend have dismissed Pocahontas' purported role in the event, based partly on Smith's silence on the matter in his initial published account.[49] Townsend notes that on several occasions during his travels in Europe and North America, Smith reported that a young woman intervened in his behalf during a moment of peril, raising questions as to the veracity of all of these events.

In fact, whether or not Pocahontas played the specific role described in Smith's *Generall Historie* may not be particularly important. More significant, perhaps, are the indications that during his captivity at Werowocomoco, Smith was transformed into a Powhatan weroance, an interpretation that has received support from several scholars.[50] Williamson and Gleach have both explored this idea in persuasive ways.[51] Williamson suggests that Wahunsenacawh adopted Smith in order to establish a political alliance with the English cemented through the creation of a father–son relationship between Wahunsenacawh and Smith. In this reading, Wahunsenacawh's offer of Capahosic and of abundant corn placed him in the superior position as creditor to the English. Rather than a potential love interest, Pocahontas became Smith's sister, an interpretation that accords well with their subsequent interaction.

The early events at Werowocomoco represent Wahunsenacawh's efforts to, in effect, *colonize* the English by creating lasting economic and political dependencies through the metaphor of kinship and gifts of food. In a similar vein, the English sought to confer a subservient status on Wahunsenacawh through the power of ritual in his coronation ceremony, an effort Wahunsenacawh seems to have grasped (and resisted) all too well. The struggles and negotiations between the English and the Powhatan from 1607 to 1609, reflected in long speeches, material exchanges, threatened violence, and ceremony, meant that Werowocomoco became a locus of new social connections and novel cultural categories important in the early colonial history of the Chesapeake. Wahunsenacawh sought copper, iron tools, and swords from the English, while the colonists desperately needed food. By obtaining valuable gifts from the English, Wahunsenacawh enhanced his ability to exercise regional authority and, briefly, to expand this authority. Judging from his rhetoric at Werowocomoco, the arrival of the English "strangers" initially played into Wahunsenacawh's efforts to expand the "Powhatan" label to include all residents in the Virginia Tidewater region, including the English. A ritualized space, Werowocomoco played a role in the events that transformed John Smith into a Powhatan weroance, even as Smith may not have completely understood this change in his social personhood. Now, with knowledge of Werowocomoco's deep history as a landscape of power, Smith's transformation at the town takes on a new resonance.

Werowocomoco as a Virginia Algonquian Space

Combined with documentary references to Werowocomoco, the archaeological record of trench features, architectural structures, and taskscapes within Werowocomoco offers some indications of how visitors experienced the town. Viewed from a dugout canoe on the river, Werowocomoco between AD 1200 and 1609 stood apart from the surrounding forests as an area largely cleared of trees. Starting at a landing along the bay, a visitor to the settlement began with domestic spaces lining the waterfront. The dense scatter of post stains in this area of the settlement traces the four-centuries-long building and rebuilding of houses within a persistent place. Judging from the diversity of material culture recovered from this area—pottery, stone tools, and fire-cracked rock, as well as abundant charcoal and charred plant materials—this domestic zone hosted a wide range of the activities performed daily in a horticultural community. After passing through the domestic spaces along the riverfront, a visitor to Werowocomoco walking in an easterly direction into the settlement's interior faced an open space lacking built structures extending 100 meters to the northeast. Beyond this area, the visitor continuing into the site interior encountered a series of trenches and berms. A gap in the two outer trenches opened to a large area enclosed by the trenches. Within this space, 100 meters east of the ditch opening, was a large structure, significantly longer and wider than other houses in the town. The visitor continuing into this structure entered a building with interior spaces separated by screens.

This arrangement of space, with its progression from domestic areas to a less accessible zone associated with priests and chiefly elites, appears in other important Algonquian settlements in the region. Spatial arrangements that allowed weroances or quioccosuks (i.e., priests) to observe visitors as they approached an important location also appear in early documentary references. At Kiskiak areas for processing oysters and clams lined the lower, embayed portion of Indian Field Creek near its mouth. Domestic spaces with midden deposits and the post stains of house patterns lined the tops of bluffs overlooking the creek. Kiskiak's interior spaces included a series of concentric trench features located 350 meters from the waterfront, a spatial arrangement with parallels at Werowocomoco.

Another important place in the Powhatan world, Uttamussak, was home to the chief Pamunkey priests. The settlement was marked by three massive temples located deep in the woods on hills overlooking the Pamunkey River. Uttamussak's temples were visited only by priests and weroances, "nor the Salvages dare not goe up the river in boats by it, but they solemnly cast some peece of copper, white beads, or *Pocones* into the river, for feare their *Okee* should be offended and revenged of them."[52] Such sacred places appear to have been infused with manitou, the spirit-force manifested in powerfully dangerous locations and people.[53]

Several aspects of Werowocomoco's spatial organization also have parallels in the North Carolina Algonquian settlement of Secota (or Secoton), illustrated by colonist John White in a watercolor painting of the town. White's depiction of Secota has been dismissed by some scholars as a Europeanized imagining of the Native world in coastal North Carolina.[54] No doubt this characterization has some merit, particularly in terms of the wide, straight avenue running through Secota, which has no parallels in the archaeological record. Yet completely dismissing this imagery may be unwise. White was a careful observer whose paintings captured cultural details otherwise lost. Like Secota, Werowocomoco and Kiskiak included residential zones close to the riverfront. Moving away from the river in the Secota imagery, an area of planted fields is followed by round plots for prayer, feasting, and ceremony centered on a small circle in the interior of the settlement marked by upright posts with carved faces. White's annotation here describes "a Ceremony in their prayers with strange iesturs and songs dancing about posts carved on the topps lyke mens faces." Opposite the dance circle, a structure marks the location where "the Tombe of their Herounds standeth."

The interior zone of the Werowocomoco and Kiskiak sites includes ditch features that echo this circular arrangement. A small circular feature along the southeastern edge of the site (feature 952) may inscribe a similar space at Werowocomoco. On the whole, a transition from domestic space to spaces associated with ceremony and chiefly elites appears in both the archival and archaeological evidence.

Werowocomoco and the Virginia Algonquian Spatial Imaginary

Early colonial encounters at Werowocomoco highlight differences in English and Virginia Algonquian conceptions of social space, revealing that colonial chroniclers overlooked ritualized spaces and failed to appreciate

Figure 6.12. John White's painting of Secoton. © Trustees of the British Museum.

the meaningful dimensions of spaces that they experienced firsthand.[55] Though Smith visited Werowocomoco several times and described his experiences there in some detail, he wrote nothing of the landscape features identified archaeologically at the site. The only apparent reference to the trenches at Werowocomoco appears on early maps of the region—the Zuñiga Chart and the *Dartmouth Map of Virginia*. Colonists' accounts provide important details of the Virginia Algonquian cultural landscape, though they emphasize prominent leaders, pivotal events, leadership structures, and military capacities. Werowocomoco's trenches, narrow enough to step across, do not appear to have served a defensive function, except perhaps in a spiritual sense that resonated with Virginia Algonquians.

While the landscape features at Werowocomoco escaped the notice of colonial chroniclers, the archaeological evidence from across the Chesapeake highlights an association between similar trenches and ritualized spaces. A discussion of one such space and its use in the Algonquian Chesapeake appears in accounts of a ceremony held at Quiyoughcohanock (KWEE-aw-kuh-HAAN-awk), a Virginia Algonquian town on the south side of the James. In 1608 the residents of Quiyoughcohanock staged a Huskanaw—a Virginia Algonquian rite of passage designed to "make black boys" who would become weroances, priests, or cockarouses (respected warriors and councilors). Colonist William White witnessed the event, and other colonial chroniclers echoed his description in their written accounts.[56] Virginia Algonquian communities staged a Huskanaw periodically within different chiefly towns throughout the region. The ceremony commenced with a feast held at the edge of the woods during which initiates were painted white and instructed by sacred practitioners who were painted black and adorned with antlers. For several days the boys danced in two groups around a circuit measuring a quarter mile, led by a weroance and encouraged by repeated beatings.[57] The initiates were subsequently brought deep into the forest and given hallucinogens. There they were confined, living nearly naked in all types of weather, in a pen fashioned from a bentwood framework. After a period of nine months, the surviving boys were reborn into town life, where they reportedly remembered nothing of their former selves.[58] A term translated as "he has a new body," the Huskanaw transformed boys into quioccosuks. They became quioccosuks through spiritual contact orchestrated by antler-wearing men and signaled by black, a color associated with Powhatan priests.[59] Colonists reported that Powhatan priests were "able to make a truer judgment of things" due to their considered instruction in the region's history and their considerable knowledge of the natural world.[60] The initial stage of the Huskanaw ritual occurred at the town's edge and was centered on a large circular track that enclosed a series of dances, feasts, and other rites. Like Quiyoughcohanock, Werowocomoco emerges from the early colonial narratives as a place of ceremony, with events that featured antler wearers and men painted black. Werowocomoco's spaces included curving trenches that measured roughly a quarter mile in diameter situated along the boundaries of the settlement at the forest edge, landscape features resembling the ritual circuits around which Huskanaw initiates traveled. At Quiyoughcohanock such areas, located at the edges of settled space, held the first stage of a rite of passage performed by antler-wearing men painted black. A similar association with quioccosuks and the Huskanaw appears likely for Werowocomoco.

Like other towns in Tidewater Virginia, Werowocomoco served as a focus of social life for much of the year from the thirteenth century through contact. Riverine towns gathered Virginia Algonquians from spring through late fall, after which individual households moved their dwellings away from the riverine settlements to hunt and forage in interior, upland settings. A period of transition between these two phases of social life in September through November was reserved for the "chiefe feasts and sacrifices," celebrated in the towns of weroances.[61] The fall harvest brought together communities dispersed along the Chesapeake's waterways for ceremonies and feasts:

> The greatest Annual Feast they have, is at the time of their Corn-gathering, at which they revel several days together. To these they universally contribute, as they do to the gathering in the Corn. On this occasion they have their greatest variety of Pastimes, and more especially of their War-Dances, and Heroick Songs; in which they boast, that their Corn being now gather'd, they have store enough for their Women and Children; and have nothing to do, but to go to War, Travel, and to seek out for New Adventures.[62]

It was during this period in the fall of 1608 when Smith witnessed a performance of women wielding weapons, led by one adorned with antlers. The spatial and temporal dimensions of Virginia Algonquian social life converged on prominent riverine towns, particularly during these rites of fall. As a place marking the transition from horticultural activities to interior hunting camps, Werowocomoco anchored the annual cycle and oriented female and male labor. Other Tidewater towns also served a similar role on the cultural landscape, yet the built environment and history of spaces associated with Werowocomoco from AD 1200 to 1609 set the town apart.

While much of its past significance no doubt remains lost today, it is clear that Werowocomoco and other chiefly centers in the Chesapeake contributed to the meaningful dimension of social space within the Virginia Algonquian landscape.[63] Werowocomoco's archaeological record, in addition to historical descriptions, indicates that the town was a prominent location well before Wahunsenacawh arrived there, and the site remains a powerful place today. The earliest construction of trench features at Werowocomoco preceded Wahunsenacawh's rise to power as the Powhatan paramount chief by more than three centuries. Wahunsenacawh moved from Powhatan, a town on the western edges of the Virginia Algonquian world, to Werowocomoco considerably later, during the sixteenth century. Initially an outsider to the town, Wahunsenacawh relocated to Werowocomoco as he became Mamanatowick and as he consolidated chiefly authority through warfare, intimidation, strategic marriages, and regional alliances. Wahunsenacawh's house at Werowocomoco was evidently located within an earthwork enclosure constructed much earlier.

A persistent place for centuries, the "Place of the antler wearers" included ritualized spaces and events orchestrated by priests trained in the social and natural histories of Tsenacomacoh. The history of the Powhatan chiefdom and Werowocomoco's long biography indicate that it was not Wahunsenacawh who made Werowocomoco a powerful place. Rather, it was Werowocomoco that transformed Wahunsenacawh into a powerful leader.

Chapter 7

Persistent Places in Colonial Tsenacomacoh

A year after Wahunsenacawh's departure from Werowocomoco, James-town's governor, Thomas Gates, ordered the 60 surviving colonists to evacuate the fort.[1] The Paspahegh and other Virginia Algonquians living near the fort had refused to trade with the colonists and sniped at any-one venturing beyond the disintegrating palisade.[2] Unable to acquire badly needed provisions or to safely raise their own crops, the settlers suffered se-vere famine in the "starving time" of 1609 to 1610.[3] At one point during this period 17 colonists slipped away from the fort, stole a boat, and made their way to Kecoughtan, never to return. Other colonists venturing beyond the fort were found slain, their mouths stuffed full of bread in an act read by the colonists as a sign of contempt and scorn, "thatt others mighte expectt the Lyke when they shold come to seeke for breade and reliefe amongste them."[4] With summer approaching, the colonists decided to give up, aban-don the fort, and make their way down the James. While waiting for the tide to turn, the departing colonists met a new English supply fleet travel-ing up the river. The three ships carried 300 colonists, provisions, arms, and Thomas West, the newly appointed governor of the colony. Gates' evacuation order was rescinded the next day.

Known today as Lord De La Warr (or Delaware), the new governor in-stituted a strict military regime and set about rebuilding James Fort's tri-angular palisade, storehouse, and chapel.[5] De La Warr also set in motion a brutal offensive against the Powhatan chiefdom, drawing on his experi-ences as a commander in Ireland.[6] A third Englishman named Thomas—Thomas Dale—arrived the following year, and as deputy governor he issued a set of regulations that became known as the "Lawes Divine, Morall, and Martiall."[7] Under the leadership of De La Warr, Gates, and Dale, the newly strengthened garrison began to assault Native towns near James Fort, killing residents, seizing food stores, and burning houses. During these attacks, heavily armored raiding parties from James Fort fired muskets en masse.

At Kecoughtan near the James River's mouth, the governor's men lured the town's residents into the open with a performance of drumming before killing or wounding all those they could fire upon.[8] De La Warr issued an ultimatum to Wahunsenacawh—return all English property and subjects or face war—delivered by a Paspahegh man whose hand had been cut off while a prisoner at James Fort. Wahunsenacawh replied with his own demand, insisting that the Tassantasses confine themselves to James Fort. The English governor ordered his men to attack the town of Paspahegh, where they once again burned houses, cut down the corn, and killed 65 to 75 residents. After capturing one of the Paspahegh weroance's wives and her children, "a Cowncell beinge called itt was Agreed upon to putt the Children to deathe the wch was effected by Throweinge them overboard and shoteinge owtt their Braynes in the water."[9] The colonists later executed the weroance's wife by the sword at Jamestown, over De La Warr's objections. De La Warr had preferred to see her burned alive.[10] On another occasion the colonists forced the Nansemond out of their island settlement, burned their houses, ransacked their temples, removed the corpses of their dead weroances from their tombs, and carried away the pearls and copper accompanying their bodies.[11] Such violence and desecration ignited what scholars have termed the First Anglo-Powhatan War, a period of raids and counter-raids that lasted four years, until 1614.[12]

Wahunsenacawh's brother Opechancanough launched the Second Anglo-Powhatan War. In 1621, three years after Wahunsenacawh's death, Opechancanough called Virginia Algonquians from across the coastal Chesapeake to gather for the "taking up of Powhatan's bones."[13] This ceremony echoes other events recorded in the colonial archives whereby American Indians in the Chesapeake returned to burial grounds and collected human remains in order to reinter them, at times within new settlements removed from the original graves. The Nanticoke, Algonquian speakers from the Eastern Shore across the Chesapeake Bay, gathered bones of the deceased from ossuaries several times during the 1700s in order to bring them to new settlement locations.[14] Writing of the mid-eighteenth century, Thomas Jefferson described a party of Monacan Indians who visited a burial mound in central Virginia: "They went through the woods directly to it, without any instructions or enquiry, and having staid about it some time, with expressions which were construed to be those of sorrow, they returned to the high road, which they had left about half a dozen miles to pay this visit, and pursued their journey."[15] As Jeffrey Hantman and his colleagues have pointed out, such journeys invoked memories of sacred spaces and of ancestors buried in nearby towns that were no longer occupied.[16]

The taking up of Powhatan's bones occurred at a pivotal moment in Tsenacomacoh's long history. The ceremony marked a change in Wahunsenacawh's status: from paramount chief to ancestor. Opechancanough's status had changed as well. Now the effective leader of the Powhatan polity, Opechancanough assumed a new name—Mangopeesomon.[17] The taking up of Powhatan's bones also marked a decisive shift in Virginia Algonquians' collective response to the Tassantasses' expanding settlement within the Chesapeake. On the morning of March 22, 1622, several hundred Virginia Algonquian men walked calmly into English settlements, unarmed in order to avoid raising alarm.[18] By this time the colonists had established tobacco plantations on the prime lands along the James, from the river's mouth to the fall line, in some cases taking over fields recently cleared and tended by Virginia Algonquians.[19] The first commercial crop of Orinoco tobacco had shipped to England in 1613, ushering in an era when tobacco profits drew growing numbers of English planters and indentured servants to the Chesapeake.[20] The Virginia Algonquian visitors seized iron tools and attacked colonists within plantations along the James River. Breaking with past Virginia Algonquian practices, they killed English women and children alongside the men. While the number of settlers in the region had been gradually increasing, the deaths of 347 of the 1,240 in Virginia came close to breaking the colony.

In the first thorough study of these events, historian Frederick Fausz recast the attacks, previously referred to as the 1622 "massacre," as an "uprising."[21] The uprising, Fausz suggests, was triggered in part by the death of Nemattenew, a Virginia Algonquian warrior who led an early revitalization movement among the Virginia Algonquians.[22] Ethnohistorian Frederic Gleach has also reexamined the 1622 attacks and the subsequent 1644 uprising—led again by Opechancanough/Mangopeesomon.[23] Seeking to understand the attacks from a Virginia Algonquian perspective, Gleach has suggested that both were in fact "coups"—blows struck by Mangopeesomon and other Powhatan leaders who understood their positions as morally superior to that of the Tassantasses.[24] The attacks, in this reading, were essentially "military corrections" intended to reproach the interlopers and to prompt them to recognize the impropriety of their behavior.[25] After the 1622 coup the Virginia Algonquians decided to retreat to their riverine towns rather than press the attack, even though the few remaining colonists were vulnerable to annihilation.

Viewed from the perspective of Tsenacomacoh's deep history, the 1622 and 1644 assaults appear as efforts to regain access to critical pathways and persistent places in the Virginia Algonquian landscape. The expansion of English settlements along the James and lower York during the first two decades after 1607, then along the remainder of the York, Rappahannock, and Potomac from 1630 to 1650, forced Virginia Algonquians from towns centered on the same spaces, a process richly documented by ethnohistorian Helen Rountree.[26] With the establishment of the "headright" system in 1618, wealthy colonists acquired vast tracts of land in return for covering the travel expenses of laborers and indentured servants brought to the Chesapeake.[27] By establishing dispersed farms in locations with direct river access that facilitated waterborne trade, English colonists effectively mimicked Virginia Algonquian settlement patterns. In the process, the colonists usurped the central spaces of Tsenacomacoh and disrupted key waterborne links used for centuries.

During the precolonial era, dwelling in the Chesapeake was framed by a riverine waterscape organized around horticultural towns along the bluffs and neck lands overlooking estuarine streams. Riverine corridors connected everyday taskscapes that included horticultural towns, wetland resources, and fishing grounds. Ritualized places—quioccosans, burial grounds, feasting locales, and chiefly towns—gathered residents from dispersed riverine communities for seasonal events vital to social life within Tsenacomacoh. The Treaty of 1646 and the 1677 Treaty of Middle Plantation formally limited Native settlement to areas north of the York River and west of the Blackwater, a tributary to Albemarle Sound south of the James.[28] The resulting refugee communities of Virginia Algonquians no longer had access to centuries-old towns, gardens, fisheries, and hunting grounds fundamental to the annual cycle. Barred from ancestral ossuaries, gathering places, and ceremonial spaces, Virginia Algonquians struggled to reconstitute events crucial to traditional institutions.

The Kiskiak, for example, left their town sometime before 1627, when Jamestown's colonial council ordered Englishmen to occupy the location.[29] In the wake of the 1622 revolt and English counter-raids, the Kiskiak first moved north of the York River, settling along the Piankatank River on land reserved for their use. Court records document colonists' repeated harassment of the Kiskiak and efforts to force them from this new home.[30] Though the Treaty of Middle Plantation sought to limit such tactics by prohibiting English settlement within three miles of a Native town, the Kiskiak's Piankatank reservation lands were surveyed for an English patent by 1683. Starting near the old Kiskiak town on the lower York, the colonists constructed a palisade line that ran the entire width of the peninsula from the York to the James, in 1634.[31] The James-York peninsula, an area that represented the core of Tsenacomacoh and the Powhatan tributary network, quickly became fortified English territory. More important than its role as a defensive feature was the way the 1634 palisade redefined social space for Virginia Algonquians and for the English. The James-York peninsula was increasingly recognized as English territory, a process that fractured pathways and interrupted the regional mobility that had been central to Tsenacomacoh. Rather than defining the *boundaries* of English colonial space as originally intended, the palisade line quickly became its *center*. In the words of historian Philip Levy, the palisade came to represent "the conceptual and cartographic spine of a rambling line of plantations—some of the colony's most impressive—which began to grow along its length almost as soon as the wall went up."[32]

This chapter draws the study to a conclusion by arguing for the enduring power of place in the *spatial imaginary* of Native communities in the colonial Chesapeake. Despite the violent ruptures and community displacements that followed English colonial expansion in the Chesapeake, Native groups returned to important places to bury ancestors, sacrifice animals, and inter objects of social importance, even after the residential population had departed. Coupled with the revolts of 1622 and 1644, the continuation of such practices into the colonial era contradicts a narrative of acculturation, abandonment, and disappearance.

Making Pilgrimages and Memorializing Places

During the early colonial era, Virginia Algonquians returned to burial grounds and settlements that, on first glance, appear to have been abandoned. The archaeological record of these visits—brief, ephemeral, and episodic—offers only limited traces of these events. With the refined chronologies now available from the Potomac Creek, Werowocomoco, and Buck Farm sites, though, it seems that Native groups returned to important locations *after* residential populations were no longer present. Indeed, Smith and Strachey noted that Native groups visited places with deep histories, at times constructing memorials and offering sacrifices in these locations.[33] Even in the face of formal treaties and English statutes that restricted Native movement in the seventeenth-century Chesapeake, Virginia Algonquians continued to travel to locations whose significance was remembered from the past. Writing early in the eighteenth century, Robert Beverley described Virginia Indians who returned to "celebrated places" to erect circles of posts, wooden pillars painted red and adorned with shell beads, and stones piled in a pyramid:

> When they travel by any of these Altars, *they take great care to instruct their Children and Young people in the particular occasion and time of their erection*, and recommend the respect which they ought to have for them; so that their careful observance of these Traditions, proves as good a Memorial of such Antiquities, as any Written Records.[34]

Such memorials provided a linkage to and record of the past for Virginia Algonquian communities. While centuries of intensive agricultural practices in the region have erased these stone altars and wooden posts, hints of Virginia Algonquian memory work may still be seen in the colonial Chesapeake's archaeological record. The Potomac Creek site in the Potomac River drainage, for example, appears as a persistent place in the region's cultural landscape, with evidence of Native activities there from the fourteenth through the seventeenth century. As discussed in chapter 3, the site represented a large, fortified town during the fourteenth century, when a substantial population lived at the location. Several ossuaries at the site date to between AD 1400 and 1560, when the settlement served as a palisaded mortuary center arranged around a large structure, likely a charnel house.[35] The Patawomeck subsequently established a new settlement close to the Potomac Creek site at Indian Point (site 44ST1) late in the sixteenth century. The old Patawomeck town remained in use, though, as a collective burial ground through the early seventeenth century. Ossuaries I and IV contained European trade goods—including copper and glass objects, scissors, hand-wrought iron nails, scrap iron, and glazed tile, materials that postdate the arrival of English colonists in the Chesapeake. The Potomac Creek site, transformed by Native communities several times from AD 1300 through the early 1600s, documents the continuing memories of a place with a deep history in the Chesapeake.

Werowocomoco has a similarly lengthy history of placemaking and remaking, though here this process has continued even after Native communities no longer resided in the vicinity of Purtan Bay. Documentary references suggest that at least some of Werowocomoco's residents remained at the location for a brief period after Wahunsenacawh's departure in 1609, greeting a raiding party of colonists with threats and hostility.[36] The archaeological record indicates that this population did not remain at Werowocomoco long. The site includes almost no evidence of Native settlement dating after 1609. The earliest English settlement on lands in this portion of the York River drainage began during the late 1630s, a process that intensified a decade later. By 1650 colonists patented thousands of acres every year, and numerous settlers began to construct houses and to plant tobacco fields. The first written record of the Werowocomoco site's location after 1609 comes from 1652, when William Roberts secured a patent for the land.[37] The land records, tax history, and archaeological survey results, though, suggest that the initial English occupation along Purtan Bay began somewhat later, during the final decades of the seventeenth century.

A seventeenth-century burial represents an exception to the overall absence of Native activity at Werowocomoco after 1609 and provides a poignant reminder of the enduring power of place in the memories of Virginia Algonquians. The human remains and associated objects are important elements of the site's history and powerful symbols for contemporary Native communities in Virginia.[38] The burial included the poorly preserved bones and teeth of a Native American child aged two to four years, though materials associated with this child included European-produced metal objects and glass beads. While the precise chronology of the interment is unclear, there are indications in the associated materials that the burial occurred *af-*

ter 1609, during a period when neither Native residents nor English settlers lived at Werowocomoco.[39]

Objects associated with the burial included an iron lathing hammer, a copper-alloy skillet, a copper-alloy spoon, copper-alloy beads, two copper-alloy "King's Touch" tokens, and several thousand white and blue glass beads.[40] These include materials central to early colonial exchange relations in the Chesapeake—copper, glass, and iron—as well as objects that embody the red, white, and blue/black colors that recur throughout Powhatan ceremonial practices. The two copper-alloy tokens were stamped on one side with a crown above an entwined rose and thistle, identical to the motif used on the halfpenny acknowledging the union of England and Scotland during the reign of James I. The copper tokens were originally produced for an English royal ceremony that imbued the monarch with healing powers.[41] The tokens found at Werowocomoco are pierced in the middle with two holes, suggesting they were modified to be used on a necklace. Copper-alloy beads in the form of short tubes were also part of the associated grave goods.[42] Given the proximity of the copper beads, tokens, and glass beads, the objects were probably strung together on a complex necklace.

The greatest number of artifacts associated with the burial, just under 4,000, consisted of small white and blue glass beads and one large chevron bead.[43] The white and blue bead varieties found at Werowocomoco have been recovered from early to middle seventeenth-century sites in the Middle Atlantic and Northeast. The white bead varieties found with the burial at Werowocomoco constitute only 1 percent of the Early Fort period (1607–1623) assemblage at Jamestown, and 4 percent of the Post-Fort period (1624–1660) assemblage.[44] The large, spherical chevron bead recovered with the Werowocomoco burial has a starlike pattern, apparent when viewed from the ends. Chevron beads associated with Dutch-supplied Polychrome Horizon assemblages dating to AD 1609–1624 are found within Iroquois sites in New York dating circa AD 1620–1650.[45]

These glass bead varieties offer some indications of the Werowocomoco burial's date. The chevron bead has been recovered from contexts ranging from 1609 to 1650. The small white bead variety (IVa11) recovered from Werowocomoco appears within Early Fort period contexts at Jamestown in small numbers but is more prevalent during the later Post-Fort period (AD 1624–1660). The beads associated with the burial point toward a post-1609 date for the interment. The materials included with the burial came

Table 7.1. Beads recovered from Werowocomoco site burial

Kidd Variety	Description	Estimated Count	Examined	Mean Diameter (mm)	Mean Length (mm)
IVa11	Very small–small, circular, 3-layer white beads (C/W/C)	3629	823	2.41	1.49
IVa11*	Very small–small, circular, 3-layer white beads (W/C/W)	2	2	2.41	1.45
IIa56	Very small–small, circular, translucent dark blue beads	319	20	2.63	1.5
IVk*	Large, spherical, 3-layer translucent dark blue beads (B/W/B)	1	1	8.76	7.89

*Variant on the bead category represented by the alphanumeric.
Source: Lapham 2004.

from sources beyond the known Virginia Algonquian world, and possibly beyond the world of English colonists, given the enigmatic origins of the chevron bead. This variety of burial goods, unusual for the Chesapeake, marks the death of a person of considerable importance, and a child with ties to Werowocomoco. The burial also appears to have marked a return to Werowocomoco after the residential population left the location. No other burials have been identified at Werowocomoco, despite a systematic survey and extensive testing of the site, raising the question of whether the residents collected the bones of ancestors following Wahunsenacawh's departure from the town. Even with the departure of Wahunsenacawh and Werowocomoco's other residents circa 1609, the town's spaces retained an importance in the memories of Virginia Algonquians.

The archaeological record of at least one additional location in the Chesapeake suggests that Native communities returned to ancestral places for commemorative events. The Buck Farm site included a small palisaded enclosure with a single human interment and eleven animal burials. As discussed in chapter 5, the site may have represented a quioccosan destroyed late in the sixteenth century. During the seventeenth and eighteenth centuries, after the palisade had burned to the ground, the site was no longer occupied. The site's archaeological record does not offer any indications of an English colonial residence or farmstead in the vicinity. A radiocarbon assay from one of the animal burials at the site, though, produced a historic-period result, suggesting that the pig burial (Burial 3) postdates the seventeenth century.[46]

Burial 3 was but one of three pigs, seven dogs, and one bird buried within the palisaded enclosure at the Buck Farm site. All of these burials contained the complete, articulated skeletal remains of an animal. Associated with Native pottery and lithic debitage, the dogs were all buried during the precontact era. In fact, Native communities in the Chesapeake often buried dogs within settlements and near burial grounds during the Late Woodland period. In her study of dog burials within Native sites in the Chesapeake, Jennifer Fitzgerald identified archaeological patterning suggesting that dog burials within Native sites linked to human mortuary ceremonies, public feasts, and boundary spaces that included the entrances to houses and palisaded enclosures.[47] Colonial accounts and ethnographic studies suggest that Native Americans of the Eastern Woodlands sacrificed dogs to accompany deceased humans, serve as proxy victims, or otherwise act as messengers to the spirit world.[48]

Burial 3's radiocarbon results indicate that the pig interment dates to the period after the Chickahominy had been forced from their homeland along the river bearing their name. Sixteenth-century Spanish colonists introduced pigs to the southeastern landscape, and English settlers later allowed pigs to roam the forests of the Chesapeake region. After the introduction of pigs, some American Indian groups in the Eastern Woodlands, including the Lenape, regularly incorporated the animals into their subsistence practices, at times substituting pigs for dogs during ceremonial occasions.[49] The pig burials at Buck Farm may, of course, relate to English settlement that began along the Chickahominy during the mid-seventeenth century. However, the absence of a historic-period component at the site from the seventeenth through the nineteenth century points in other directions.

Chickahominy Indians who returned to the site in the colonial era may have sacrificed and buried the pigs. Colonial-era accounts reference Virginia Algonquian sacrifices on several occasions, with offerings that included animals, pearls, shell beads, tobacco, puccoon, copper, and human life.[50] At times stones were tossed into rivers in order to "Sacrifice to Running Streams, which by the perpetuity of their Motion, typifie the Eternity of God."[51] Perhaps the most prominent reference to a sacrifice in the early colonial accounts may be found in the origin story, excerpted

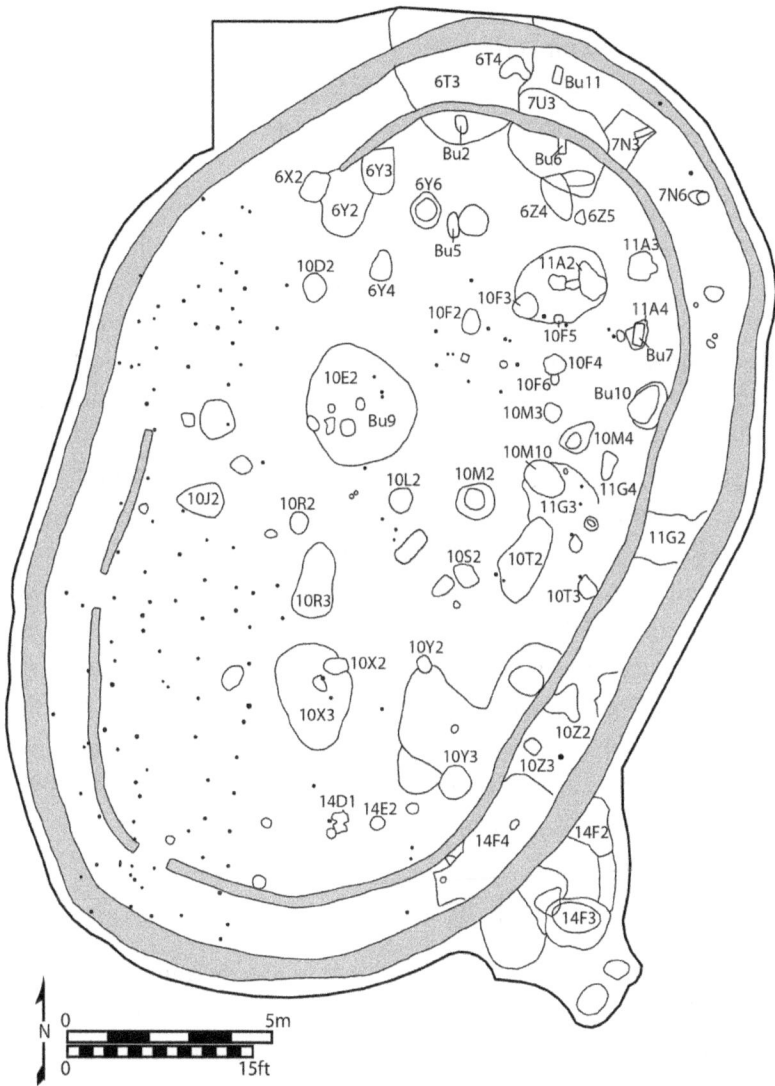

Figure 7.1. Buck Farm site plan.

in chapter 3, whereby the killing of the first deer brought both fertility and social order to the region. Virginia Algonquians offered sacrifices to give thanks and to avoid divine punishments.[52] By the colonial era, documentary sources indicate that Native groups made such sacrifices on memorial altars and within places associated with past events.[53] Historical accounts of the Nanticoke and Monacan provide additional references confirming that Native communities in the region returned to former settlements to perform ceremonies and to retrieve ancestors' remains.[54] Chickahominy Indians may have likewise revisited a place with a deep history on the Virginia Algonquian landscape to renew connections to an important place.

During the early seventeenth century, the Patawomeke returned to a centuries-old burial ground at the Potomac Creek site. Located near their principal town, the Potomac Creek site continued to represent a place where the Patawomeck completed ossuary mortuary rituals that now included trade goods acquired from the English. At Werowocomoco, a Native child was buried with glass beads, copper, and iron objects during the seventeenth century. By this time, though, no one lived at Werowocomoco. Later still, the Chickahominy seem to have returned to a formerly palisaded compound to bury several animals, events that echoed practices of the precolonial era. Much like the Monacans' travel to a mound in central Virginia and the Nanticoke's return to Eastern Shore ossuaries, such visits appear to have involved pilgrimages—special journeys to a sacred place— and performances of commemoration.[55] The documentary references and evidence from Potomac Creek, Werowocomoco, and Buck Farm hint that Virginia Algonquians returned to persistent places for pilgrimages, performances, and sacrifices, asserting enduring attachments to "celebrated places" during the early colonial era.[56]

Dwelling in Tsenacomacoh

This study has examined Tsenacomacoh's deep history from the spread of forager-fishers who used shell-tempered pottery to the commemoration of persistent places during the colonial era. I have framed the changes over time evident in the archaeological record in terms of representations of social space in the Chesapeake, Native spatial practices within the James and York River valleys, and the meaningful dimension of space within Werowocomoco and other Virginia Algonquian towns. English chroniclers' representations of colonized landscapes in maps and in narrative accounts dominate contemporary understandings of the Native societies in the Chesapeake. Still, we catch glimpses of Virginia Algonquian representations of space in the divination ceremony performed by Pamunkey priests and in Powhatan's Mantle. The resulting maps offer complementary Native representations of Tsenacomacoh, framed by priests on the one hand and by the chiefly elite on the other.

Other Virginia Algonquian representations of social space appear in the names of places lining the waterways of the Chesapeake estuary. Most Algonquian place-names in the Chesapeake accentuate a riverine or estuarine perspective that references the configuration of waterways and their relationship to land. Place-names that depart from this prevailing practice, from the "Hill of priestly divination" (Powhatan) to the "Place of the antler wearers" (Werowocomoco) echo histories of placemaking in the Algonquian Chesapeake. The names of places and people outside Tsenacomacoh diverged sharply from those of the Virginia Algonquian waterscape, highlighting a Virginia Algonquian sense of place centered on estuarine settings, waterborne travel, and the interface between land and water.

A history of Algonquian spatial practices within Tsenacomacoh seems to begin during the Middle Woodland period with forager-fishers who created persistent places during seasonal aggregations focused on fishing and shellfish harvesting. Circa AD 200 the archaeological record features a different set of materials, settlement practices, and subsistence orientations across the coastal Chesapeake, pointing toward a new mode of dwelling more closely oriented to the estuarine system. Historical linguistic studies trace the arrival and spread of Algonquian speech communities in the Chesapeake to this period, though this evidence is not without ambiguity. On the lower James and York Rivers, foragers and fishers produced ceramics tied to distinct communities of practice, highlighting interaction and social diversity at Tsenacomacoh's origins. Seasonal gatherings in riverfront settings produced middens with deep accumulations of shell, faunal remains, and (in some locations) decorated ceramics used in large-scale feasts.

The Chickahominy River's archaeological record traces the development of a riverine landscape of connected places from the sixth through the sixteenth centuries AD. Starting circa AD 500, mortuary ceremonies created ossuaries in the drainage interior. Downstream, in the central portion of the river valley, dispersed residential settlements appeared after AD 1300 along the riverfront bluffs and neck lands overlooking the river. Horticulture assumed a modest importance in subsistence patterns at the same time, as forager-fishers augmented their diets with maize. From AD 1300 through the early seventeenth century, residents of the Chickahominy drainage shifted their subsistence practices away from reliance on wild plants and fish toward domesticated plants and terrestrial fauna.

During these centuries the lower portion of the Chickahominy drainage saw the construction of a small, palisaded enclosure—possibly a priest's compound—surrounding a series of animal burials. Downstream, residents of the Chickahominy drainage feasted around massive pits used for food consumption events that they celebrated on an impressive scale. Chickahominy coalescence was channeled by these subsistence and settlement changes and by a linked network of locations for social gatherings within the drainage.

Werowocomoco's archaeology reveals a biography of place that began with the clearing of forests and the building of a horticultural town during the thirteenth century AD. Residents expanded a small earthwork enclosure in the settlement's interior circa AD 1350 with the construction of two much longer trenches. The trenches delineated an area that represents the closest thing in the Algonquian Chesapeake to monumental space. Werowocomoco's residents constructed a large structure behind these trenches by 1607, quite likely Wahunsenacawh's residence, based on its size, location, configuration, chronology, and associated copper from James Fort. Werowocomoco enters the documentary record as a settlement that, like other Virginia Algonquian towns, oriented the annual calendar and anchored seasonal movement. Werowocomoco, though, stood apart as the place with ritualized spaces where Wahunsenacawh became paramount chief, where John Smith became a weroance, and where antler-wearing wise men hosted ceremonies. As the hub of the Powhatan tributary network, Werowocomoco represented both a Native political center and a place of colonial entanglements during the early seventeenth century.

Across the James and York River valleys, spatial practices and temporal rhythms were keyed to such riverine locations used for centuries. These persistent places oriented the ways Virginia Algonquians dwelled in Tidewater Virginia, initially around shell middens and prime fishing grounds used seasonally, and later within horticultural towns occupied for much of the year. Ritualized spaces, including ossuaries and trench enclosures, gathered people for events that oriented the annual cycle and that allowed Virginia Algonquian communities to persist. From the ossuary burials along the Chickahominy arranged around a fire, to the trenches at Werowocomoco, Kiskiak, and Buck Farm, circular and concentric forms frequently appeared in these spaces. The Pamunkey priests' divination ceremony likewise generated concentric circles, using maize-based imagery to represent Tsenacomacoh and to encompass the Tassantasses. Powhatan's Mantle also drew upon circular imagery, though here it appears as a claim to regional sovereignty and a statement of chiefly power. At Werowocomoco, spaces marked by concentric earthworks played a role in the origins of the Powhatan chiefdom and in events that incorporated the Tassantasses and their materials. Unlike English maps of the region, Virginia Algonquian representations of social space emphasized centers attached to exterior rings, each with a distinct relationship to the core.

Tsenacomacoh incorporated outside elements throughout the Algonquian history of the Chesapeake, starting well before colonist John Smith or any other "stranger" reached Werowocomoco. Tsenacomacoh's archaeological record points to an eventful past framed by the arrival of Algonquian-speaking fishers circa AD 100 and their interactions with indigenous foragers. As Native communities established horticultural towns in riverine settings from the thirteenth through the sixteenth century AD, valued objects from Tsenacomacoh's periphery, including shell beads, began to flow into these settlements.[57] During the sixteenth century, exchange relations brought copper objects mined from the Blue Ridge Mountains or from the Great Lakes region into the Chesapeake and its political networks.[58] By the end of the 1500s, Wahunsenacawh's rise to paramount status culminated with his relocation from the edges of Tsenacomacoh to Werowocomoco, a ceremonial center and "Place of the antler wearers." Even after their displacement from riverine settlements in Tsenacomacoh, Virginia Algonquians returned to burial grounds, residential towns, and ceremonial spaces, signaling the enduring memories of place in the Virginia Algonquian spatial imaginary. These colonial-era pilgrimages and performances incorporated materials—copper objects, glass beads, iron implements, and animals—brought from outside Tsenacomacoh.

Viewed through a long lens, the Virginia Algonquian past brings into focus a history of emplacement and displacement stretching across more than 1,500 years. This record highlights the enduring power of place throughout a deep history of dwelling along the Chesapeake's waterways.

Epilogue

March 31, 2009

A U.S. district court judge ruled that the Army Corps of Engineers acted arbitrarily and capriciously when it approved a permit for a reservoir in King William County, Virginia.[1] The judge declared that the corps made egregious errors when it found that the proposed reservoir was the least damaging alternative, that it would not cause substantial harm to Tidewater Virginia's rivers, and that the reservoir was in the public interest.[2]

The proposed King William Reservoir was to provide freshwater for Newport News and other communities on the lower James-York peninsula.[3] The City of Newport News' plans for the project included a water intake and pumping station on the Mattaponi River to withdraw up to 75 million gallons of water per day. A dam on Cohoke Mill Creek would impound freshwater in a 1,500-acre area between the Mattaponi and Pamunkey Rivers, destroying hundreds of wetland acres and miles of streams in the process. If completed, the reservoir's construction would trigger the most extensive destruction of wetlands since the passage of the Clean Water Act in 1972. The reservoir's location placed it close to both the Mattaponi and Pamunkey Reservations, and the water intake would be positioned immediately upstream of the Mattaponi Reservation.

The Mattaponi Tribe fought the King William Reservoir project from its beginnings, partnering in a long and complicated history of administrative and judicial review with environmental conservation groups and other Virginia tribes, including the Pamunkey and Upper Mattaponi.[4] The Virginia Marine Resources Commission initially denied the project permit in 2003 upon hearing from this coalition and from expert testimony of the detrimental impact of the water intake and salinity changes on shad populations. Under threat of litigation from Newport News, the commission then reversed that decision, and the project went forward.

The City of Newport News' request for a federal permit under the Clean Water Act was also initially denied. In their opposition to the federal permit for the reservoir, the Mattaponi pointed out that the location of the project's water intake on the Mattaponi River violated the three-mile buffer zone established by the 1677 Treaty of Middle Plantation. In the interest of establishing a secure and lasting peace with Virginia's tribes, the seventeenth-century treaty states that "noe English, shall seate or plant nearer then three miles of any Indian towne, and whosoever hath made or shall make any encroachment upon their Lands shall be removed from thence."[5]

The tribe also objected to the reservoir's destruction of over 150 archaeological sites that included Native burial grounds and sacred places. A study of the project's impact on traditional cultural properties (i.e., places with deep religious and cultural importance to a community) conducted by my William and Mary colleagues Kathleen Bragdon and Danielle Moretti-Langholtz identified several such properties in the reservoir's pathway, including the Mattaponi River itself.[6] In his remarks to the public hearing on the federal permit, Mattaponi chief Carl Custalow noted:

> These places have tremendous emotional and symbolic significance for the tribe. Not only have they been important to us for centuries, but also because they represent some of the last remaining physical links we have with our ancestors. Other sites have already been wiped out by development from hundreds of years of encroachment. If the King William Reservoir is built, we will lose an historic and culture heritage that these sites represent.[7]

Convinced by such arguments, the corps' district commander recommended denying the permit. Virginia's governor James Gilmore then requested that the Army Corps of Engineers take the permitting decision out of the hands of the local district commander so that the review process could be shifted to the North Atlantic Division headquarters.[8] In a familiar pattern, the division engineer reversed the district commander's decision after the governor's intervention. The Mattaponi then joined a suit filed in U.S. district court to stop the reservoir.

The judge's final ruling in March 2009 overturned the Army Corps of Engineers' permitting decision and resulted in the termination of the project. Rather than relying on treaty obligations, federal Indian law, or the National Historic Preservation Act's protection of historic sites and traditional cultural properties, the decision depended upon environmental and administrative law. Still, the result represents a victory for the Mattaponi and other Virginia tribes. Reservoir opponents overcame an administrative process initially driven by political and economic considerations rather than fairness and the law, with decisions that were frequently reversed for dubious reasons. While playing a central role in this process, the Mattaponi asserted that seventeenth-century treaty obligations still matter today and that tribal sovereignty remains intact in Tsenacomacoh even after the demise of the Powhatan chiefdom. By insisting on the enduring power of place in the contemporary Chesapeake, the Mattaponi also underscored the connection between places associated with the Native past and the aspirations of a contemporary tribe. The Mattaponi River and its annual shad run served as central motifs in the Mattaponi's opposition to the reservoir.[9] The river continues to orient Mattaponi navigation through the Chesapeake landscape, figuratively and literally.

June 21, 2013

Representatives from Virginia's Native communities returned to Werowocomoco for a ceremony dedicating a conservation easement on the land. After almost a decade of investigations at the site, Chickahominy tribal chief Stephen Adkins observed,

> The archaeological discoveries and attendant interpretations . . . ripped to shreds the Anglo-centric term "pre-history" as it relates to the *history* of this land and its indigenous people prior to the arrival of the invaders in 1607. Today we honor the polity, social order, economic enterprise, religious customs, agricultural prowess, engineering feats, and craftsmanship of our ancestors.[10]

The dedication event provided an opportunity for Native leaders to make a new pilgrimage to Werowocomoco. The 58-acre conservation easement preserves the site's archaeological record, only a modest portion of which has been subject to investigation to date. The easement also prompted an effort to incorporate Werowocomoco into the National Park Service's Captain John Smith Chesapeake National Historic Trail, a water-based trail stretching 3,000 miles along the Bay and its tributaries. In a region where many heritage sites focus on English settlements, colonial towns, plantation settings, and the battlefields of the Revolutionary and Civil Wars, the effort to give Werowocomoco a role in a historic trail represents a noteworthy development. The historic trail tracing the waterways of the Chesapeake estuary provides an opportunity to reimagine Native spaces and their importance in Tsenacomacoh's waterscape of connected places.

The Mattaponi's prominent role in the opposition to the King William Reservoir and the Virginia tribes' participation in the Werowocomoco project represent significant, positive changes in the Chesapeake's contemporary landscape. And yet the Mattaponi's assertions of treaty obligations and of enduring attachments to ancestral places were largely brushed aside in the administrative and judicial decisions relating to the King William Reservoir project. Should the Werowocomoco site be included in the National Park system, its role will likely be framed in terms of events centered on Smith and other English colonists. Werowocomoco is slated to become a part of the "Captain John Smith Chesapeake National Historic Trail." Perhaps one day, though, the site might become the hub of a trail with even deeper roots in the Chesapeake, the "Historical Waterscape of Tsenacomacoh."

Even as Native communities have reclaimed a more prominent place in the Chesapeake landscape and a greater role in representations of their past, the colonial archive still places constraints on efforts to link the past to the present, and the present to the future. For Native communities in the Chesapeake, Tsenacomacoh's deep history represents a powerful basis from which to contest narratives centered solely on colonial history and government policies that have denied their existence. Giving voice to such aspirations during the Werowocomoco dedication, Pamunkey Tribal Museum director Ashley Spivey noted,

What began here at Werowocomoco needs to continue as the future of this Native place is decided. Virginia Indians have a stake in this history and thus take our experiences at Werowocomoco and look to the future to reclaim our rightful place at the table as participants in researching and presenting our pasts, our histories, our cultures, our places, and our stories.[11]

Notes

Prologue

1. Smith 1986a:45–53; Smith 1986c:212–14; Smith 1986d:146–51.
2. Barbour 1967:222.
3. Strachey 1953:29.
4. Bragdon 1996:184.
5. Smith 1986b:174.
6. Stern 1952; Tooker 1895a, 1901.
7. For example, Busby 2010; Dawdy 1995; Hantman 2010; Moore 1993; Potter 1993; Rice 2007; Rountree and Davidson 1997.
8. Smith 1986a:35.
9. Smith 1986a:53; Smith 1986c:213–14; Smith 1986d:150–51.
10. Fogelson 1989:143.
11. For example, Horn 2005; Kelso 2006; Kupperman 2007; Price 2003.
12. Smith 1986a:59; Smith 1986d:149–50.
13. Gleach 1995, 1997:120; Williamson 1992; Williamson 2003:226.
14. Smith 1986a:69.
15. Williamson 2003:226–28.
16. Gleach 1997:113–15.
17. Smith 1986a:59.
18. Fogelson 1989:142.
19. Halbwachs 1992.
20. Augé 1995.
21. Fogelson 1989.
22. For example, Nabokov 2002.
23. Quinn 1955:854.
24. Geary 1953.
25. Barbour 1971:296–97; Tooker 1894b:178, 1904a:467.
26. Feld and Basso 1996.
27. Basso 1996:5; King 2012.
28. Basso 1996:71; Heidegger 1971; Ingold 1993; Smith 2003.

Chapter 1. Dwelling in Tsenacomacoh

1. Feest 1990; Potter 1993; Rountree 1989; Turner 1985.

2. Cf. Gamble 2013; Shryock and Smail 2011.

3. For example, Bourdieu 1970; Certeau 1984; Foucault 1986; Gupta and Ferguson 1992; Lefebvre 1991; Soja 1989; Warf and Arias 2009.

4. Sheller and Urry 2006:216.

5. Lefebvre 1991.

6. Hubbard and Kitchin 2011:6.

7. Sauer 1925:46.

8. Thomas 2001:173

9. Sewell 2005:363–64.

10. Ashmore 2002:1177; Schlanger 1992.

11. For example, Steward 1937; Willey 1953; Flannery 1976.

12. Knapp and Ashmore 1999:2.

13. Rodning 2010.

14. David and Thomas 2008:38.

15. Balée and Erickson 2006; Thompson and Waggoner 2013.

16. Balée 2006:75; Crumley 1994:9.

17. Balée 2013:144.

18. Thompson and Waggoner 2013:2.

19. Erickson 2008; Heckenberger 2005; Heckenberger et al. 2003; Meggers 1971, 2003.

20. Heckenberger 2005; Heckenberger et al. 2003:1711.

21. Heidegger 1982; Husserl 2001; Johnson 2012; Merleau-Ponty 2011; Smith 2013.

22. Heidegger 1962.

23. Heidegger 1971.

24. Ingold 2000:153–288.

25. Ingold 2006:14.

26. Ingold 1993.

27. Fowles 2010.

28. For example, Ferguson and Colwell-Chanthaphonh 2006; Lelièvre 2012.

29. Snead 2008:20

30. Halttunen 2011.

31. Cronon 1983.

32. White 1991.

33. For example, Curtin et al. 2001; Rountree et al. 2007; Rice 2009.

34. Halttunen 2011:532.

35. The Werowocomoco Research Groups is a collaborative team of archaeologists and a cultural anthropologist from the Virginia Department of Historic Resources (E. Randolph Turner, now retired), the College of William and Mary (Danielle Moretti-Langholtz and myself), and the Fairfield Foundation (David Brown and Thane Harpole).

36. Gallivan et al. 2005. For a discussion of the "biography of place," see Ashmore 2002.

37. McCary and Barka 1977.

38. Gallivan et al. 2009.

39. Tooker 1895a, 1901.

40. Hantman 1990, 2010.

41. Lightfoot 1995.

42. For example, Bragdon 1996; Ethridge and Shuck-Hall 2009; Ferris 2009; Jordan 2008; Liebmann 2012; Lightfoot 2005; Loren 2008; Rodning 2009; Silliman 2005.

43. Cobb 2005.

44. Gallivan and Moretti-Langholtz 2007.

45. Nabokov 2002.

46. Gallivan et al. 2011.

47. Schrire 1995.

48. Cook 2003.

49. Cook 2000; Gleach 2003, 2002; Moretti-Langholtz 1998; Rountree 1990, 1993.

50. Deloria 1970:39.

51. For example, Rountree 1989; Rountree and Turner 2002.

52. For example, Axtell 2001; Smith et al. 2002; Fausz 1988; Horn 2005; Hudson and Tesser 1994; Rice 2007.

53. For example, Busby 2010; Dent 1995; Gallivan 2003; Hantman 1993; Moore 1993; Turner 1976.

54. For example, Potter 1993:139.

55. Binford 1964.

56. Turner 1985, 1986, 1992, 1993.

57. Potter 1993.

58. Williamson 1992:368–69.

59. Williamson 2003:202–55.

60. Gleach 1997:3.

61. Mallios 2006.

62. Hantman 2008.

63. For example, Fandos 2015; Wade 2013.

64. Horning 2006; Mallios and Straube 2000.

65. For example, Kelso 2006.

66. Kupperman 2007.

67. Klein and Sanford 2004:72.

68. For example, Hatfield 2008; Richter 2007.

69. For example, Hantman et al. 2000; Kerber 2006.

70. For example, Atalay 2012; Colwell-Chanthaphonh and Ferguson 2008; Kerber 2006; Riggs 2002; Swidler 1997; Watkins 2000.

71. These include the Eastern Chickahominy, Chickahominy, Mattaponi, Monacan, Nansemond, Nottoway, Cheroenhaka Nottoway, Pamunkey, Patawomeck, Rappahannock, and Upper Mattaponi.

72. The two officially recognized groups are the Piscataway Indian Nation and the Piscataway Conoy Tribe. The Piscataway Conoy petition for recognition includes the Piscataway Conoy Confederacy and Subtribes plus the Cedarville Band of the Piscataway.

73. Koenig 2007:117.

74. Blume 2006; Custer 2005; Petraglia et al. 2002.

75. Final Determination for Federal Acknowledgment of the Pamunkey Indian Tribe, 80 Federal Register 39144 (July 8, 2015).

76. Heim 2015; Heim 2016.

77. Custer et al. 1990; Hughes and Henry 2006:113; Rountree and Turner 2002:227–29.

78. Moretti-Langholtz 1998.

79. Gallivan 2007; Gallivan et al. 2009; Gallivan et al. 2005.

80. Lefebvre 1991.

81. For example, Thompson 2009.

82. Ethridge and Shuck-Hall 2009.

Chapter 2. Mapping the Terrain

1. Smith 1986a:63–79, 1986c:215–17. Since the term *Powhatan* is ambiguous, I will refer to the man as Wahunsenacawh, and the Algonquian-speaking people of coastal Virginia as Virginia Algonquians, following a practice introduced by Christian Feest (1978). I use the term *Powhatan* primarily to refer to the political structures of the paramount chiefdom.

2. Smith 1986a:69.

3. Barbour 1986 1:121.

4. Archer 1910:xli.

5. Waselkov 2006.

6. Pargellis 1959:232.

7. Cosgrove 1999:9.

8. Stephenson and McKee 2000:28.

9. For example, Blansett 2005; Ford 1924; Harley 1988; Hatfield 2003; McCary 1957; Waselkov 1998.

10. Barbour 1986 1:123–24; Harriot 1972.

11. Smith 1986b:151.

12. Hatfield 2003.

13. Potter 1993:161–66.

14. Kupperman 1984; Mallios 2006.

15. Kupperman 2007.

16. Smith 1986a, 1986b, 1986c, 1986d.

17. Barbour 1964; Vaughan 1975.

18. Lehman 2007; Nicholls 2005; Percy 1922.

19. Smith 1986e.

20. Townsend 2004:53.

21. Smith 1986b.

22. Turner 1982.

23. Smith 1986b:162.

24. Ibid.

25. Strachey 1953:60.

26. Ibid., 70.

27. Smith 1986b:164.

28. Potter and Waselkov 1994.

29. Archer 1910; Percy 1922; Spelman 1998; Strachey 1953.

30. Smith 1986b:157.

31. Ibid., 165.

32. For example, Lederer et al. 1958; Lawson 1967.

33. Bushnell 1922, 1930; Griffin 1945; Goddard 2005:15–19; Mooney 1894:26–27.

34. Hantman 1990, 1993.

35. Strachey 1953:87.

36. Brown 1890:183–90; Stephenson and McKee 2000:33.

37. Barbour 1969:238.

38. For example, Barbour 1969:69–71, 77–78, 114–23, 236–37.

39. Brown 1890:183–84.

40. Ibid., 461; Goldman 2011.

41. Brown 1890:971.

42. Goldman 2011:439.

43. Ibid.

44. Turner and Opperman 1993:72.

45. Kelso 2006:22.

46. Smith 1986d:126.

47. Certeau 1984:118–22.

48. Boelhower 2003.

49. Mauss 2000.

50. Mallios 2006.

51. Barbour 1971:288.

52. Smith 1986d:150. A trencher is a circular platter or a slice of bread, scooped out to be used as a plate.

53. Waselkov 1998, 2006.

54. Waselkov 2006:445.

55. Smith 2011.

56. Williamson 2003.

57. Bushnell 1907; Tradescant 1925; Waselkov 2006:453–57, 1998.

58. Bushnell 1907:38.

59. Feest 1983.

60. Waselkov 2006:453–55.

61. Smith 1986b:173–74.

62. For example, Speck 1917.

63. Fogelson and Brightman 2002:311. In the Mississippian region, moieties labeled Red and White signified war and peace, and some Siouan groups organized themselves into Earth and Sky moieties, each composed of several clans (Miller 2002:140).

64. Woodard and Moretti-Langholtz 2009.

65. Miller 1979:797.

66. Bloom 1939:266.

67. Turner 1976:176.

68. Strachey 1953:63; Turner 1976:133.

69. Smith 1986b:173.

70. For example, Feest 1966:7–8; Mouer 1981:17; Potter 1993:152; Rountree 1989:149; Turner 1985:210.

71. Binford 1964; Feest 1966; Rountree 2005:28–29; Rountree and Turner 2002:42–44; Woodard 2008.

72. Egloff and Potter 1982; Turner 1993:84–88.

73. Gleach 1995.

74. Smith 1986d:149–50.

75. Barbour 1972:42.

76. Turner 1976:117; Gleach 1997:42.

77. Gleach 1997:36.

78. Gleach 1997:120, 1995.

79. Williamson 2003:227.

80. Strachey 1953:81.

81. Tyler 1907:20.

82. Spelman 1998:486–87.

83. Beverley 1947:153.

84. Grumet 2001.

85. Peirce 1991; Preucel 2006; Preucel and Bauer 2001.

86. Peirce's semiotic comprises a complex theory of knowledge with its own unique and densely meaningful jargon, and my effort to borrow some of this language does not come close to capturing its nuance or conveying its analytical power. Central to his theory are a series of three-part (or triadic) relations, starting with the relation between signs, objects, and "interpretants." An interpretant is the effect of a sign on someone who reads or comprehends it. People may understand the sign/object relation in several different ways, but actors are always an integral part of the semiotics process. As a result, the sign-object relation (i.e., the meanings of things) may be variable and multiple. Rather than a set of static structural codes or arbitrary relations between sign and signifier, Peircean semiotics centers on dynamic cultural conventions derived from the flow of changing social conventions.

87. Preucel 2010:249.

88. Lorant 1965:274–75.

89. Pitt and Taylor 2009.

90. Binford 1964; Potter 1993; Turner 1976.

91. Turner 1986; Gallivan 2003.

92. Earle 1997.

93. Ibid., 70–73.

94. Ibid., 73–75.

95. Feinman and Neitzel 1984.

96. For example, Emerson 1997; Pauketat 2004.

97. Smith 1986b:169.

98. Crumley 1995:3.

Chapter 3. Placemaking in the Algonquian Chesapeake

1. Strachey 1953:98–99.

2. Basso 1996:4.

3. Tooker 1906:26.

4. Tooker 1904b:679.

5. Mithun 1999:38.

6. Basso 1996:xv.

7. Bloomfield 1946; Clements 2011; Feest 1978; Goddard 1994, 1991, 1978; Rudes 2011; Siebert 1975.

8. For example, Campbell 1997:153.

9. Siebert 1975:440.

10. Smith 1986b:136–38.

11. Ibid., 139.

12. Goddard 2000.

13. Strachey 1953:183–96.

14. Barbour 1972:23.

15. Siebert 1975:292.

16. Smith 1986a:67.

17. Barbour 1971:297.

18. Tooker 1904a:467.

19. Barbour 1971:302.

20. Tooker 1905b:525.

21. For example, Strachey 1953:189.

22. Percy 1998:93.

23. White 1998.

24. Williamson 2003.

25. Rountree 1989:14; Barbour 1971:296.

26. Tooker 1894b:179–80.

27. Ibid., 180.

28. Potter 1993; Dent 2003; Dent and Jirikowic 2001.

29. Blanton et al. 1999.

30. Ibid., 102–4.

31. Potter 1993:126–32.

32. Cissna 1986:31; Potter 1993:132.

33. Blanton et al. 1999:92–98.

34. Rice 2007.

35. Hantman 1990, 1993.

36. Smith 1986b:165–67, 1986c:200, 1986d:158–59.

37. Goddard 2005:15–19; Mooney 1894:22, 26–27.

38. Goddard 2005:17; Tooker 1895b. James Mooney (1894:22) similarly notes that several Virginia Piedmont place-names appear to be Algonquian, though he suggested that the names "Monacan" and "Mannahoac" may in fact be rough approximations of Siouan terms that were garbled in transcription. Mooney suggested that the prefixes to

these names may relate to the Siouan root *mo-* or *ma-,* a locative that signifies earth. Re-assessing the linguistic evidence from the Virginia Piedmont in the broader context of the Southeast, Ives Goddard (2005:17) has more recently concluded that the Monacan and Mannahoac spoke Siouan dialects related to Crow and Mandan, yet the Piedmont place-names that John Smith used on this map were likely Algonquian.

39. Goddard 2005:17.

40. Barbour 1971:291; Tooker 1895b:380.

41. Tooker 1895a:261.

42. Smith 1986d:246–47.

43. Woodard 2008.

Chapter 4. Arrival in the Wide Land

1. Gallivan and Blouet 2001.

2. Blanton 1992; Custer 1989a; McLearan 1992; Stewart 1992.

3. Dent 1995:235–42; Potter 1993:48–102.

4. Blanton and Pullins 2004:91.

5. Hayden 2009a.

6. Rountree 1989:88.

7. Carr and Maslowski 1995; Maslowski 1996; Minar 2001.

8. Johnson and Speedy 1992; Klein 2003; Custer 2004.

9. Hayden 2009b.

10. Dietler and Herbich 1998.

11. Rountree 1998.

12. For example, Sassaman and Rudolphi 2001.

13. Originally developed by cognitive anthropologists Jean Lave and Etienne Wenger (1991), the community of practice framework is useful in considering the relationship between materials and social groups by highlighting the learning networks and social-ization processes of crafting traditions.

14. For example, Kelly 2013:137–65; Sassaman 2004; Thompson and Andrus 2011.

15. Binford 2001:147–51; Whallon 2006.

16. Fitzhugh et al. 2011.

17. Wiessner 1983.

18. Sassaman and Holly 2011.

19. Sassaman 2010.

20. Egloff and Potter 1982.

21. Feathers 2009; Herbert 2008.

22. Anadromous fish spend most of their lives in salt water but migrate to freshwater tributaries to spawn. These include sturgeon and shad in the Chesapeake estuary.

23. Opperman 1992; Barber and Madden 2006; Heinsman and Duncan 2006; Stew-art 1998.

24. Blanton and Pullins 2004.

25. Luckenbach et al. 1987; Fiedel 2013, 1999, 1994, 1987; Denny 1991, 2003. Mito-chondrial DNA studies also document a large amount of gene flow between Eastern

Algonquian groups and Eastern Siouan populations, raising the possibility that Algonquian migrants intermarried with Siouan communities that had deeper roots in the region (Malhi et al. 2001).

26. For example, Custer 1989a; Hutchinson 2002; Stewart 1990.

27. Potter 1993:139.

28. Blanton et al. 1999:242.

29. Underwood et al. 2003.

30. It is also important to note that rising sea levels have inundated an unknown number of Archaic period (12,000 BC–1000 BC) sites to the east, limiting access to the archaeology from this interval. Tidal wetlands that may have attracted large, Archaic-period settlements were located beyond the NWSY and are currently submerged as a result of Holocene-era sea-level rise that created the Chesapeake estuary (Blanton 1996).

31. Egloff and Potter 1982.

32. There is evidence of earlier shell-tempered wares that appeared sporadically on the Eastern Shore and in the Dismal Swamp area, though Mockley ceramics appear to represent the beginnings of a widespread, Middle Atlantic shell-tempered ceramic tradition that was sustained through contact (Dent 1995:235–43; Herbert 2008; Rick and Lowery 2013).

33. McLearan 1992:41.

34. Curry and Kavanagh 1991.

35. Blanton 1992:68.

36. Blanton and Pullins 2004:91. These groups bear some resemblance to the settlement practices associated with different ends of the hunter-gatherer spectrum proposed by Lewis Binford in his classic article "Willow Smoke and Dogs' Tails" (Binford 1980; Blanton 1992). Binford suggested that foragers—highly mobile generalists—practice "residential" mobility. Foragers establish a series of base camps during the year, obtain food in close proximity, and move on as needed in an annual round. Collectors, by contrast, practice what Binford referred to as "logistical" mobility. They do so by establishing more substantial base camps with durable food processing and storage facilities. Such base camps serve as hubs for task groups that hunt, gather, and (especially in the Chesapeake) fish for resources as they become available. Sites associated with Varina ceramics share elements of the forager model, while those associated with Mockley ceramics more closely approximate the collector model.

37. Klein 2003.

38. Hayden 2009a, 2009b.

39. Cronin et al. 2010; Cronin et al. 2005; Cronin et al. 2003.

40. Turner and Opperman 1993; Underwood et al. 2003:392.

41. Barbour 1971:288; Strachey 1953:69; Tooker 1905a:63.

42. Lewis and Loomie 1953; Mallios 2006, 2007.

43. Lewis and Loomie 1953:42.

44. Richter 2007:36–42.

45. Beverley 1947:51; Bridenbaugh 1980.

46. Rountree 2005:27.

47. Ibid., 26–29.

48. Smith 1986a:79.

49. Rountree 1990:116–17.

50. Within the two westernmost units (TU 40 and 41), ceramics near the midden base (i.e., below the shell-rich deposits) include a small number (n = 20) of grog-tempered Croaker Landing sherds dating to the Early Woodland period (1000 BC–500 BC). Such ceramics, first identified at the Croaker Landing site located upstream on the York, were built with slabs of clay pressed together at right angles and tempered with crushed bits of previously fired ceramics (Egloff et al. 1988). Middle Woodland Varina and Mockley vessels, constructed using the more common coil-and-scrape method, appear in sequence above the Early Woodland layer.

51. For example, Waselkov 1982.

52. Seriation is a relative dating method in which artifacts from different contexts are placed in chronological order.

53. Jenkins 2012.

54. Mann et al. 2009.

55. Harding et al. 2008; Harding et al. 2010; Rick and Lockwood 2013.

56. Blanton et al. 2005:62–65.

57. Jones 2005.

58. Ibid., E3.

59. Ibid., E10.

60. Walsh 2010.

61. Brush 2001.

62. Carr et al. 1991; Craven 2006; Earle 1988; Walsh 2010:357–58; Wennersten 1996.

63. Cronon 1983; Erickson 2008.

64. Smith 1986b:162; Strachey 1953:60.

65. Hulton 1984:73; Strachey 1953:127; Bushnell 1913:535; Wennersten 1981.

66. Smith 1986a:37.

67. Smith 1986c:245.

68. Hulton 1984:73.

69. Strachey 1953:127.

70. Bushnell 1913:536.

71. Smith's (1986b:162–63) description of the seasonal round in his *Map of Virginia* notes that colonial-era Virginia Algonquians ate oysters as a backup to the fish and nuts that comprised staples during May and June: "But to mend their diet, some disperse in small companies and live upon fish, beasts, crabs, oysters, land Torteyses, strawberries, mulberries, and such like." Smith's reference to late-spring consumption of oysters is, on first glance, somewhat surprising, since oysters begin to spawn with May's warmer water temperatures, a reproductive process that continues through the summer months. As oysters shift their energy into reproduction, meat quality declines—fertile oysters turn thin and soft. This annual process is behind the adage that oysters should not be eaten in months whose names lack an "R" (i.e., May through August). The "small companies" consuming these oysters during the seventeenth century likely differed from those generating the substantial Middle Woodland–era shell deposits at locations

including Kiskiak. The oysters that served as a backstop to the fish and nuts commonly consumed during this part of the annual round may well have been roasted and smoked for preservation. Indeed, Smith concludes this passage with a description of meat-smoking practices that preserved food "till scarce times."

72. Barber and Madden 2006; Opperman 1992; Heinsman and Duncan 2006.

73. Opperman 1992.

74. Cross 1956:1344.

75. Stewart 1998.

76. Steadman 2008.

77. Stewart 1998:175–77.

78. Hantman and Gold 2000.

79. Steadman 2008.

80. Feasting definition from Dietler 2010:65. See also Dietler and Hayden 2010; Hayden and Villeneuve 2011; Joyce and Henderson 2007; Mills 2004.

81. For example, Blitz 1993; Maxham 2000; Pauketat et al. 2002; Potter 2000; Welch and Scarry 1995.

82. Plog 1985.

83. T-tests comparing rim diameter ($t = $ -2.224, $p = $ .032, $n = $ 40) and profile diameter ($t = $ -2.328, $p = $ .025, $n = $ 40) indicate that differences between mean values are statistically significant.

84. Stewart 1998.

85. Luckenbach et al. 1987; Fiedel 2013, 1999, 1994, 1990; 1987; Denny 1991, 2003.

86. Gleach 1997:25; Potter 1993:3–4.

87. Anthony 1990; Burmeister 2000; Snow 2002.

88. Bellwood 2001; Frachetti 2011; McConvell 2010.

89. For example, Bernardini 2008.

90. Cissna 1986:31; Feest 1978:240; Potter 1993:132.

91. Fiedel 1990:222.

92. Bloomfield 1946.

93. Siebert 1967.

94. Goddard 1994; Campbell 1997:152–53.

95. Siebert 1975.

96. Ibid., 440–41.

97. Luckenbach et al. 1987; Fiedel 2013, 1999, 1994, 1990; 1987; Denny 1991, 2003.

98. Luckenbach et al. 1987:10.

99. Swadesh 1959, 1955, 1952.

100. Luckenbach et al. 1987:13.

101. Ibid.,16.

102. Fiedel 1999, 1990.

103. Fiedel 1994.

104. Denny 2003.

105. For example, Potter 1993:2.

106. Campbell 2004; Hymes 1960; Rankin 2006:564. Glottochronology assumes that a language's basic vocabulary is replaced at a constant rate over time, allowing estimates

for the date two related languages diverged based on a measure of similarity between word lists. In fact, historical analyses of the best-documented languages indicate that words are replaced at rates that vary according to cultural and historical context.

107. Bellwood 2001:194; Brown 2006:661.

108. Luckenbach et al. 1987:8. Mindful of the method's limitations, archaeologists continue to draw upon glottochronology as a valuable line of evidence that is independent from the material record (for example, Renfrew et al. 2000). Indeed, studies that employ glottochronology have had some success with limited time spans and by considering corroborating evidence from the archaeological and paleoethnobotanical records (for example, Brown 2006).

109. For example, Hornborg 2005; Bellwood and Renfrew 2002.

Chapter 5. The Coarse-Pounded Corn People

1. McCary and Barka 1977; Gallivan et al. 2009.

2. Moretti-Langholtz 1998; Rountree 1990; Stern 1952.

3. Adkins 2009; Fitzgerald 2009; Gallivan 2009; Golenishcheva-Coonan 2009; Hayden 2009b; Mahoney 2009; McKnight 2009d; Shephard 2009; Woodard and Moretti-Langholtz 2009.

4. Hamor 2007:1160; Woodard and Moretti-Langholtz 2009.

5. For example, Fennell 2007; Meskell 2002; Mullins and Paynter 2000; Voss 2008; Weik 2009.

6. Moore 1994, 2001; Voss 2008:1.

7. Weber 1978:389.

8. Ibid.

9. Kohl 1998.

10. Barth 1969.

11. Hu 2013:372.

12. For example, Voss 2008, 2012:303; Hornborg 2005.

13. Haley and Wilcoxon 2005:432.

14. For example, Hill 1996a; Sider 1994.

15. Cipolla 2013; Sturtevant 1971; Voss 2012:304.

16. Ethridge and Shuck-Hall 2009.

17. For example, Hill 1996b.

18. Strachey 1953:61–62.

19. Ferguson and Whitehead 1992:21–22.

20. Feest 1978:67–68.

21. Woodard and Moretti-Langholtz 2009.

22. Smith 1986c:39–43

23. Smith 1986d:246–47.

24. Stern 1952.

25. Rountree and Turner 2002:177–210.

26. Stern 1952:193.

27. Gallivan et al. 2009:15–38.

28. Ibid., 57–110.

29. Curry 1999; Gold 2004.

30. For example, Blick 2000; Dunham 1999; Dunham et al. 2003; Jirikowic 1990; Shaffer 2005.

31. Spelman 1998:491.

32. Seeman 2011; Tooker 1991; Trigger 1990.

33. Hall 1997:35–36; Thwaites 1959:10:277–316.

34. Hall 1997:38.

35. The radiocarbon assays for the ossuary features on the Chickahominy relied on direct dates of human bone, rather than on radiocarbon assays drawn from associated wood charcoal. Native sites in the Chesapeake often saw multiple occupations, and the presence of wood charcoal from several different occupations can result in a misleading chronology when dated.

36. For example, Blick 2000; Curry 1999; Ubelaker 1974.

37. Ubelaker 1974.

38. Curry 1999:74.

39. Blick 2000.

40. Curry 1999:10.

41. Dunham et al. 2003.

42. Jirikowic 1990:370.

43. Hantman 1990:684.

44. Gallivan et al. 2009:63–88.

45. While unusual in the Chickahominy drainage, several of the decorative motifs have appeared on other sites across the coastal Middle Atlantic. For example, Custer 1987.

46. Blanton et al. 1999; Snow 1994:30.

47. Shephard 2009.

48. Beverley 1947:137.

49. Hall 1976.

50. Smith 1986c:212, 239.

51. Strachey 1953:73.

52. For example, Binford 1964; Turner 1976; Potter 1993.

53. McKnight and Gallivan 2008.

54. Potter 1993:172.

55. For example, Dore 2011; Gold 1994; Hart et al. 2007; Messner 2011.

56. Larsen 1997:270–301.

57. Isotopes are simply alternative forms of a chemical element. All isotopes of an element, including carbon, share the same number of protons and electrons, but isotopes differ in the number of neutrons present. For example, carbon-12 has six protons and six neutrons, while carbon-14 (a much rarer isotope of carbon) has six protons and eight neutrons.

58. Hutchinson 2002; Hutchinson et al. 1998; Hutchinson and Norr 2006; Schoeninger 2009.

59. Upon receiving our initial report summarizing the results of the survey, includ-

ing the sites discussed above, the Chickahominy Tribal Council asked that we expand our analysis to gauge the importance of maize in the precontact diet of their ancestors. As descendants of the "Coarse-pounded Corn People," the Chickahominy Tribal Council hoped to learn more about the history of corn-based horticulture in the Chickahominy drainage. The resulting study, funded by the Virginia Department of Historic Resources, examined human bone chemistry from 10 different burial contexts along the Chickahominy River.

60. Trimble 1996:55–56; Tykot 2006:134.

61. Trimble 1996:59.

62. Dore 2011; McKnight and Gallivan 2009.

Chapter 6. The Place of the Antler Wearers

1. Gallivan et al. 2005:36–49.

2. Brown 1890:151,188.

3. Smith 1986a:63, 1986b:173; Strachey 1953:57.

4. Gallivan et al. 2005:2–7.

5. For example, Blume 2006; Hantman et al. 2000; Hughes and Henry 2006; Kerber 2006; Petraglia and Cunningham 2006; Petraglia et al. 2002; Riggs 2002.

6. Nicholas 2008:1660.

7. For example, Atalay 2012; Colwell-Chanthaphonh 2009; Colwell-Chanthaphonh and Ferguson 2008; Nicholas 2010; Phillips and Allen 2010; Preucel and Cipolla 2008; Silliman 2008; Smith and Wobst 2005; Swidler 1997; Watkins 2000.

8. Gallivan and Moretti-Langholtz 2007.

9. The spatial imaginary is the third axis in Henri Lefebvre's (1991) model of social space.

10. Smith 1986a:63.

11. Smith 1986b:173; Strachey 1953:57.

12. Mook 1943.

13. Barbour 1969:104–7. Tindall described himself in a letter as "gunner to Prince Henry," and later references note that he was a master mariner (Mook 1943:373).

14. Brown 1890:151, 188; Gray 1934; Lewis and Loomie 1953:242; McCary 1981; Montague 1972; Mook 1943; Noël Hume 1994:225; Rountree 1990:41; Tyler 1901.

15. This second map's exact origins are unknown, though it was found in the collection of George Legge, Baron Dartmouth, an English military commander who served kings Charles II and James II of England during the latter half of the seventeenth century (Kraus 1967:43–46). Other Dartmouth collection maps date to the reign of James I, the English king when Jamestown was established. Over 70 Native settlements are denoted by semicircles on the map, with labels applied only to Werowocomoco and to "Monacon, Enemyes to Powaton" adjacent to a location in the James River piedmont. No English settlements are identified on the map, suggesting that the map may date to the earliest years of English colonization in the Chesapeake.

16. Gallivan et al. 2013:29.

17. Gallivan 2003:116.

18. Turner 1992:110–12.

19. Spelman 1998:487.

20. Smith 1986a:51.

21. Ibid., 69.

22. Barbour 1986 1:69n.175; Rountree 2005:252n.25.

23. Potter 2006; Hantman 1990.

24. Earle 1997:70–73; Beck 2013:196.

25. Earle 1997:73–75; Beck 2013:196, 210.

26. Trench features similar to those identified at Werowocomoco are rare in the Chesapeake, though Native communities across much of Eastern North America have a long history of marking important places with ditches, ridges, mounds, shell rings, and earthwork enclosures. The earliest such effort dates to approximately 3500 BC, when hunter-gatherers at the Watson Brake site in northern Louisiana constructed an oval formation of 11 mounds, connected by ridges to form an oval nearly 900 feet (270 m) across (Saunders et al. 2005). Archaic-period hunter-gatherers constructed a range of other monumental landscapes in the Southeast, notably the massive complex of ridges and mounds at the Poverty Point site built between 1650 and 700 BC (Kidder 2002; Sassaman 2010). In interior portions of the Eastern Woodlands centered on the Ohio River Valley, earthen enclosures, effigy mounds, circular wooden screens, and burial mounds associated with Adena and Hopewell sites marked places of ceremony between 1000 BC and AD 500 (for example, Carr and Case 2005). From AD 800 to 1500, communities across a vast portion of the Midwest and southeast fell under the sway of a Mississippian tradition marked by hierarchical chiefdoms, platform mound centers, Southeastern Ceremonial Complex iconography, and intensive maize agriculture (for example, Emerson 1997; Pauketat 2009). The Chesapeake region's archaeological record indicates that these mound-building or earthwork-constructing peoples had only limited and indirect contacts with the Native communities in the coastal Chesapeake (for example, Custer 1989b:262–75; Dent 1995:231–35; Lowery 2012; Potter 1993:214).

27. Blanton et al. 2005:50–53.

28. Beta-323136, conventional date: 450 bp ±30, median probability: AD 1440.

29. Blanton et al. 1999; Potter 1993:121.

30. Blanton et al. 1999:95.

31. Ibid., 91–98.

32. Smith 1986a:43–59, 1986c:212–13, 1986d:146–51.

33. Smith 1986d:150.

34. Smith 1986c:147, 1986d:104.

35. Smith 1986a:53–64.

36. Smith 1986d:151.

37. Smith 1986d:151.

38. Smith 1986a:63–79, 1986c:215–17.

39. Orli 2008:17.

40. Smith 1986c:235–36, 1986d:182–83.

41. Smith 1986c:237.

42. Smith 1986d:184

43. Smith 1986c:245–50, 1986d:205–6.

44. Orli 2008:21.

45. Smith 1986d:195.

46. Smith 1986c:250–56, 1986d:199–206.

47. Silliman 2005.

48. Barbour 1986:lxiii–lxiv.

49. Rountree 1990:38–39; Townsend 2004:52–56.

50. For example, Barbour 1970:23–26.

51. Gleach 1997:120; Williamson 2003.

52. Smith 1986d:122.

53. Bragdon 1996:184.

54. Lorant 1965.

55. Cf. Norman and Kelly 2004.

56. White 1998; Smith 1986b:171–72; Strachey 1953:98–100.

57. White 1998:138.

58. Beverley 1947:209.

59. Gerard 1907; White 1998:140–41.

60. Beverley 1947:213.

61. Smith 1986b:157.

62. Beverley 1947:210.

63. Lefebvre (1991:33) refers to this as the "representational spaces," the third dimension in his model of social space alongside representations of space and spatial practices.

Chapter 7. Persistent Places in Colonial Tsenacomacoh

1. West 1998; Governor and Council of Virginia 1998.

2. Kupperman 2007:254–60

3. Herrmann 2011; Kupperman 1979.

4. Nicholls 2010:246–47.

5. Horn 2005:180–83; Smith 1986d:234–37.

6. Brown 1883.

7. Strachey 1969.

8. Horn 2005:185–86.

9. Nicholls 2010:253–54.

10. Fausz 1977:277; Nicholls 2010:254.

11. Nicholls 2010:244–45.

12. Fausz 1990.

13. Gleach 1997:146; Virginia Council 1935:10.

14. Shaffer 2005:141.

15. Jefferson 1955:97–98.

16. Hantman 2003.

17. Gleach 1997:146.

18. Beverley 1947:51–55; Smith 1986d:293.

19. Fausz 1977:281–82; Rountree 1990:66–67.

20. Walsh 2010:38.

21. Fausz 1977.

22. Ibid., 353–59.

23. Gleach 1997:148–58, 174–83.

24. Ibid., 4.

25. Fausz 1977:49, 130, 200.

26. Rountree 1990:89–127.

27. Walsh 2010:111.

28. Rountree 1990:87–89, 100. An exhibit at the Pamunkey Museum and Cultural Center interprets the ramifications of these treaties in more detail.

29. Rountree 1990:79.

30. Ibid., 117.

31. Levy 2004.

32. Ibid., 229.

33. Smith 1986d:123–24; Strachey 1953:93.

34. Beverley 1947 :213. Italics added.

35. Blanton et al. 1999:97.

36. Smith 1986c:256.

37. Gallivan et al. 2005:38.

38. After consultation with the Werowocomoco Research Group and property owners, the project's Virginia Indian Advisory Board recommended an inventory of the remains and associated grave goods, to be followed by reburial.

39. Though the Native American Graves Protection and Repatriation Act (NAG-PRA) did not yet apply to Virginia's tribes, the research team's policy on human remains operated as if it did. The burial was excavated prior to the Werowocomoco Research Group's involvement at the site. Our goal has been to implement a plan for the human remains and associated material that balances respect for the Virginia Indian community's wishes regarding an ancestor while also meeting our obligations as stewards of archaeological information from the site. The Virginia Indian advisors to the project have expressed a strong sense that the objects represent items sacred to Powhatan descendants. Under NAGPRA, the materials would likely be accorded the status of associated funerary objects. Given the strong convictions of the representatives from contemporary Native communities, it is also possible that the materials would today be considered objects of cultural patrimony. Objects of cultural patrimony have ongoing historical, traditional, or cultural importance central to a tribe, rather than being the property of an individual tribal member. Upon completion of an inventory, the Werowocomoco Research Group and landowners delegated decisions pertaining to the reinterment of the remains and associated objects to the Virginia Indian Advisory Board.

40. Gallivan et al. 2005:39–44.

41. Excavations at James Fort have recovered similar tokens (Straube 2004). A similar set of 18 tokens, pierced and constituting a necklace, was excavated from a seventeenth-century ossuary on the banks of Piscataway Creek in Maryland (Ferguson 1940).

42. The beads were made of thin pieces of rolled copper. Several of the beads have a

fibrous thread inside them, which suggests that they were held together in a necklace. An analysis of the thread from several of the beads indicates the fibers are linen flax of probable European origin (Williams 2005).

43. Gallivan et al. 2005:41–44; Lapham 2004.

44. Lapham 2001.

45. Fitzgerald et al. 1995.

46. Beta-249895, conventional date: 110 bp ±40, two-sigma range: 1677–1954.

47. Fitzgerald 2009.

48. Kerber 1997.

49. Fitzgerald 2009:109.

50. Williamson 2003:234. *Puccoon* is an Algonquian term for dye and refers to several plants from which Native communities produced a red dye.

51. Beverley 1947:213.

52. Williamson 2003:234.

53. Beverley 1947:213; Smith 1986d:123–24; Strachey 1953:93.

54. Bushnell 1920, 1930.

55. Pilgrimage is a challenging process to study, in part because of the very mobility that it entails. In their classic treatise of Christian pilgrimage, Victor and Edith Turner (1978) framed pilgrimage as a rite of passage that allows people to move from their everyday lives and spaces to places and states of heightened spirituality. In the process, Christian travelers encounter others on pilgrimage and lose their individual identity to a feeling of collective unity or "communitas." In colonized settings, places of revisitation and ceremony may be viewed by indigenous communities in a shifting way as once sacred, now desacralized, and later resacralized in a new way (Scott and Simpson-Housley 2001). Some Native American pilgrimages seek to access cosmological or sacred power in order to contest colonial hegemony, albeit through distinctly different cultural and historical frames (e.g., Astor-Aguilera and Jarvenpa 2008). Recently, studies of pilgrimage in the postcolonial world have emphasized the often-contested quality of pilgrimage sites from Stonehenge to Wounded Knee that figure in debates about boundaries, identities, and sovereignty (for example, Badone and Roseman 2004).

56. Archaeological studies of pilgrimage in Native North America have identified evidence of pilgrimage in the deep past, typically focusing on the monumental spaces of spectacular sites such as Poverty Point, Cahokia, and Chaco Canyon. Pilgrims evidently traveled considerable distances to acquire materials, including basalt and red cedar, to bring back to Cahokia as tokens of pilgrimages or vision quests (Kelley and Brown 2012). In Chaco Canyon the great houses of Ancestral Pueblo societies may have attracted thousands of individuals from the surrounding region for seasonal fairs and ceremonies. This scenario has not, however, stood up well to detailed scrutiny of the expected accumulations of ceramic and faunal debris, which points instead toward smaller-scale events and feasting on a household scale (Plog and Watson 2012). Another recent study examined pathways to ritual sites in Mexico, illustrating a landscape that included places of pilgrimage with short-term, ephemeral use and others used persistently over long durations (Claassen 2011). Finally, a recent archaeological study comparing evidence from Chaco Canyon and Cahuachi in the Nasca region of Peru

argues that pilgrimages provided an opportunity for pilgrims to transmit a "costly signal" of their commitment to a religious system and its associated values (Kantner and Vaughn 2012). On the whole, pilgrimage appears to be of considerable importance in the study of cultural landscapes, though it is also difficult to assess archaeologically.

57. Klein and Sanford 2004.

58. Hantman 1990.

Epilogue

1. Kennedy 2009.

2. Ibid., 128–30.

3. Dussias 2011; Kinney 2008.

4. Dussias 2011:54–101.

5. Vaughan 1979:111.

6. Bragdon and Moretti-Langholtz 1998.

7. Dussias 2011:17–18.

8. Ibid., 74.

9. Rowe 2008.

10. McClain 2013; emphasis added.

11. Ashley Atkins, e-mail message to author containing speech transcript, June 18, 2013.

References

Abbott, Lawrence E., Erica E. Sanborn, Leslie E. Raymer, Irwin Rovner, Lisa D. O'Steen
2003   *Archaeological Data Recovery at 44MC491 (Area 1): Woodland Settlement and Subsistence Practices on an Alluvial Island in the Middle of the Roanoke River Valley, John H. Kerr Reservoir.* Stone Mountain, Ga., New South Associates.

Adkins, Wayne
2009   Comments on the Chickahominy River Survey. *Journal of Middle Atlantic Archaeology* 25:141–44.

Anthony, David W.
1990   Migration in Archeology: The Baby and the Bathwater. *American Anthropologist* 92(4):895–914.

Archer, Gabriel
1910 [1607]   A Relatyon of the Discovery of Our River, from *James Forte* into the Maine. In *Travels and Works of Captain John Smith: President of Virginia and Admiral of New England, 1580–1631,* edited by E. Arber and A. G. Bradley, xl–lv. Edinburgh: John Grant.

Ashmore, Wendy
2004   Social Archaeologies of Landscape. In *A Companion to Social Archaeology,* edited by L. Meskell and R. W. Preucel, 255–71. Malden, Mass.: Blackwell.
2002   "Decisions and Dispositions": Socializing Spatial Archaeology. *American Anthropologist* 104(4):1172–83.

Ashmore, Wendy, and Arthur Bernard Knapp
1999   *Archaeologies of Landscape: Contemporary Perspectives.* Oxford: Blackwell.

Astor-Aguilera, Miguel, and Robert Jarvenpa
2008   Comparing Indigenous Pilgrimages: Devotion, Identity, and Resistance in Mesoamerica and North America. *Anthropos* 103(2):482–506.

Atalay, Sonya
2012   *Community-Based Archaeology: Research with, by, and for Indigenous and Local Communities.* Berkeley: University of California Press.

Augé, Marc
1995   *Non-places: Introduction to an Anthropology of Supermodernity.* London: Verso.

Axtell, James

2001 *Natives and Newcomers: The Cultural Origins of North America*. New York: Oxford University Press.

Badone, Ellen, and Sharon R. Roseman

2004 *Intersecting Journeys: The Anthropology of Pilgrimage and Tourism*. Urbana: University of Illinois Press.

Balée, William L.

2013 *Cultural Forests of the Amazon: A Historical Ecology of People and Their Landscapes*. Tuscaloosa: University of Alabama Press.

2006 The Research Program of Historical Ecology. *Annual Review of Anthropology* 35:75–98.

Balée, William L., and Clark L. Erickson

2006 Time, Complexity, and Historical Ecology. In *Time and Complexity in Historical Ecology: Studies in the Neotropical Lowlands*, edited by William L. Balée and Clark L. Erickson, 1–17. New York: Columbia University Press.

Barber, Michael B., and Michael J. Madden

2006 The Maycock's Point (44PG40) Beach Collection: The Implications of Controlled Survey in a Disturbed Context or Time and Tide Wait for No Man. *Quarterly Bulletin of the Archeological Society of Virginia* 61(2):61–81.

Barbour, Philip L., ed.

1986 *The Complete Works of Captain John Smith (1580–1631)*. 3 vols. Chapel Hill: University of North Carolina Press.

1969 *The Jamestown Voyages under the First Charter, 1606–1609*. London: Cambridge University Press.

1964 *The Three Worlds of Captain John Smith*. Boston: Houghton Mifflin.

Barbour, Philip L.

1972 The Earliest Reconnaissance of the Chesapeake Bay Area: Captain John Smith's Map and Indian Vocabulary, Part II. *The Virginia Magazine of History and Biography* 80(1):21–51.

1971 The Earliest Reconnaissance of the Chesapeake Bay Area: Captain John Smith's Map and Indian Vocabulary. *The Virginia Magazine of History and Biography* 79(3):280–302.

1970 *Pocahontas and Her World*. Boston: Houghton Mifflin.

1967 Chickahominy Place Names in Captain John Smith's "True Relation." *Names* 15:216–27.

Barth, Fredrik

1969 *Ethnic Groups and Boundaries: The Social Organization of Culture Difference*. Boston: Little, Brown.

Basso, Keith H.

1996 *Wisdom Sits in Places: Landscape and Language among the Western Apache*. Albuquerque: University of New Mexico Press.

Beck, Robin

2013 *Chiefdoms, Collapse, and Coalescence in the Early American South*. New York: Cambridge University Press.

Bellwood, Peter

2001　Early Agriculturalist Population Diasporas? Farming, Languages, and Genes. *Annual Review of Anthropology* 30:181–207.

Bellwood, Peter S., and Colin Renfrew

2002　*Examining the Farming/Language Dispersal Hypothesis*. Oxford: McDonald Institute for Archaeological Research.

Bender, Barbara

1998　*Stonehenge: Making Space*. New York: Berg.

Bernardini, Wesley

2008　Identity as History: Hopi Clans and the Curation of Oral Tradition. *Journal of Anthropological Research* 64(4):483–509.

Beverley, Robert

1947 [1705]　*The History and Present State of Virginia*. Chapel Hill: University of North Carolina Press.

Binford, Lewis R.

2001　*Constructing Frames of Reference: An Analytical Method for Archaeological Theory Building Using Hunter-Gatherer and Environmental Data Sets*. Berkeley: University of California Press.

1980　Willow Smoke and Dogs' Tails: Hunter-Gatherer Settlement Systems and Archaeological Site Formation. *American Antiquity* 45(1):4–20.

1964　Archaeological and Ethnohistorical Investigation of Cultural Diversity and Progressive Development among Aboriginal Cultures of Coastal Virginia and North Carolina. Ph.D. diss., Department of Anthropology, University of Michigan, Ann Arbor.

Blansett, Lisa

2005　John Smith Maps Virginia: Knowledge, Rhetoric, and Politics. In *Envisioning an English Empire: Jamestown and the Making of the North Atlantic World*, edited by R. Appelbaum and J. W. Sweet, 68–91. Philadelphia: University of Pennsylvania Press.

Blanton, Dennis

1996　Accounting for Submerged Mid-Holocene Archaeological Sites in the Southeast: A Case Study from the Chesapeake Estuary, Virginia. In *Archaeology of the Mid-Holocene Southeast*, edited by K. E. Sassaman and D. G. Anderson, 200–221. Gainesville: University Press of Florida.

1992　Middle Woodland Settlement Systems in Virginia. In *Middle and Late Woodland Research in Virginia: A Synthesis*, edited by T. R. Reinhart and M. E. Hodges, 65–96. Richmond: Dietz Press.

Blanton, Dennis B., and Stevan C. Pullins

2004　*Middle Woodland Settlement and Environment in the Chisel Run/Powhatan Creek Drainage: Archaeological Data Recovery at Sites 44jc127 and 44jc850 Associated with the Route 199 Project, James City County, Virginia*. William and Mary Center for Archaeological Research, Williamsburg. Richmond: Virginia Department of Transportation.

Blanton, Dennis B., Stevan C. Pullins, and Veronica L. Deitrick

1999　*The Potomac Creek Site (44ST2) Revisited*. Volume 10. Richmond, Va. Prepared by William and Mary Center for Archaeological Research. Williamsburg: Virginia Department of Historic Resources.

Blanton, Dennis B., John R. Underwood, Courtney Birkett, David W. Lewes, and William H. Moore

2005 *Archaeological Evaluation of Eight Prehistoric-Native American Sites at Naval Weapons Station Yorktown, Virginia.* Williamsburg: William and Mary Center for Archaeological Research.

Blick, Jeffrey P.

2000 The Quiyoughcohannock Ossuary Ritual and the Huron Feast of the Dead: A Case for Cultural Diffusion? Sixth Internet World Congress for Biomedical Sciences, Ciudad Real, Spain, 2000.

Blitz, John H.

1993 Big Pots for Big Shots: Feasting and Storage in a Mississippian Community. *American Antiquity* 58(1):80–96.

Bloom, Leonard

1939 The Cherokee Clan: A Study in Acculturation. *American Anthropologist* 41(2): 266–68.

Bloomfield, Leonard

1946 Algonquian. In *Linguistic Structures of Native America*, edited by H. Hoijer, 85–129. New York: Wenner Gren Foundation for Anthropological Research.

Blume, Cara Lee

2006 Working Together: Developing Partnerships with American Indians in New Jersey and Delaware. In *Cross-Cultural Collaboration: Native Peoples and Archaeology in the Northeastern United States*, edited by J. E. Kerber, 197–211. Lincoln: University of Nebraska Press.

Boelhower, William

2003 Mapping the Gift Path: Exchange and Rivalry in John Smith's *A True Relation*. *American Literary History* 15(4):655–82.

Bourdieu, Pierre

1970 The Berber House or the World Reversed. *Social Science Information* 9(1):151–70.

Bragdon, Kathleen J.

1996 *Native People of Southern New England, 1500–1650*. Norman: University of Oklahoma Press.

Bragdon, Kathleen J., and Danielle Moretti-Langholtz

1998 *Powhatan's Legacy: Traditional Cultural Property Study for the Proposed Regional Raw Water Study Group's Water Supply Reservoir, King William County, Virginia.* Williamsburg: College of William and Mary.

Bridenbaugh, Carl

1980 *Jamestown, 1544–1699*. New York: Oxford University Press.

Brown, Alexander

1890 *The Genesis of the United States*. Boston: Houghton, Mifflin.

1883 Sir Thomas West, Third Lord De La Warr. *Magazine of American History with Notes and Queries* 9:18–30.

Brown, Cecil H.

2006 Prehistoric Chronology of the Common Bean in the New World: The Linguistic Evidence. *American Anthropologist* 108(3):507–16.

Brush, Grace Somers

2001 Forests before and after the Colonial Encounter. In *Discovering the Chesapeake: The History of an Ecosystem*, edited by P. D. Curtin, G. S. Brush, and G. W. Fisher, 40–59. Baltimore: Johns Hopkins University Press.

Burmeister, Stefan

2000 Archaeology and Migration: Approaches to an Archaeological Proof of Migration. *Current Anthropology* 41(4):539–67.

Busby, Virginia Roche

2010 *Transformation and Persistence: The Nanticoke Indians and Chicone Indian Town in the Context of European Contact and Colonization*. Ph.D. diss., Department of Anthropology, University of Virginia, Charlottesville.

Bushnell, David I.

1930 *The Five Monacan Towns in Virginia, 1607 (with 14 Plates)*. Washington, D.C.: Smithsonian Institution.

1922 The Native Tribes of Virginia. *Virginia Magazine of History and Biography* 30(2):123–32.

1920 *Native Cemeteries and Forms of Burial East of the Mississippi*. Washington, D.C.: U.S. Government Printing Office.

1913 Notes on the Indians of Maryland, 1706–1706. *American Anthropologist* 15(3): 535–36.

1907 Virginia from Early Records. *American Anthropologist* 9(1):31–44.

Campbell, Lyle

1997 *American Indian Languages: The Historical Linguistics of Native America*. New York: Oxford University Press.

2004 *Historical Linguistics: An Introduction*. Cambridge, Mass.: MIT Press.

Carr, Christopher, and D. Troy Case

2005 *Gathering Hopewell: Society, Ritual, and Ritual Interaction*. New York: Kluwer Academic/Plenum.

Carr, Christopher, and Robert F. Maslowski

1995 Cordage and Fabrics: Relating Form, Technology, and Social Process. In *Style, Society and Person: Archaeological and Ethnological Perspectives*, edited by C. Carr and J. E. Neitzel, 297–344.

Carr, Lois Green, Russell R. Menard, and Lorena S. Walsh

1991 *Robert Cole's World: Agriculture and Society in Early Maryland*. Chapel Hill: University of North Carolina Press.

Certeau, Michel de

1984 *The Practice of Everyday Life*. Berkeley: University of California Press.

Cipolla, Craig N.

2013 *Becoming Brothertown: Native American Ethnogenesis and Endurance in the Modern World*. Tucson: University of Arizona Press.

Cissna, Paul B.

1986 The Piscataway Indians of Southern Maryland: An Ethnohistory from Pre-European Contact to the Present. Ph.D. diss., Department of Anthropology, American University, Washington, D.C.

Claassen, Cheryl

2011 Waning Pilgrimage Paths and Modern Roadscapes: Moving through Landscape in Northern Guerrero, Mexico. *World Archaeology* 43(3):493–504.

Clements, William M.

2011 Translating Context and Situation: William Strachey and Powhatan's "Scornful Song." In *Born in the Blood: On Native American Translation*, edited by B. Swann, 398–418. Lincoln: University of Nebraska Press.

Cobb, Charles R.

2005 Archaeology and the "Savage Slot": Displacement and Emplacement in the Premodern World. *American Anthropologist* 107(4):563–74.

Colwell-Chanthaphonh, Chip

2009 *Inheriting the Past: The Making of Arthur C. Parker and Indigenous Archaeology.* Tucson: University of Arizona Press.

Colwell-Chanthaphonh, Chip, and T. J. Ferguson

2008 *Collaboration in Archaeological Practice: Engaging Descendant Communities.* Lanham, Md.: AltaMira Press.

2006 Memory Pieces and Footprints: Multivocality and the Meanings of Ancient Times and Ancestral Places among the Zuni and Hopi. *American Anthropologist* 108(1):148–62.

Cook, Samuel R.

2003 Anthropological Advocacy in Historical Perspective: The Case of Anthropologists and Virginia Indians. *Human Organization* 62(2):193–201.

2000 *Monacans and Miners: Native American and Coal Mining Communities in Appalachia.* Lincoln: University of Nebraska Press.

Cosgrove, Denis

1999 Introduction: Mapping Meaning. In *Mappings*, edited by D. Cosgrove, 1–23. London: Reaktion Books.

Craven, Avery

2006 *Soil Exhaustion as a Factor in the Agricultural History of Virginia and Maryland, 1606–1860.* Columbia: University of South Carolina Press.

Cronin, Thomas M., Gary S. Dwyer, Takahiro Kamiya, Sara Schwede, and Debra A. Willard

2003 Medieval Warm Period, Little Ice Age and 20th Century Temperature Variability from Chesapeake Bay. *Global and Planetary Change* 36(1):17–29.

Cronin, Thomas M., K. Hayo, Robert C. Thunell, Gary S. Dwyer, Casey Saenger, and Debra A. Willard

2010 The Medieval Climate Anomaly and Little Ice Age in Chesapeake Bay and the North Atlantic Ocean. *Palaeogeography, Palaeoclimatology, Palaeoecology* 297(2): 299–310.

Cronin, Thomas M., Robert C. Thunell, Gary S. Dwyer, Casey Saenger, M. E. Mann, Cheryl Vann, and R. R. Seal

2005 Multiproxy Evidence of Holocene Climate Variability from Estuarine Sediments, Eastern North America. *Paleoceanography* 20(4):PA4006.

Cronon, William

1983 *Changes in the Land: Indians, Colonists, and the Ecology of New England.* New York: Hill and Wang.

Cross, Dorothy

1956 *Archaeology of New Jersey.* Vol. 2, *The Abbott Farm.* Trenton: Archaeological Society of New Jersey and the New Jersey State Museum.

Crumley, Carole L.

1995 Heterarchy and the Analysis of Complex Societies. *Archeological Papers of the American Anthropological Association* 6(1):1–5.

1994 *Historical Ecology: Cultural Knowledge and Changing Landscapes.* Santa Fe: School of American Research Press.

Curry, Dennis C.

1999 *Feast of the Dead: Aboriginal Ossuaries in Maryland.* Crownsville: Maryland Historic Trust.

Curry, Dennis C., and Maureen Kavanagh

1991 The Middle to Late Woodland Transition in Maryland. *North American Archaeologist* 12(1):3–28.

Curtin, Philip D., Grace Somers Brush, and George Wescott Fisher

2001 *Discovering the Chesapeake: The History of an Ecosystem.* Baltimore: Johns Hopkins University Press.

Cusick, James G.

1998 *Studies in Culture Contact: Interaction, Culture Change, and Archaeology.* Carbondale: Center for Archaeological Investigations, Southern Illinois University.

Custer, Jay F.

2005 Ethics and the Hyperreality of the Archaeological Thought World. *North American Archaeologist* 26(1):3–27.

2004 Cultural Context and Cordage Twist Direction. *North American Archaeologist* 25(2):139–52.

1989a The Woodland I–Woodland II Transition in the Delmarva Peninsula and Southeast Pennsylvania. *North American Archaeologist* 11(3):273–87.

1989b *Prehistoric Cultures of the Delmarva Peninsula: An Archaeological Study.* Newark: University of Delaware Press.

1987 Late Woodland Ceramics and Social Boundaries in Southeastern Pennsylvania and the Northern Delmarva Peninsula. *Archaeology of Eastern North America* 15:13–27.

Custer, Jay F., Karen R. Rosenberg, Glenn Mellin, and Arthur Washburn

1990 A Re-examination of the Island Field Site (7k-F-17), Kent County, Delaware. *Archaeology of Eastern North America* 18:145–212.

David, Bruno, and Julian Thomas

2008 Landscape Archaeology: Introduction. In *Handbook of Landscape Archaeology*, edited by B. David and J. Thomas, 27–43. Walnut Creek, Calif.: Left Coast Press.

Dawdy, Shannon Lee

1995 The Meherrin's Secret History of the Dividing Line. *North Carolina Historical Review* 72(4):385–415.

Deloria, Vine

1970 *We Talk, You Listen: New Tribes, New Turf.* New York: Macmillan.

Denny, J. Peter

2003 Archaeological Signs of Eastern Algonquian. In *Essays in Algonquian, Catawban, and Siouan Linguistics in Memory of Frank T. Siebert, Jr.*, edited by B. A. Rudes and D. J. Costa, 15–35. Winnipeg: University of Manitoba Press.

1991 The Algonquian Migration from Plateau to Midwest: Linguistics and Archaeology. In *Papers of the 22nd Algonquian Conference*, edited by W. Cowan, 103–24. Ottawa: Carleton University Press.

Dent, Richard J.

2003 Excavations at a Late Woodland Village in the Middle Atlantic Valley: Theory and Practice at the Winslow Site. *Journal of Middle Atlantic Archaeology* 19:3–24.

1995 *Chesapeake Prehistory: Old Traditions, New Directions.* New York: Plenum Press.

Dent, Richard J., and Christine A. Jirikowic

2001 Accokeek Creek: Chronology, the Potomac Creek Complex, and Piscataway Origins. *Journal of Middle Atlantic Archaeology* 17:39–58.

Dietler, Michael

2010 Theorizing the Feast: Rituals of Consumption, Commensal Politics, and Power in African Contexts. In *Feasts: Archaeological and Ethnographic Perspectives on Food, Politics, and Power*, edited by M. Dietler and B. Hayden, 65–114. Tuscaloosa: University of Alabama Press.

Dietler, Michael, and Brian Hayden

2010 *Feasts: Archaeological and Ethnographic Perspectives on Food, Politics, and Power.* Tuscaloosa: University of Alabama Press.

Dietler, Michael, and Ingrid Herbich

1998 Habitus, Techniques, Style: An Integrated Approach to the Social Understanding of Material Culture and Boundaries. In *The Archaeology of Social Boundaries*, edited by M. T. Stark, 232–63. Washington, D.C.: Smithsonian Institution Press.

Dore, Berek J.

2011 Dietary Bioarchaeology: Late Woodland Subsistence within the Coastal Plain of Virginia. Master's thesis, Department of Anthropology, College of William and Mary, Williamsburg, Va.

Dunham, Gary H.

1999 Making Territory: Burial Mounds in Interior Virginia. In *Material Symbols: Culture and Economy in Prehistory*, edited by J. E. Robb, 112–30. Carbondale: Center for Archaeological Investigations, Southern Illinois University.

Dunham, Gary H., Debra L. Gold, and Jeffrey L. Hantman

2003   Collective Burial in Late Prehistoric Virginia: Excavation and Analysis of the Rapidan Mound. *American Antiquity* 68(1):109–28.

Dussias, Allison M.

2011   Protecting Pocahontas's World: The Mattaponi Tribe's Struggle against Virginia's King William Reservoir Project. *American Indian Law Review* 36(1):1–123.

Earle, Carville

1988   The Myth of the Southern Soil Miner: Macrohistory, Agricultural Innovation, and Environmental Change. In *The Ends of the Earth: Perspectives on Modern Environmental History*, edited by D. Worster, 175–210. Cambridge: Cambridge University Press.

Earle, Timothy K.

1997   *How Chiefs Come to Power: The Political Economy in Prehistory.* Stanford, Calif.: Stanford University Press.

Egloff, Keith T., Mary Ellen N. Hodges, Jay F. Custer, Keith R. Doms, and Leslie D. McFaden

1988   *Archaeological Investigations at Croaker Landing.* Richmond: Virginia Department of Conservation and Historic Resources.

Egloff, Keith T., and Stephen R. Potter

1982   Indian Ceramics from Coastal Plain Virginia. *Archaeology of Eastern North America* 10:95–117.

Emerson, Thomas E.

1997   *Cahokia and the Archaeology of Power.* Tuscaloosa: University of Alabama Press.

Erickson, Clark L.

2008   Amazonia: The Historical Ecology of a Domesticated Landscape. In *Handbook of South American Archaeology*, edited by H. Silverman and W. H. Isbell, 157–83. New York: Springer.

Ethridge, Robbie Franklyn, and Sheri Marie Shuck-Hall

2009   *Mapping the Mississippian Shatter Zone: The Colonial Indian Slave Trade and Regional Instability in the American South.* Lincoln: University of Nebraska Press.

Fandos, Nicholas

2015   Unearthing Jamestown's Leaders, and a Mystery. *New York Times*, July 28, 2015, A13.

Fausz, J. Frederick

1990   An "Abundance of Blood Shed on Both Sides": England's First Indian War, 1609–1614. *Virginia Magazine of History and Biography* 98(1):3–56.

1988   Merging and Emerging Worlds: Anglo-Indian Interest Groups and the Development of the Seventeenth-Century Chesapeake. In *Colonial Chesapeake Society*, edited by L. G. Carr, P. D. Morgan, and J. B. Russo, 47–98. Chapel Hill: University of North Carolina Press.

1977   The Powhatan Uprising of 1622: A Historical Study of Ethnocentrism and Cultural Conflict. Ph.D. diss., College of William and Mary, Williamsburg, Va.

Feathers, James K.

2009   Problems of Ceramic Chronology in the Southeast: Does Shell-Tempered Pottery Appear Earlier than We Think? *American Antiquity* 74(1):113–42.

Feest, Christian F.

1990   *The Powhatan Tribes.* New York: Chelsea House.

1983   Powhatan's Mantle. In *Tradescant's Rarities: Essays on the Foundation of the Ashmolean Museum, 1683,* edited by A. MacGregor, 130–35. Oxford: Clarendon Press.

1978   Virginia Algonquians. In *Handbook of North American Indians,* edited by B. G. Trigger, 235–70. Washington, D.C.: Smithsonian Institution.

1966   Powhatan: A Study in Political Organization. *Wiener volkerkundliche Mitteilungen* 13:69–83.

Feinman, Gary, and Jill Neitzel

1984   Too Many Types: An Overview of Sedentary Prestate Societies in the Americas. In *Archaeology Method and Theory,* edited by M. Schiffer, 39–102. New York: Academic Press.

Feld, Steven, and Keith H. Basso

1996   *Senses of Place.* Santa Fe: School of American Research Press.

Fennell, Christopher

2007   *Crossroads and Cosmologies: Diasporas and Ethnogenesis in the New World.* Gainesville: University Press of Florida.

Ferguson, Alice L., and T. Dale Stewart

1940   An Ossuary near Piscataway Creek with a Report on the Skeletal Remains. *American Antiquity* 6:4–18.

Ferguson, R. Brian, and Neil L. Whitehead

1992   *War in the Tribal Zone: Expanding States and Indigenous Warfare.* Santa Fe: School of American Research Press.

Ferguson, T. J., and Chip Colwell-Chanthaphonh

2006   *History Is in the Land: Multivocal Tribal Traditions in Arizona's San Pedro Valley.* Tucson: University of Arizona Press.

Ferris, Neal

2009   *The Archaeology of Native-Lived Colonialism: Challenging History in the Great Lakes.* Tucson: University of Arizona Press.

Fiedel, Stuart J.

2013   Are Ancestors of Contact Period Ethnic Groups Recognizable in the Archaeological Record of the Early Late Woodland? *Archaeology of Eastern North America* 41:221–29.

1999   Algonquians and Iroquoians: Taxonomy, Chronology, and Archaeological Implications. In *Taming the Taxonomy: Toward a New Understanding of Great Lakes Archaeology,* edited by R. F. Williamson and C. M. Watts, 193–204. Toronto: Eastend Books.

1994   Some Inferences concerning Proto-Algonquian Economy and Society. *Northeast Anthropology* 48:1–9.

1990   Middle Woodland Algonquian Expansion: A Refined Model. *North American Archaeologist* 11(3):209–30.

1987   Algonquian Origins: A Problem in Archaeological-Linguistic Correlation. *Archaeology of Eastern North America* 15 (1):1–11.

Fitzgerald, Jennifer A.

2009   Late Woodland Dog Ceremonialism on the Chickahominy and Beyond. *Journal of Middle Atlantic Archaeology* 25:105–10.

Fitzgerald, William R., Dean H. Knight, and Allison Bain

1995   Untanglers of Matters Temporal and Cultural: Glass Beads and the Early Contact Period Huron Ball Site. *Canadian Journal of Archaeology* 19:117–38.

Fitzhugh, Ben, S. Colby Phillips, and Erik Gjesfjeld

2011   Modeling Variability in Hunter-Gatherer Information Networks: An Archaeological Case Study from the Kuril Islands. In *Information and Its Role in Hunter-Gatherer Band Adaptations*, edited by R. Whallon, W. Lovis, and R. Hitchcock, 85–115. Los Angeles: UCLA Cotson Institute for Archaeology.

Flannery, Kent V.

1976   *The Early Mesoamerican Village*. New York: Academic Press.

Fogelson, Raymond D.

1989   The Ethnohistory of Events and Nonevents. *Ethnohistory* 36(2):133–47.

Fogelson, Raymond D., and Robert A. Brightman

2002   Totemism Reconsidered. In *Anthropology, History, and American Indians: Essays in Honor of William Curtis Sturtevant*, edited by W. C. Sturtevant, W. L. Merrill, and I. Goddard, 305–14. Washington, D.C.: Smithsonian Institution Press.

Ford, Worthington Chauncey

1924   Captain John Smith's Map of Virginia, 1612. *Geographical Review* 14(3):433–43.

Foucault, Michel

1986   Of Other Spaces. *Diacritics* 16(1):22–27.

Fowles, Severin

2010   The Southwest School of Landscape Archaeology. *Annual Review of Anthropology* 39:453–68.

Frachetti, Michael D.

2011   Migration Concepts in Central Eurasian Archaeology. *Annual Review of Anthropology* 40:195–212.

Gallivan, Martin D.

2009   The Chickahominy River Survey: Native Settlement in Tidewater Virginia, AD 200–1600. *Journal of Middle Atlantic Archaeology* 25:73–83.

2007   Powhatan's Werowocomoco: Constructing Place, Polity, and Personhood in the Chesapeake, C.E. 1200–C.E. 1609. *American Anthropologist* 109(1):85–100.

2003   *James River Chiefdoms: The Rise of Social Inequality in the Chesapeake*. Lincoln: University of Nebraska Press.

Gallivan, Martin, Michael F. Blakey, Shannon S. Mahoney, Christopher J. Shephard, Meredith A. Mahoney, Jennifer A. Fitzgerald, Anna K. Hayden, Justine W. Mc-Knight, Nadejda Golenishcheva-Coonan, Jennifer H. Ogborne, Brian E. Heinsman, Cyndi M. Volbrecht, Sarah E. Heinsman, and P. Brendan Burke

2009   *The Chickahominy River Survey: Native Communities in Tidewater Virginia, AD 200–1600. Department of Anthropology Archaeological Research Report #3*. Williamsburg, Va.: College of William and Mary.

Gallivan, Martin, and Helen Blouet

2001 Middle Woodland Settlement in the Interior Coastal Plain: Excavations at 44JC1052 and 44JC1053. *Quarterly Bulletin of the Archeological Society of Virginia* 56(3):127–35.

Gallivan, Martin D., Thane Harpole, David A. Brown, Danielle Moretti-Langholtz, and E. Randolph Turner III

2005 *The Werowocomoco Research Project: Background and 2003 Archaeological Field Season Results.* Volume 15. Richmond: Virginia Department of Historic Resources.

Gallivan, Martin D., and Danielle Moretti-Langholtz

2007 Civic Engagement at Werowocomoco: Reasserting Native Narratives from a Powhatan Place of Power. In *Archaeology as a Tool of Civic Engagement*, edited by B. J. Little and P. A. Shackel, 47–66. Lanham, Md.: AltaMira.

Gallivan, Martin, Danielle Moretti-Langholtz, and Buck Woodard

2011 Collaborative Archaeology and Strategic Essentialism: Native Empowerment in Tidewater Virginia. *Historical Archaeology* 45(1):10–23.

Gallivan, Martin, E. Randolph Turner III, Justine Woodard McKnight, David A. Brown, Thane Harpole, and Danielle Moretti-Langholtz

2013 *The Werowocomoco Research Project: 2004–2010 Field Seasons. Department of Anthropology Archaeological Research Report #3.* Williamsburg, Va.: College of William and Mary.

Gamble, Clive

2013 *Settling the Earth: The Archaeology of Deep Human History.* New York: Cambridge University Press.

Geary, James A.

1953 Strachey Vocabulary of Indian Words Used in Virginia. In *The Historie of Travell into Virginia Britania*, edited by L. B. Wright and V. Freund, 208–14. London: Cambridge University Press.

Gerard, William R.

1907 Virginia Indian's Contribution to English. *American Anthropologist* n.s. 9:87–112.

Gleach, Frederic W.

2003 Pocahontas at the Fair: Crafting Identities at the 1907 Jamestown Exposition. *Ethnohistory* 50(3):419–45.

2002 Anthropological Professionalization and the Virginia Indians at the Turn of the Century. *American Anthropologist* 104(2):499–507.

1997 *Powhatan's World and Colonial Virginia: A Conflict of Cultures.* Lincoln: University of Nebraska Press.

1995 Mimesis, Play, and Transformation in Powhatan Ritual. In *Papers of the Twenty-Sixth Algonquian Conference*, edited by D. Pentland, 114–23. Winnipeg: University of Manitoba.

Goddard, Ives

2005 The Indigenous Languages of the Southeast. *Anthropological Linguistics* 47(1):1–60.

2000 The Use of Pidgins and Jargons on the East Coast of North America. In *The Lan-*

guage Encounter in the Americas, 1492–1800: A Collection of Essays, edited by E. G. Gray and N. Fiering, 61–78. New York: Berghahn Books.

1994 The West-to-East Cline in Algonquian Dialectology. In *Papers of the 25th Algonquian Conference*, edited by W. Cowan, 187–211. Ottawa: Carleton University.

1991 Algonquian Linguistic Change and Reconstruction. In *Patterns of Change, Change of Patterns: Linguistic Change and Reconstruction Methodology*, edited by P. Baldi, 55–70. Berlin: Mouton de Gruyter.

1978 Eastern Algonquian Languages. In *Handbook of North American Indians: Northeast*, edited by B. G. Trigger, 70–77. Washington, D.C.: Smithsonian Institution.

Gold, Debra L.

2004 *The Bioarchaeology of Virginia Burial Mounds.* Tuscaloosa: University of Alabama Press.

Goldman, William S.

2011 Spain and the Founding of Jamestown. *William and Mary Quarterly* 68(3):427–50.

Golenishcheva-Coonan, Nadejda

2009 Wild Animals in Domesticated Landscapes: Patterns of Subsistence in Middle and Late Woodland Virginia Coastal Plain. *Journal of Middle Atlantic Archaeology* 25:125–32.

Governor and Council of Virginia

1998 [1610] Letter to the Virginia Company. In *Jamestown Narratives: Eyewitness Accounts of the Virginia Colony*, edited by E. W. Haile, 454–64. Champlain, Va.: Roundhouse.

Gray, Arthur

1934 Purtan, the Site of Werowocomico. *Virginia Magazine of History and Biography* 42:116–22.

Gregory, Leverett B.

1983 Zoned Pottery from the Hatch Site [Weyanoke Old Town] (44PG51) in Prince George County, Virginia. *The Chesopiean: A Journal of North American Archaeology* 21(4):2–8.

Griffin, James B.

1945 An Interpretation of Siouan Archaeology in the Piedmont of North Carolina and Virginia. *American Antiquity* 10(4):321–30.

Grumet, Robert Steven

2001 *Voices from the Delaware Big House Ceremony.* Norman: University of Oklahoma Press.

Gupta, Akhil, and James Ferguson

1992 Beyond "Culture": Space, Identity, and the Politics of Difference. *Cultural Anthropology* 7(1):6–23.

Halbwachs, Maurice

1992 *On Collective Memory.* Chicago: University of Chicago Press.

Haley, Brian D., and Larry R. Wilcoxon

2005 How Spaniards Became Chumash and Other Tales of Ethnogenesis. *American Anthropologist* 107(3):432–45.

Hall, Robert L.

1997   *An Archaeology of the Soul: North American Indian Belief and Ritual*. Urbana: University of Illinois Press.

1976   Ghosts, Water Barriers, Corn, and Sacred Enclosures in the Eastern Woodlands. *American Antiquity* 41(3):360–64.

Halttunen, Karen

2011   Grounded Histories: Land and Landscape in Early America. *William and Mary Quarterly* 68(4):513–32.

Hamor, Ralph

2007   [1615] A True Discourse of the Present Estate of Virginia, and the Success of the Affaires There till the 18 of June 1614. In *Captain John Smith: Writings with Other Narratives of Roanoke, Jamestown, and the First English Settlements of America*, edited by J. P. Horn, 1115–68. New York: Library of America.

Hantman, Jeffrey L.

2010   Long-Term History, Positionality, Contingency, Hybridity: Does Rethinking Indigenous History Reframe the Jamestown Colony? In *Across a Great Divide: Continuity and Change in Native North American Societies, AD 1400–1900*, edited by L. Scheiber and M. Mitchell, 42–60. Tucson: University of Arizona Press.

2008   Jamestown's 400th Anniversary: Old Themes, New Words, New Meanings for Virginia Indians. In *Archaeologies of Placemaking: Monuments, Memories, and Engagement in Native North America*, edited by P. Rubertone, 217–41. Walnut Creek, Calif.: Left Coast Press.

2003   *"With Expressions Construed to Be Those of Sorrow": Secondary Burial Ritual and Resettlement in the Colonial Era*. Paper Presented at the Annual Meeting of the Society for American Archaeology, Milwaukee.

1993   Powhatan's Relations with the Piedmont Monacans. In *Powhatan Foreign Relations, 1500–1722*, edited by H. C. Rountree. Charlottesville: University Press of Virginia.

1990   Between Powhatan and Quirank: Reconstructing Monacan Culture and History in the Context of Jamestown. *American Anthropologist* 92(3):676–90.

Hantman, Jeffrey L., and Debra Gold

2000   The Woodland in the Middle Atlantic: Ranking and Dynamic Political Stability. In *The Woodland Southeast*, edited by D. G. Anderson and R. C. Mainfort Jr. Tuscaloosa: University of Alabama Press.

Hantman, Jeffrey L., Karenne Wood, and Diane Shields

2000   Writing Collaborative History: How the Monacan Nation and Archaeologists Worked Together to Enrich Our Understanding of Virginia's Native Peoples. *Archaeology* 53(5):56–59.

Harding, Juliana M., Roger Mann, and Melissa J. Southworth

2008   Shell Length-at-Age Relationships in James River, Virginia, Oysters (*Crassostrea Virginica*) Collected Four Centuries Apart. *Journal of Shellfish Research* 27(5): 1109–15.

Harding, Juliana M., Howard J. Spero, Roger Mann, Gregory S. Herbert, and Jennifer L. Sliko

2010   Reconstructing Early 17th Century Estuarine Drought Conditions from James-
        town Oysters. *Proceedings of the National Academy of Sciences* 107(23):10549–54.

Harley, J. B.

1988   Silences and Secrecy: The Hidden Agenda of Cartography in Early Modern Eu-
        rope. *Imago Mundi* 40(1):57–76.

Harriot, Thomas

1972 [1588]   *A Briefe and True Report of the New Found Land of Virginia.* New York:
        Dover.

Hart, John P., William A. Lovis, Janet K. Schulenberg, and Gerald R. Urquhart

2007   Paleodietary Implications from Stable Carbon Isotope Analysis of Experimental
        Cooking Residues. *Journal of Archaeological Science* 34(5):804–13.

Hatfield, April Lee

2004   *Atlantic Virginia: Intercolonial Relations in the Seventeenth Century.* Philadelphia:
        University of Pennsylvania Press.

2003   Spanish Colonization Literature, Powhatan Geographies, and English Percep-
        tions of Tsenacommacah/Virginia. *Journal of Southern History* 69(2):245–82.

Hayden, Anna

2009a   Middle Woodland Cordage Twist on the Chickahominy and James Rivers. *Jour-
        nal of Middle Atlantic Archaeology* 25:97–104.

2009b   *Cordage Twist and Ceramic Style in the Chesapeake: Evaluating the Evidence for
        Middle Woodland Population Movements.* Undergraduate honors thesis, College
        of William and Mary, Williamsburg, Va.

Hayden, Brian, and Suzanne Villeneuve

2011   A Century of Feasting Studies. *Annual Review of Anthropology* 40:433–49.

Heckenberger, Michael

2005   *The Ecology of Power: Culture, Place, and Personhood in the Southern Amazon,
        AD 1000–2000.* New York: Routledge.

Heckenberger, Michael J., Afukaka Kuikuro, Urissapa Tabata Kuikuro, J. Christian Rus-
        sell, Morgan Schmidt, Carlos Fausto, and Bruna Franchetto

2003   Amazonia 1492: Pristine Forest or Cultural Parkland? *Science* 301:1710–14.

Heidegger, Martin

1982   *The Basic Problems of Phenomenology.* Bloomington: Indiana University Press.

1971   Building Dwelling Thinking. In *Poetry, Language, Thought,* 141–60. New York:
        Harper and Row.

1962   *Being and Time.* London: SCM Press.

Heim, Joe

2015   Federal Recognition Put on Hold for Virginia's Pamunkey Indian Tribe. *Wash-
        ington Post,* October 8.

2016   Virginia's Pamunkey Withstand Challenge to Tribe's Federal Recognition. *Wash-
        ington Post,* February 1.

Heinsman, Brian E., and Joshua F. Duncan

2006   The Maycock's Point Site: A Synthesis and Assessment of Research. Prepared by
        the William and Mary Department of Anthropology for the Virginia Depart-
        ment of Historic Resources,Williamsburg.

Herbert, Joseph M.

2008 The History and Practice of Shell Tempering in the Middle Atlantic: A Useful Balance. *Southeastern Archaeology* 27(2):265–85.

Herrmann, Rachel B.

2011 The "Tragicall Historie": Cannibalism and Abundance in Colonial Jamestown. *William and Mary Quarterly* 68(1):47–74.

Hill, Jonathan David, ed.

1996a *History, Power, and Identity: Ethnogenesis in the Americas, 1492–1992.* Iowa City: University of Iowa Press.

Hill, Jonathan David

1996b Introduction: Ethnogenesis in the Americas, 1492–1992. In *History, Power, and Identity: Ethnogenesis in the Americas, 1492–1992,* edited by J. D. Hill, 1–19. Iowa City: University of Iowa Press.

Horn, James P. P.

2005 *A Land as God Made It: Jamestown and the Birth of America.* New York: Basic Books.

Hornborg, Alf

2005 Ethnogenesis, Regional Integration, and Ecology in Prehistoric Amazonia: Toward a System Perspective. *Current Anthropology* 46(4):589–620.

Horning, Audrey

2006 Archaeology and the Construction of America's Jamestown. *Post-Medieval Archaeology* 40(1):1–27.

Hu, Di

2013. Approaches to the Archaeology of Ethnogenesis: Past and Emergent Perspectives. *Journal of Archaeological Research* 21(4):371–402.

Hubbard, Phil, and Rob Kitchin

2011 *Key Thinkers on Space and Place.* Los Angeles: Sage.

Hudson, Charles M., and Carmen Chaves Tesser

1994 *The Forgotten Centuries: Indians and Europeans in the American South, 1521–1704.* Athens: University of Georgia Press.

Hughes, Richard B., and Dixie L. Henry

2006 Forging New Partnerships: Archaeologists and the Native People of Maryland. In *Cross-Cultural Collaboration: Native Peoples and Archaeology in the Northeastern United States,* edited by J. E. Kerber, 112–29. Lincoln: University of Nebraska Press.

Hulton, Paul H.

1984 *America, 1585: The Complete Drawings of John White.* Chapel Hill: University of North Carolina Press.

Husserl, Edmund

2012 *Ideas: General Introduction to Pure Phenomenology.* New York: Routledge.

2001 *Logical Investigations.* New York: Routledge.

Hutchinson, Dale L.

2002 *Foraging, Farming, and Coastal Biocultural Adaptation in Late Prehistoric North Carolina.* Gainesville: University Press of Florida.

Hutchinson, Dale L., Clark Spencer Larsen, Margaret J. Schoeninger, and Lynette Norr

1998   Regional Variation in the Pattern of Maize Adoption and Use in Florida and Georgia. *American Antiquity* 63(3):397–416.

Hutchinson, Dale L., and Lynette Norr

2006   Nutrition and Health at Contact in Late Prehistoric Central Gulf Coast Florida. *American Journal of Physical Anthropology* 129(3):375–86.

Hymes, Dell H.

1960. Lexicostatistics So Far. *Current Anthropology* 1:3–44.

Ingold, Tim

2006   Rethinking the Animate, Re-animating Thought. *Ethnos* 71(1):9–20.

2000   *The Perception of the Environment: Essays on Livelihood, Dwelling and Skill.* New York: Routledge.

1993   The Temporality of the Landscape. *World Archaeology* 25(2):152–74.

Jefferson, Thomas

1955 [1787]   *Notes on the State of Virginia*, edited by W. Peden. Chapel Hill: University of North Carolina Press.

Jenkins, Jessica

2012   Oyster Shell from Midden Deposits at Kiskiak. Paper delivered at the Middle Atlantic Archaeological Conference, Virginia Beach.

Jirikowic, Christine A.

1990   The Political Implications of a Cultural Practice: A New Perspective on Ossuary Burial in the Potomac Valley. *North American Archaeologist* 11:353–74.

Johnson, Matthew

2012   Phenomenological Approaches in Landscape Archaeology. *Annual Review of Anthropology* 41:269–84.

2007   *Ideas of Landscape.* Malden, Mass.: Blackwell.

Johnson, William C., and D. Scott Speedy

1992   Cultural Continuity and Change in the Middle and Late Woodland Periods in the Upper James Estuary, Prince George County, Virginia. *Journal of Middle Atlantic Archaeology* 8:91–107.

Jones, John G.

2005   Appendix E: Pollen Analysis: Site 44YO2. In *Archaeological Evaluation of Eight Prehistoric-Native American Sites at Naval Weapons Station Yorktown, Virginia*, edited by D. B. Blanton, E1-E11. Williamsburg, Va.: William and Mary Center for Archaeological Research.

Jordan, Kurt A.

2008   *The Seneca Restoration, 1715–1754: An Iroquois Local Political Economy.* Gainesville: University Press of Florida.

Joyce, Rosemary A., and John S. Henderson

2007   From Feasting to Cuisine: Implications of Archaeological Research in an Early Honduran Village. *American Anthropologist* 109(4):642–53.

Kantner, John, and Kevin J. Vaughn

2012   Pilgrimage as Costly Signal: Religiously Motivated Cooperation in Chaco and Nasca. *Journal of Anthropological Archaeology* 31 (1):66–82.

Kelly, John E., and James A. Brown

2012 In Search of Cosmic Power: Contextualizing Spiritual Journeys between Cahokia and the St. Francois Mountains. In *Archaeology of Spiritualities*, edited by K. Rountree, C. Morris, and A.A.D. Peatfield, 107–29. One World Archaeology. New York: Springer.

Kelly, Robert L.

2013 *The Lifeways of Hunter-Gatherers: The Foraging Spectrum*. Cambridge: Cambridge University Press.

Kelso, William M.

2006 *Jamestown, the Buried Truth*. Charlottesville: University of Virginia Press.

Kennedy, Henry

2009 *Alliance to Save the Mattaponi v. U.S. Army Corps of Eng'rs*, 606 F. Supp. 2d 121 (D.D.C. 2009).

Kerber, Jordan E., ed.

2006 *Cross-Cultural Collaboration: Native Peoples and Archaeology in the Northeastern United States*. Lincoln: University of Nebraska Press.

Kerber, Jordan E.

1997 Native American Treatment of Dogs in Northeastern North America: Archaeological and Ethnohistorical Perspectives. *Archaeology of Eastern North America* 25:81–95.

Kidder, Tristram R.

2002 Mapping Poverty Point. *American Antiquity* 67(1):89–101.

King, Julia A.

2012 *Archaeology, Narrative, and the Politics of the Past: The View from Southern Maryland*. Knoxville: University of Tennessee Press.

Kinney, Adam F.

2008 The Tribe, the Empire, and the Nation: Enforceability of Pre-Revolutionary Treaties with Native American Tribes. *Case Western Reserve Journal of International Law* 39:897–925.

Klein, Michael J.

2003 Ceramics, Style, and Society in the Potomac Valley of Virginia. *Journal of Middle Atlantic Archaeology* 19:25–35.

Klein, Michael J., and Doug W. Sanford

2004 Analytical Scale and Archaeological Perspectives on the Contact Era in the Northern Neck of Virginia. In *Indian and European Contact in Context: The Mid-Atlantic Region*, edited by D. B. Blanton and J. A. King, 47–73. Gainesville: University Press of Florida.

Knapp, A. Bernard, and Wendy Ashmore

1999 Archaeological Landscapes: Constructed, Conceptualized, Ideational. In *Archaeologies of Landscape: Contemporary Perspectives*, edited by W. Ashmore and A. B. Knapp, 1–23. Oxford: Blackwell.

Koenig, Alexa

2007 Federalism and the State Recognition of Native American Tribes. *Santa Clara Law Review* 48 (1):79.

Kohl, Philip

1998 Nationalism and Archaeology: On the Constructions of Nations and the Reconstructions of the Remote Past. *Annual Review of Anthropology* 27:223–46.

Kraus, Hans

1967 *Monumenta Cartographica*. New York: H. P. Kraus.

Kupperman, Karen Ordahl

2007 *The Jamestown Project*. Cambridge: Belknap Press of Harvard University Press.

1984 *Roanoke, the Abandoned Colony*. Totowa, N.J.: Rowman and Allanheld.

1979 Apathy and Death in Early Jamestown. *Journal of American History* 66(1):24–40.

Lapham, Heather A.

2004 Glass Beads from the Ripley Collection. Manuscript on file at the Department of Anthropology, College of William and Mary, Williamsburg, Va.

2001 More than "a Few Blew Beads": The Glass and Stone Beads from Jamestown Rediscovery's 1994–1997 Excavations. *Journal of the Jamestown Rediscovery Center* 1.

Larsen, Clark Spencer

1997 *Bioarchaeology: Interpreting Behavior from the Human Skeleton*. New York: Cambridge University Press.

Lave, Jean, and Etienne Wenger

1991 *Situated Learning: Legitimate Peripheral Participation*. New York: Cambridge University Press.

Lawson, John

1967 [1709] *A New Voyage to Carolina*. Chapel Hill: University of North Carolina Press.

Lederer, John, William Patterson Cumming, and John Winthrop

1958 [1672] *The Discoveries of John Lederer*. Charlottesville: University of Virginia Press.

Lefebvre, Henri

1991 *The Production of Space*. Cambridge: Blackwell.

Lehman, Forrest K.

2007 Settled Place, Contested Past: Reconciling George Percy's "A Trewe Relacyon" with John Smith's "Generall Historie." *Early American Literature* 42(2):235–61.

Lekson, Stephen H.

2009 A New Deal for Chaco Canyon? Review of Ruth Van Dyke, "The Chaco Experience: Landscape and Ideology at the Center Place." *Current Anthropology* 50(4):579–80.

Lelièvre, Michelle A.

2012 Ajiwisin (you move from one place to another): Mobility, Emplacement and Politics in (Post-)colonial Nova Scotia. Ph.D. diss., Department of Anthropology, University of Chicago.

Levy, Philip

2004 A New Look at an Old Wall. Indians, Englishmen, Landscape, and the 1634 Palisade at Middle Plantation. *Virginia Magazine of History and Biography* 112(3):226–65.

Lewis, Clifford Merle, and Albert J. Loomie

1953 *The Spanish Jesuit Mission in Virginia, 1570–1572*. Chapel Hill: University of North Carolina Press.

Liebmann, Matthew

2012 *Revolt: An Archaeological History of Pueblo Resistance and Revitalization in 17th Century New Mexico.* Tucson: University of Arizona Press.

Lightfoot, Kent G.

2005 *Indians, Missionaries, and Merchants: The Legacy of Colonial Encounters on the California Frontiers.* Berkeley: University of California Press.

1995 Culture Contact Studies: Redefining the Relationship between Prehistoric and Historical Archaeology. *American Antiquity* 60(2):199–217.

Lorant, Stefan, ed.

1965 *The New World: The First Pictures of America.* New York: Duell, Sloan and Pearce.

Loren, Diana DiPaolo

2008 *In Contact: Bodies and Spaces in the Sixteenth- and Seventeenth-Century Eastern Woodlands.* Lanham, Md.: AltaMira Press.

Lowery, Darrin L.

2012 The Delmarva Adena Complex: A Study of the Frederica Site, Kent County, Delaware. *Archaeology of Eastern North America* 40:27–57.

Luckenbach, A. H., Wayne E. Clark, and R. S. Levy

1987 Rethinking Cultural Stability in Eastern North American Prehistory: Linguistic Evidence from Eastern Algonquian. *Journal of Middle Atlantic Archaeology* 3:1–33.

MacGregor, Arthur

1983 *Tradescant's Rarities: Essays on the Foundation of the Ashmolean Museum, 1683.* Oxford: Clarendon Press.

Mahoney, Shannon S.

2009 Mortuary Practices of the Chickahominy: Late Woodland Ceremonial Processes in Tidewater Virginia. *Journal of Middle Atlantic Archaeology* 25:133–40.

Malhi, Ripan S., Beth A. Schultz, and David G. Smith

2001 Distribution of Mitochondrial DNA Lineages among Native American Tribes of Northeastern North America. *Human Biology* 73(1):17–55.

Mallios, Seth

2007 The Apotheosis of Ajacan's Jesuit Missionaries. *Ethnohistory* 54(2):223–44.

2006 *The Deadly Politics of Giving: Exchange and Violence at Ajacan, Roanoke, and Jamestown.* Tuscaloosa: University of Alabama Press.

Mallios, Seth W., and Beverley A. Straube

2000 *1999 Interim Report on the APVA Excavations at Jamestown, Virginia.* Richmond: Association for the Preservation of Virginia Antiquities.

Mann, Roger, Juliana M. Harding, and Melissa J. Southworth

2009 Reconstructing Pre-colonial Oyster Demographics in the Chesapeake Bay, USA. *Estuarine, Coastal and Shelf Science* 85(2):217–22.

Maslowski, Robert F.

1996 Cordage Twist and Ethnicity. In *A Most Indispensable Art: Native Fiber Industries from Eastern North America,* edited by J. B. Petersen, 88–99. Knoxville: University of Tennessee Press.

Mauss, Marcel

2000 [1950] *The Gift: The Form and Reason for Exchange in Archaic Societies.* New York: W. W. Norton.

Maxham, Mintcy D.

2000 Rural Communities in the Black Warrior Valley, Alabama: The Role of Commoners in the Creation of the Moundville I Landscape. *American Antiquity* 65(2):337–54.

McCary, Ben C.

1981 The Location of Werowocomoco. *Quarterly Bulletin of the Archaeological Society of Virginia* 36:77–93.

1957 *John Smith's Map of Virginia: With a Brief Account of Its History.* Williamsburg: Virginia 350th Anniversary Celebration Corp.

McCary, Ben C., and Norman F. Barka

1977 The John Smith Map of Virginia and Zuñiga Maps in Light of Recent Archaeological Investigations along the Chickahominy River. *Archaeology of North America* 5:73–89.

McClain, Joseph

2013 Werowocomoco Ceremony: America Didn't Begin in 1607. *William & Mary.* June 24, 2013. http://www.wm.edu/news/stories/2013/werowocomoco-ceremony-america-didnt-begin-in-1607.php. Accessed January 15, 2016.

McConvell, Patrick

2010 The Archaeo-Linguistics of Migration. In *Migration History in World History: Multidisciplinary Approaches*, edited by J. Lucassen, L. Lucassen, and P. Manning, 155–87. Leiden: Brill.

McKnight, Justine W.

2013 Paleoethnobotanical Analysis. In *The Werowocomoco Research Project: 2004–2010 Field Seasons. Department of Anthropology Archaeological Research Report #3*, edited by M. Gallivan, 38–51. Williamsburg, Va.: College of William and Mary.

2010a Analysis of Flotation-Recovered Archeobotanical Remains from the Claggett Retreat Site (18FR25), Frederick County, Maryland. *Maryland Archaeology* 46(1, 2):38–46.

2010b Report on the Analysis of Flotation-Recovered and Waterscreen-Recovered Archeobotanical Remains from the Hughes Site (18MO1), Montgomery County, Maryland. Prepared for the Potomac River Archaeology Survey, American University, Washington, D.C.

2009a Pilot Archeobotanical Analysis of Three Sample Types from a Single Context at the Cumberland Site (18CV171) with Direct Radiocarbon Dating of Maize Remains. Prepared for the Maryland Archaeological Conservation Laboratory, Jefferson Patterson Park and Museum, St. Leonard, Maryland.

2009b Direct Dating of Maize from the Thomas Point Shell Midden. Prepared for the Maryland Archaeological Conservation Laboratory, Jefferson Patterson Park and Museum, St. Leonard, Maryland.

2009c Study of a Pocket of Cultigens and Direct Dating of Common Bean (*Phaseolus vulgaris*) from a Late Woodland Context at the Rosenstock Site 18FR18, Frederick County, Maryland. Prepared for the Maryland Archaeological Conservation Laboratory, Jefferson Patterson Park and Museum, St. Leonard, Maryland.

2009d Archeobotanical Evidence from the Chickahominy in a Chesapeake Context. *Journal of Middle Atlantic Archaeology* 25:119–24.

2001 Report of Archeobotanical Remains. In *The Fisher Site Revisited: Archaeology at a Montgomery Focus Village on the Potomac River*, edited by S. C. Pullins and D. Lewes. William and Mary Center for Archaeological Research, Williamsburg, Va.

McKnight, Justine W., and Martin D. Gallivan

2008 The Virginia Archeobotanical Database Project: A Preliminary Synthesis of Chesapeake Ethnobotany. *Quarterly Bulletin of the Archeological Society of Virginia* 62(4):181–89.

McLearan, Douglas C.

1992 Virginia's Middle Woodland Period: A Regional Perspective. In *Middle and Late Woodland Research in Virginia: A Synthesis*, edited by T. R. Reinhart and M. E. Hodges, 39–63. Richmond: Dietz Press.

Meggers, Betty J.

2003 Revisiting Amazonia circa 1492. *Science* 302:2067–70.

1971 *Amazonia: Man and Culture in a Counterfeit Paradise*. Chicago: Aldine-Atherton.

Merleau-Ponty, Maurice

2011 *Phenomenology of Perception*. New York: Routledge.

Meskell, Lynn

2002 The Intersections of Identity and Politics in Archaeology. *Annual Review of Anthropology* 31:279–301.

Messner, Timothy C.

2011 *Acorns and Bitter Roots: Starch Grain Research in the Prehistoric Eastern Woodlands*. Tuscaloosa: University of Alabama Press.

Miller, Jay

2002 Kinship, Family Kindreds, and Community. In *A Companion to American Indian History*, edited by P. J. Deloria and N. Salisbury, 139–53. Malden, Mass.: Blackwell.

1979 A Strucon Model of Delaware Culture and the Positioning of Mediators. *American Ethnologist* 6(4):791–802.

Mills, Barbara J., ed.

2004 *Identity, Feasting, and the Archaeology of the Greater Southwest*. Boulder: University Press of Colorado.

Minar, Cynthia J.

2001 Motor Skills and the Learning Process: The Conservation of Cordage Final Twist Direction in Communities of Practice. *Journal of Anthropological Research* 57(4):381–405.

Mithun, Marianne

1999 *The Languages of Native North America*. Cambridge: Cambridge University Press.

Montague, Ludwell Lee

1972 Powhatan's Chimney, Gloucester County. *Discovery* 4(3):6–10.

Mook, Maurice A.

1943 The Ethnological Significance of Tindall's Map of Virginia, 1608. *William and Mary College Quarterly Historical Magazine* 23(4):371–408.

Mooney, James

1894 Siouan Tribes of the East. In *Ethnology Bureau Bulletin* No. 22. U.S. Government Printing Office.

Moore, John H.

2001 Ethnogenetic Patterns in Native North America. In *Archaeology, Language, and History*, edited by J. E. Terrell, 31–56. Westport, Conn.: Bergin and Garvey.

1994 Putting Anthropology Back Together Again: The Ethnogenetic Critique of Cladistic Theory. *American Anthropologist* 96(4):925–48.

Moore, Larry

1993 Piscataway, Doeg, and the Potomac Creek Complex. *Journal of Middle Atlantic Archaeology* 9:117–38.

Moretti-Langholtz, Danielle

1998 Other Names I Have Been Called: Political Resurgence among Virginia Indians in the Twentieth Century. Ph.D. diss., Department of Anthropology, University of Oklahoma, Norman.

Mouer, L. Daniel

1981 Powhatan and Monacan Settlement Hierarchies. *Archeological Society of Virginia* 1 and 2:1–21.

Mullins, Paul R., and Robert Paynter

2000 Representing Colonizers: An Archaeology of Creolization, Ethnogenesis, and Indigenous Material Culture among the Haida. *Historical Archaeology* 34(3): 73–84.

Nabokov, Peter

2002 *A Forest of Time: American Indian Ways of History.* New York: Cambridge University Press.

Nassaney, Michael S.

2001 The Historical-Processual Development of Late Woodland Societies. In *The Archaeology of Traditions: Agency and History before and after Columbus*, edited by T. R. Pauketat, 157–73. Gainesville: University Press of Florida.

Nicholas, George P.

2010 Seeking the End of Indigenous Archaeology. In *Bridging the Divide: Indigenous Communities and Archaeology into the 21st Century*, edited by C. Phillips and H. Allen, 233–52. Walnut Creek, Calif.: Left Coast Press.

2008 Native Peoples and Archaeology. In *The Encyclopedia of Archaeology*, edited by D. Pearsall, 1660–69, vol. 3. Oxford: Elsevier.

Nicholls, Mark

2005 George Percy's "Trewe Relacyon": A Primary Source for the Jamestown Settlement. *Virginia Magazine of History and Biography* 113(3):212–75.

Nöel Hume, Ivor

1994 *The Virginia Adventure: Roanoke to James Towne, An Archaeological and Historical Odyssey.* New York: Knopf.

Norman, Neil L., and Kenneth G. Kelly

2004 Landscape Politics: The Serpent Ditch and the Rainbow in West Africa. *American Anthropologist* 106(1):98–110.

Ogborne, Jennifer H.

2004 Chickahominy Stylistic Expression: Preliminary Motif Analysis of Ceramics of the Chickahominy River Drainage. Master's thesis, Department of Anthropology, College of William and Mary, Williamsburg, Va.

Opperman, Antony F.

1992 *Middle Woodland Subsistence at Maycock's Point (44PG40), Prince George County, Virginia.* Master's thesis, University of Tennessee, Knoxville.

Orli, Richard J.

2008 The Identity of the 1608 Jamestown Craftsmen. *Polish American Studies* 65(2): 17–26.

Pargellis, Stanley

1959 An Account of the Indians in Virginia. *William and Mary Quarterly* 16(2):228–43.

Pauketat, Timothy R.

2009 *Cahokia: Ancient America's Great City on the Mississippi.* New York: Viking.

2004 *Ancient Cahokia and the Mississippians.* New York: Cambridge University Press.

2001a Practice and History in Archaeology: An Emerging Paradigm. *Anthropological Theory* 1(1):73–98.

2001b A New Tradition in Archaeology. In *The Archaeology of Traditions: Agency and History before and after Columbus*, edited by T. R. Pauketat, 1–6. Gainesville: University Press of Florida.

Pauketat, Timothy R., Lucretia S. Kelly, Gayle J. Fritz, Neal H. Lopinot, Scott Elias, and Eve Hargrave

2002 The Residues of Feasting and Public Ritual at Early Cahokia. *American Antiquity* 67(2):257–79.

Peirce, Charles S.

1991 *Peirce on Signs: Writings on Semiotic.* Chapel Hill: University of North Carolina Press.

Percy, George

1998 [1625] Observations Gathered out of a Discourse of the Plantation of the Southerne Colonie in Virginia by the English, 1606. In *Jamestown Narratives: Eyewitness Accounts of the Virginia Colony, the First Decade, 1607–1617*, edited by E. W. Haile, 85–100. Champlain, Va.: Roundhouse.1922 [1625] A Trewe Relacyon of the Proceedings and Occurentes of Momente Which Have Happened in Virginia. *Tyler's Quarterly Magazine* 3:260–82.

Petraglia, Michael D., Susan L. Bupp, Sean P. Fitzell, and Kevin W. Cunningham

2002 *Hickory Bluff: Changing Perceptions of Delmarva Archaeology.* Delaware Department of Transportation Archaeology Series No. 175. Dover.

Petraglia, Michael D., and Kevin Cunningham

2006 Native American Collaboration in Delmarva: New Meanings and an Expanded Approach to Delaware Archaeology. In *Cross-Cultural Collaboration: Native Peo-*

ples and Archaeology in the Northeastern United States, edited by J. E. Kerber, 213–32. Lincoln: University of Nebraska Press.

Phillips, Caroline, and Harry Allen

2010 *Bridging the Divide: Indigenous Communities and Archaeology into the 21st Century.* Walnut Creek, Calif.: Left Coast Press.

Pitt, Ken, and Jeremy Taylor

2009 *Finsbury's Moated Manor, Medieval Land Use and Later Development in the Finsbury Square Area, Islington.* London: Museum of London Archaeology.

Plog, Stephen

1985 Estimating Vessel Orifice Diameters: Measurement Methods and Measurement Error. In *Decoding Prehistoric Ceramics*, edited by B. A. Nelson, 243–53. Carbondale: Southern Illinois University Press.

Plog, Stephen, and Adam S. Watson

2012 The Chaco Pilgrimage Model: Evaluating the Evidence from Pueblo Alto. *American Antiquity* 77(3):449–77.

Potter, James M.

2000 Pots, Parties, and Politics: Communal Feasting in the American Southwest. *American Antiquity* 65(3):471–92.

Potter, Stephen R.

2006 Early English Effects on Virginia Algonquian Exchange and Tribute in the Tidewater Potomac. In *Powhatan's Mantle: Indians in the Colonial Southeast*, edited by G. A. Waselkov, P. H. Wood, and T. Hatley, 215–42. Lincoln: University of Nebraska Press.

1993 *Commoners, Tribute, and Chiefs: The Development of Algonquian Culture in the Potomac Valley.* Charlottesville: University Press of Virginia.

Potter, Stephen R., and Gregory A. Waselkov

1994 Whereby We Shall Enjoy Their Cultivated Places. In *Historical Archaeology of the Chesapeake*, edited by P. Shackel and B. J. Little, 23–33. Washington, D.C.: Smithsonian Institution Press.

Preucel, Robert W.

2006 *Archaeological Semiotics.* Malden, Mass.: Blackwell.

Preucel, Robert W., and Alexander A. Bauer

2001 Archaeological Pragmatics. *Norwegian Archaeological Review* 34(2):85–96.

Preucel, Robert W., and Craig N. Cipolla

2008 Indigenous and Postcolonial Archaeologies. In *Archaeology and the Postcolonial Critique*, edited by M. Liebmann and U. Z. Rizvi, 129–40. Lanham, Md.: AltaMira Press.

Price, David A.

2003 *Love and Hate in Jamestown: John Smith, Pocahontas, and the Heart of a New Nation.* New York: Knopf.

Quinn, David B.

1955 *The Roanoke Voyages, 1584–1590: Documents to Illustrate the English Voyages to North America under the Patent Granted to Walter Raleigh in 1584.* London: Hakluyt Society.

Rankin, Robert L.

2006   Siouan Tribal Contacts and Dispersions Evidenced in the Terminology for Maize and Other Cultigens. In *Histories of Maize: Multidisciplinary Approaches to the Prehistory, Linguistics, Biogeography, Domestication, and Evolution of Maize*, edited by J. E. Staller, R. H. Tykot, and B. F. Benz, 564–77. Boston: Elsevier Academic Press.

Renfrew, Colin, April M. S. McMahon, R. L. Trask, and McDonald Institute for Archaeological Research

2000   *Time Depth in Historical Linguistics.* 2 vols. Cambridge: McDonald Institute for Archaeological Research.

Rice, James D.

2009   *Nature and History in the Potomac Country: From Hunter-Gatherers to the Age of Jefferson.* Baltimore: Johns Hopkins University Press.

2007   Escape from Tsenacommacah: Chesapeake Algonquians and the Powhatan Menace. In *The Atlantic World and Virginia, 1550–1624*, edited by P. C. Mancall, 97–142. Chapel Hill: University of North Carolina Press.

Richter, Daniel K.

2007   Tsenacommacah and the Atlantic World. In *The Atlantic World and Virginia, 1550–1624*, edited by P. C. Mancall, 29–65. Chapel Hill: University of North Carolina Press.

Rick, Torben C., and Rowan Lockwood

2013   Integrating Paleobiology, Archeology, and History to Inform Biological Conservation. *Conservation Biology* 27(1):45–54.

Rick, Torben, and Darrin Lowery

2013   Accelerator Mass Spectrometry 14C Dating and the Antiquity of Shell-Tempered Ceramics from the Chesapeake Bay and Middle Atlantic. *American Antiquity* 78(3):570–79.

Riggs, Brett

2002   In the Service of Native Interests: Archaeology for, by, and of Cherokee People. In *Southern Indians and Anthropologists: Culture, Politics, and Identities*, edited by L. J. Lefler and F. W. Gleach, 19–30. Athens: University of Georgia Press.

Rodning, Christopher

2010   Place, Landscape, and Environment: Anthropological Archaeology in 2009. *American Anthropologist* 112(2):180–90.

2009   Mounds, Myths, and Cherokee Townhouses in Southwestern North Carolina. *American Antiquity* 74 (4):627–63.

Rountree, Helen C., ed.

1993   *Powhatan Foreign Relations, 1500–1722.* Charlottesville: University Press of Virginia.

Rountree, Helen C.

2005   *Pocahontas, Powhatan, Opechancanough: Three Indian Lives Changed by Jamestown.* Charlottesville: University of Virginia Press.

1998   Powhatan Indian Women: The People Captain John Smith Barely Saw. *Ethnohistory* 45(1):1–29.

1990 *Pocahontas's People: The Powhatan Indians of Virginia through Four Centuries.* Norman: University of Oklahoma Press.

1989 *The Powhatan Indians of Virginia: Their Traditional Culture.* Norman: University of Oklahoma Press.

Rountree, Helen C., Wayne E. Clark, and Kent Mountford

2007 *John Smith's Chesapeake Voyages, 1607–1609.* Charlottesville: University of Virginia Press.

Rountree, Helen C., and Thomas E. Davidson

1997 *Eastern Shore Indians of Virginia and Maryland.* Charlottesville: University Press of Virginia.

Rountree, Helen C., and E. Randolph Turner

2002 *Before and after Jamestown: Virginia's Powhatans and Their Predecessors.* Gainesville: University Press of Florida.

Rowe, John Bloodworth

2008 Culture, Progress and the Media: The Shad as Synecdoche in Environmental News Coverage. *Environmental Communication* 2(3):362–78.

Rubertone, Patricia E., ed.

2008 *Archaeologies of Placemaking: Monuments, Memories, and Engagement in Native North America.* Walnut Creek, Calif.: Left Coast Press.

Rudes, Blair

2011 In the Words of Powhatan: Translation across Space and Time for *The New-World.* In *Born in the Blood: On Native American Translation,* edited by B. Swann, 189–209. Lincoln: University of Nebraska Press.

Sassaman, Kenneth E.

2010 *The Eastern Archaic, Historicized.* Lanham, Md.: AltaMira Press.

2004 Complex Hunter-Gatherers in Evolution and History: A North American Perspective. *Journal of Archaeological Research* 12(3):227–80.

Sassaman, Kenneth E., and Donald H. Holly

2011 *Hunter-Gatherer Archaeology as Historical Process.* Tucson: University of Arizona Press.

Sassaman, Kenneth E., and Wictoria Rudolphi

2001 Communities of Practice in the Early Pottery Traditions of the American Southeast. *Journal of Anthropological Research* 57(4):407–25.

Sauer, Carl Ortwin

1925 *The Morphology of Landscape.* Berkeley: University of California Press.

Saunders, Joe W., Rolfe D. Mandel, C. Garth Sampson, Charles M. Allen, E. Thurman Allen, Daniel A. Bush, James K. Feathers, Kristen J. Gremillion, C. T. Hallmark, and H. Edwin Jackson

2005 Watson Brake, a Middle Archaic Mound Complex in Northeast Louisiana. *American Antiquity* 70(4):631–68.

Schlanger, Sarah H.

1992 Recognizing Persistent Places in Anasazi Settlement Systems. In *Space, Time and Archaeological Landscapes,* edited by J. Rossignol and L. Wandsnider, 91–112. New York: Plenum.

Schoeninger, Margaret J.

2009   Stable Isotope Evidence for the Adoption of Maize Agriculture. *Current Anthropology* 50(5):633–40.

Schrire, Carmel

1995   *Digging through Darkness: Chronicles of an Archaeologist.* Charlottesville: University Press of Virginia.

Scott, Jamie S., and Paul Simpson-Housley

2001   *Mapping the Sacred: Religion, Geography and Postcolonial Literatures.* Atlanta: Rodopi.

Seeman, Erik R.

2011   *The Huron-Wendat Feast of the Dead: Indian-European Encounters in Early North America.* Baltimore: Johns Hopkins University Press.

Sewell, William Hamilton

2005   *Logics of History: Social Theory and Social Transformation.* Chicago: University of Chicago Press.

Shaffer, Gary D.

2005   Nanticoke Indian Burial Practices: Challenges for Archaeological Interpretation. *Archaeology of Eastern North America* 33:141–62.

Sheller, Mimi, and John Urry

2006   The New Mobilities Paradigm. *Environment and Planning A* 38(2):207–26.

Shephard, Christopher J.

2009   A Late Woodland Protohistoric Compound on the Chickahominy River: Multiscalar Investigations of the Buck Farm Site. *Journal of Middle Atlantic Archaeology* 25:111–18.

Shryock, Andrew, and Daniel Lord Smail, eds.

2011   *Deep History: The Architecture of Past and Present.* Berkeley: University of California Press.

Sider, Gerald

1994   Identity as History: Ethnohistory, Ethnogenesis and Ethnocide in the Southeastern United States. *Identities* 1(1):109–22.

Siebert, Frank

1975   Resurrecting Virginia Algonquian from the Dead: The Reconstituted and Historical Phonology of Powhatan. In *Studies in Southeastern Indian Languages,* edited by J. Crawford, 285–453. Athens: University of Georgia Press.

1967   The Original Home of the Proto-Algonquian People. *Contributions to Anthropology: Linguistics I (Algonquian).* Anthropological Series 78. Bulletin 214, 13–47. Ottawa: National Museum of Canada.

Silliman, Stephen W.

2008   *Collaborating at the Trowel's Edge: Teaching and Learning in Indigenous Archaeology.* Tucson: University of Arizona Press.

2005   Culture Contact or Colonialism? Challenges in the Archaeology of Native North America. *American Antiquity* 70(1):55–74.

Slattery, Richard G., and Douglas R. Woodward

1992   *The Montgomery Focus: A Late Woodland Potomac River Culture.* Rockville: Archaeological Society of Maryland.

Smith, Adam T.

2011   Archaeologies of Sovereignty. *Annual Review of Anthropology* 40:415–32.

2003   *The Political Landscape: Constellations of Authority in Early Complex Polities.* Berkeley: University of California Press.

Smith, Claire, and H. Martin Wobst

2005   *Indigenous Archaeologies: Decolonizing Theory and Practice.* New York: Routledge.

Smith, David Woodruff

2013   Phenomenology. In *The Stanford Encyclopedia of Philosophy*, edited by E. N. Zalta. Stanford, Calif.: Stanford University.

Smith, John

1986a [1608]   *A True Relation.* In *The Complete Works of Captain John Smith (1580–1631)*, edited by P. L. Barbour, 5–117, vol. 1. Chapel Hill: University of North Carolina Press.

1986b [1608]   *A Map of Virginia.* In *The Complete Works of Captain John Smith (1580–1631)*, edited by P. L. Barbour, 119–89, vol. 1. Chapel Hill: University of North Carolina Press.

1986c [1612]   *The Proceedings.* In *The Complete Works of Captain John Smith (1580–1631)*, edited by P. L. Barbour, 191–279, vol. 2. Chapel Hill: University of North Carolina Press.

1986d [1623]   *Generall Historie of Virginia.* In *The Complete Works of Captain John Smith (1580–1631)*, edited by P. L. Barbour, 5–475, vol. 2. Chapel Hill: University of North Carolina Press.

1986e [1630]   *The True Travels, Adventures, and Observations of Captaine John Smith.* In *The Complete Works of Captain John Smith (1580–1631)*, edited by P. L. Barbour, 123–252, vol. 3. Chapel Hill: University of North Carolina Press.

Smith, Marvin T., Robbie Franklyn Ethridge, and Charles M. Hudson

2002   *The Transformation of the Southeastern Indians, 1540–1760.* Jackson: University Press of Mississippi.

Snead, James E.

2008   *Ancestral Landscapes of the Pueblo World.* Tucson: University of Arizona Press.

Snow, Dean R.

2002   American Indian Migrations: A Neglected Dimension of Paleodemography. In *Anthropology, History, and American Indians: Essays in Honor of William Curtis Sturtevant*, edited by W. L. Merrill and I. Goddard, 75–83. Washington, D.C.: Smithsonian Institution Press.

1994   *The Iroquois.* Oxford, UK; Cambridge, Mass.: Blackwell.

Soja, Edward W.

1989   *Postmodern Geographies: The Reassertion of Space in Critical Social Theory.* London: Verso.

Speck, Frank G.

1917   Game Totems among the Northeastern Algonkians. *American Anthropologist* 19(1):9–18.

Spelman, Henry

1998 [1613]   Relation of Virginia. In *Jamestown Narratives: Eyewitness Accounts of the Virginia Colony*, edited by E. W. Haile, 481–95. Champlain, Va.: Roundhouse.

Steadman, Laura

2008 Uncovering the Origins of Abbott Zoned Incised Pottery in Coastal Plain Virginia: An La-Icp-Ms Study. *Journal of Middle Atlantic Archaeology* 24:79–86.

Stephenson, Richard W., and Marianne M. McKee

2000 *Virginia in Maps: Four Centuries of Settlement, Growth, and Development*. Richmond: Library of Virginia.

Stern, Theodore

1952 Chickahominy: The Changing Culture of a Virginia Indian Community. *Proceedings of the American Philosophical Society* 96(2):157–225.

Steward, Julian H.

1937 Ecological Aspects of Southwestern Society. *Anthropos* 32(1/2):87–104.

Stewart, Michael

1998 Unraveling the Mystery of Zoned Decorated Pottery: Implications for Middle Woodland Society in the Middle Atlantic Region. *Journal of Middle Atlantic Archaeology* 14:161–82.

1993 Comparison of Late Woodland Cultures: Delaware, Potomac, and Susquehanna River Valleys, Middle Atlantic Region. *Archaeology of Eastern North America* 21:163–78.

1992 Middle and Late Woodland Research in Virginia: A Synthesis. In *Observations on the Middle Woodland Period of Virginia: A Middle Atlantic Region Perspective*, edited by T. R. Reinhart and M. E. Hodges, 1–38. Richmond: Dietz Press.

1990 The Middle to Late Woodland Transition in the Lower/Middle Delaware Valley. *North American Archaeologist* 11(3):231–54.

Strachey, William

1969 [1612] *For the Colony in Virginea Britannia; Lawes Divine, Morall, and Martiall, Etc*. Charlottesville: University Press of Virginia.

1953 [1612] *The Historie of Travell into Virginia Britania*. London: Printed for the Hakluyt Society.

Straube, Beverley A.

2004 Inventory of Metal Objects Recovered from the Werowocomoco Site (44GL32), Gloucester County, Virginia. Manuscript on file at the Department of Anthropology, College of William and Mary, Williamsburg, Va.

Sturtevant, William C.

1971 Creek into Seminole. In *North American Indians in Historical Perspective*, edited by E. B. Leacock and N. Lurie, 92–128. New York: Random House.

Swadesh, Morris

1959 Linguistics as an Instrument of Prehistory. *Southwestern Journal of Anthropology* 15(1):20–35.

1955 Towards Greater Accuracy in Lexicostatistic Dating. *International Journal of American Linguistics* 21(2):121–37.

1952 Lexiocostatistic Dating of Prehistoric Ethnic Contacts. *Proceedings of the American Philosophical Society* 96:452–63.

Swidler, Nina, ed.

1997 *Native Americans and Archaeologists: Stepping Stones to Common Ground*. Walnut Creek, Calif.: AltaMira Press.

Thomas, Julian

2001 Archaeologies of Place and Landscape. In *Archaeological Theory Today*, edited by I. Hodder, 165–86. Cambridge: Polity Press.

Thompson, Victor D.

2009 The Mississippian Production of Space through Earthen Pyramids and Public Buildings on the Georgia Coast, USA. *World Archaeology* 41(3):445–70.

Thompson, Victor D., and C. Fred T. Andrus

2011 Evaluating Mobility, Monumentality, and Feasting at the Sapelo Island Shell Ring Complex. *American Antiquity* 76(2):315–43.

Thompson, Victor D., and James C. Waggoner

2013 *The Archaeology and Historical Ecology of Small Scale Economies*. Gainesville: University Press of Florida.

Thwaites, Reuben Gold, ed.

1959 *The Jesuit Relations and Allied Documents; Travels and Explorations of the Jesuit Missionaries in New France, 1610–1791*. 73 vols. New York: Pageant.

Tilley, Christopher Y.

1994 *A Phenomenology of Landscape: Places, Paths, and Monuments*. Oxford: Berg.

Tooker, Elisabeth

1991 *An Ethnography of the Huron Indians, 1615–1649*. Syracuse: Syracuse University Press.

Tooker, William Wallace

1906 The Powhatan Name for Virginia. *American Anthropologist* 8(1):23–27.

1905a Meaning of Some Indian Names in Virginia. *William and Mary Quarterly* 14(1):62–64.

1905b Some More about Virginia Names. *American Anthropologist* 7(3):524–28.

1904a Derivation of the Name Powhatan. *American Anthropologist* 6(4):464–68.

1904b Some Powhatan Names. *American Anthropologist* 6(5):670–94.

1901 *The Names Chickahominy, Pamunkey, and the Kuskarawaokes of Captain John Smith*. New York: Francis P. Harper.

1899 The Adopted Algonquian Term "Poquosin." *American Anthropologist* 1(1):162–70.

1895a The Name Chickahominy, Its Origin and Etymology. *American Anthropologist* 8(3):257–63.

1895b The Algonquian Appellatives of the Siouan Tribes of Virginia. *American Anthropologist* 8(4):376–92.

1894a On the Meaning of the Name Anacostia. *American Anthropologist* 7(4):389–393.

1894b The Algonquian Terms Patawomeke and Massawomeke. *American Anthropologist* 7(2):174–85.

Townsend, Camilla

2004 *Pocahontas and the Powhatan Dilemma*. New York: Hill and Wang.

Tradescant, John

1925 [1656] *Musaeum Tradescantianum*. London: Printed by John Grismond.

Trigger, Bruce G.

1990 *The Huron: Farmers of the North*. Fort Worth: Holt, Rinehart and Winston.

Trimble, Carmen C.

1996 Paleodiet in Virginia and North Carolina as Determined by Stable Isotope Analysis of Skeletal Remains. Master's thesis, Department of Environmental Sciences, University of Virginia, Charlottesville.

Trumbull, J. Hammond

1870   Indian Names in Virginia. *The Historical Magazine and Notes and Queries Concerning the Antiquities, History and Biography of America* 7:47–48.

Turner, E. Randolph

1993   Native American Protohistoric Interactions in the Powhatan Core Area. In *Powhatan Foreign Relations, 1500–1722*, edited by H. Rountree, 76–93. Charlottesville: University of Virginia Press.

1992   The Virginia Coastal Plain during the Late Woodland Period. In *Middle and Late Woodland Research in Virginia: A Synthesis*, edited by T. R. Reinhart and M. E. Hodges, 97–136. Richmond, Va.: Dietz Press.

1986   Difficulties in the Archaeological Identification of Chiefdoms as Seen in the Virginia Coastal Plain during the Late Woodland and Early Historic Periods. In *Late Woodland Cultures of the Middle Atlantic Region*, edited by J. F. Custer. Newark: University of Delaware Press.

1985   Socio-political Organization within the Powhatan Chiefdom and the Effects of European Contact, AD 1607–1646. In *Cultures in Contact: The Impact of European Contacts on Native American Cultural Institutions in Eastern North America, AD 1000–1800*, edited by W. W. Fitzhugh, 193–224. Washington, D.C.: Smithsonian Institution Press.

1982   A Re-examination of Powhatan Territorial Boundaries and Population, ca. AD 1607. *Quarterly Bulletin of the Archeological Society of Virginia* 37(2):45–64.

1976   *An Archaeological and Ethnohistorical Study of the Evolution of Rank Societies in the Virginia Coastal Plain*. PhD diss., Department of Anthropology, Pennsylvania State University, State College.

Turner, E. Randolph, and Anthony F. Opperman

1993   Archaeological Manifestations of the Virginia Company Period: A Summary of Surviving Powhatan and English Settlements in Tidewater Virginia, circa 1607–1624. In *The Archaeology of 17th-Century Virginia, Archeological Society of Virginia*, edited by T. R. Reinhart and D. J. Pogue, 67–104. Richmond, Va.: Dietz Press.

Turner, Victor W., and Edith L. B. Turner

1978   *Image and Pilgrimage in Christian Culture: Anthropological Perspectives*. New York: Columbia University Press.

Tykot, Robert H.

2006   Isotope Analyses and the Histories of Maize. In *Histories of Maize: Multidisciplinary Approaches to the Prehistory, Linguistics, Biogeography, Domestication, and Evolution of Maize*, edited by J. E. Staller, R. H. Tykot, and B. F. Benz, 131–42. Boston: Elsevier Academic Press.

Tyler, Lyon G.

1907   *Narratives of Early Virginia, 1606–1625*. New York: C. Scribner's Sons.

1901   Werowocomoco. *William and Mary College Quarterly* 10(1):1–4.

Ubelaker, Douglas H.

1974   *Reconstruction of Demographic Profiles from Ossuary Skeletal Samples; a Case*

Study from the Tidewater Potomac. Washington, D.C.: Smithsonian Institution Press.

Underwood, John R., Dennis B. Blanton, W. Jason Cline, David W. Lewes, and William H. Moore

2003 *Systematic Archaeological Survey of 6,000 Acres, Naval Weapons Station Yorktown, Virginia.* Williamsburg, Va.: William and Mary Center for Archaeological Research.

Vaughan, Alden T.

1979 *Early American Indian Documents: Treaties and Laws, 1607–1789.* Volume 4. Washington, D.C.: University Publications of America.

1975 *American Genesis: Captain John Smith and the Founding of Virginia.* Boston: Little, Brown.

Virginia Council

1935 Letter to Virginia Company of London [January 10, 1623]. In *The Records of the Virginia Company of London,* edited by S. M. Kingsbury, Vol. 4. Washington, D.C.: U.S. Government Printing Office.

Voss, Barbara L.

2012 A Land of Ethnogenesis: Material Culture, Power, and Identity. In *Contemporary Issues in California Archaeology,* edited by T. L. Jones and J. E. Perry, 303–18. Walnut Creek, Calif.: Left Coast Press.

2008 *The Archaeology of Ethnogenesis: Race and Sexuality in Colonial San Francisco.* Berkeley: University of California Press.

Wade, Nicholas

2013 Girl's Bones Bear Signs of Cannibalism by Starving Virginia Colonists. *New York Times,* May 1, 2013, A11.

Walsh, Lorena S.

2010 *Motives of Honor, Pleasure, and Profit: Plantation Management in the Colonial Chesapeake, 1607–1763.* Chapel Hill: University of North Carolina Press.

Warf, Barney, and Santa Arias

2009 *The Spatial Turn: Interdisciplinary Perspectives.* New York: Routledge.

Waselkov, Gregory A.

2006 Indian Maps of the Colonial Southeast. In *Powhatan's Mantle: Indians in the Colonial Southeast,* edited by G. A. Waselkov, P. H. Wood, and T. Hatley, 435–502. Lincoln: University of Nebraska Press.

1998 Indian Maps of the Colonial Southeast: Archaeological Implications and Prospects. In *Cartographic Encounters: Perspectives on Native American Mapmaking and Map Use,* edited by G. M. Lewis, 205–22. Chicago: University of Chicago Press.

1982 Shellfish Gathering and Shell Midden Archaeology. Ph.D. diss., Department of Anthropology, University of North Carolina, Chapel Hill.

Waselkov, Gregory A., P. H. Wood, and M. T. Hatley, eds.

2006 *Powhatan's Mantle: Indians in the Colonial Southeast.* Lincoln: University of Nebraska Press.

Watkins, Joe

2000 *Indigenous Archaeology: American Indian Values and Scientific Practice.* Walnut Creek, Calif.: Alta Mira Press.

Weber, Max

1978   *Economy and Society: An Outline of Interpretive Sociology*. Berkeley: University of California Press.

Weik, Terrance M.

2009   The Role of Ethnogenesis and Organization in the Development of African-Native American Settlements: An African Seminole Model. *International Journal of Historical Archaeology* 13(2):206–38.

Welch, Paul D., and C. Margaret Scarry

1995   Status-Related Variation in Foodways in the Moundville Chiefdom. *American Antiquity* 60(3):397–419.

Wennersten, John R.

1996   Soil Miners Redux: The Chesapeake Environment, 1680–1810. *Maryland Historical Magazine* 91(2):156–79.

1981   *The Oyster Wars of Chesapeake Bay*. Centreville, Md.: Tidewater.

West, Thomas

1998 [1610]   Thomas West, Lord Delaware, Letter to Salisbury, Rec'd September 1610. In *Jamestown Narratives: Eyewitness Accounts of the Virginia Colony, at the First Decade*, edited by E. W. Haile, 465–67. Champlain, Va.: Roundhouse.

Whallon, Robert

2006   Social Networks and Information: Non-"utilitarian" Mobility among Hunter-Gatherers. *Journal of Anthropological Archaeology* 25(2):259–70.

White, Richard

1991   *The Middle Ground: Indians, Empires, and Republics in the Great Lakes Region, 1650–1815*. Cambridge: Cambridge University Press.

White, William

1998 [1613]   The Black Boys Ceremony. In *Jamestown Narratives: Eyewitness Accounts of the Virginia Colony: The First Decade, 1607–1617*, edited by E. W. Haile, 138–41. Champlain, Va.: Roundhouse.

Wiessner, Polly

1983   Style and Social Information in Kalahari San Projectile Points. *American Antiquity* 48(2):253–76.

Willey, Gordon R.

1953   *Prehistoric Settlement Patterns in the Virú Valley, Peru*. Washington, D.C.: U.S. Government Printing Office.

Williams, Emily

2005   *Analysis of Fibers from the Werowocomoco Site (44GL32)*. Report on file at the William and Mary Department of Anthropology, Williamsburg, Va.

Williamson, Margaret Holmes

2003   *Powhatan Lords of Life and Death: Command and Consent in Seventeenth-Century Virginia*. Lincoln: University of Nebraska Press.

1992   Pocahontas and Captain John Smith: Examining a Historical Myth. *History and Anthropology* 5(3–4):365–402.

Woodard, Buck

2008   Degrees of Relatedness: The Social Politics of Algonquian Kinship in the Contact

Era Chesapeake. Master's thesis, Department of Anthropology, College of William and Mary, Williamsburg, Va.

Woodard, Buck, and Danielle Moretti-Langholtz

2009   "They Will Not Admitt of Any Werowance from Him to Governe over Them": The Chickahominy in Context: A Reassessment of Political Configurations. *Journal of Middle Atlantic Archaeology* 25:85–96.

Index

Page numbers in *italics* indicate illustrations.

Hayden, Anna, 77
"Headright" system, 182
Heidegger, Martin, 11
Heterarchical chiefdoms, 50
Historical anthropology: colonialism and, 15, 17, 18, 23; Kiskiak community, 13–14, 80–81; of landscapes, 13–19
Historical ecology, landscapes and, 10–11, 90
History, "cameo" theory of, 16
Hole, William, 26
Horticulture, 22, 211n59; cultigens, Coastal Plain and Piedmont sites, 134–35; horticultural practices, 30–31, 32, 132–39; Werowocomoco and, 149–53, 164
Houses: Big House ceremony or Gamwing, 45–46; king's houses, 27, 29, 44, 47, 55, 61, 62, 66, 144, 147, 161, 162, 163; sapling-framed house or yihakin, 29; settlement patterns, 30–31, 33; of Wahunsenacawh, 144, 147, 161, 162–63, 192
Hunter-gatherers. See Forager-fishers
Hunting, 53; hunting camps, 22, 32, 55, 66, 178; hunting grounds, 183
Huron community, Feast of the Dead, 118
Hurricane Floyd, 68
Huskanaw (male rite of passage), 45, 62, 176–77
Husserl, Edmund, 11

Icons, 47–48, 213n26
Identity: Opechancanough and controversy with, 79–80; social identity, 107–8
Indentured servants, 28, 182
Indexical signs, 47, 48
Indian Field Creek, 74; forager-fishers and, 73; forests and, 88–90; Kiskiak community and, 79–93; pollen data and, 87–89, 90; radiocarbon dates, 81, 83; shell-midden excavation area, 81, 82, 83, 84, 85, 86–87, 91
Indigenous archaeology, 22, 143
Ingold, Tim, 11–12
Inside, outside and, 4
Intermarriage. See Marriage
Interpretants, signs and, 204n86

James Fort, 2–3, 8, 16, 18, 28, 164
James I (King of England), 112, 168, 171, 186, 212n15
James II (King of England), 212n15

Jamestown Colony, 38, 132, 137, 144, 159, 160, 163; starvation and, 28, 166, 169, 179; Wahunsenacawh and, 166, 169–70, 180
Jefferson, Thomas, 181
Jenkins, Jessica, 83–84
Jesuit Relations, 118
Jesuits, 27, 36, 38, 79, 118
Jirikowic, Christine, 125

King Creek, 74
King's houses. See Houses
King William Reservoir, 194–96, 197
Kinship system, 49
Kiskiak community, 2, 20, 113, 147, 165, 173; archaeology, 81, 82; forest cover changes, 90; historical anthropology of, 13–14, 80–81; Indian Field Creek and, 79–93; oyster shell heights and weights, 85, 86–87; radiocarbon dates, 81, 83; shell-midden deposits, 81, 82, 83, 84, 85, 86–87, 91; site midden, 85, 91
Klein, Michael, 18, 77

Labor, 28, 32, 178
Lake Powell site, 68, 69–70
Land, 26; colonial encroachment, 28, 32, 105, 112; conservation, 196–97; "headright" system and, 182; land treaty, 112; Treaty of Middle Plantation (1677), 182, 183, 195; wetlands, 21, 63, 74, 88, 207n30. See also Placemaking
Landscapes, 6–7, 9, 21, 54; dwelling perspective on, 11–12; historical anthropology of, 13–19; historical ecology and, 10–11, 90
Language: dialects, 29, 32, 33, 54, 60, 64, 73, 99, 100, 205n38; glottochronology and, 100, 101, 209n106, 210n108; with Mannahoac and Monacan communities, 32–33; Pidgin syntax, 60; with place-names, 55–59, 63, 205n38; population movements and, 73, 98–103; suffixes, 53–54, 63. See also Algonquian
Late Archaic period (2500–1200 BC), 84, 88, 90
Late Woodland I centuries (AD 900–1200), 86, 89, 91
Late Woodland II centuries (after AD 1200), 89
Late Woodland period (AD 900–1500), 21, 124, 130, 144, 149, 188; archaeology of, 74; Chickahominy River Survey and, 106

Lave, Jean, 206n13

Laws. *See* Legislation

Lefebvre, Henri, 9, 20, 212n9, 214n63

Legge, George (Baron), 212n15

Legislation, 180; Clean Water Act (1972), 194, 195; NAGPRA, 19, 105, 143–44, 215n39; National Historic Preservation Act, 19, 105, 196

Lenape community, 19, 41, 45–46

Levy, Philip, 183

Lightfoot, Kent, 14

"Logistical" mobility, 207n36

Luckenbach, Al, 100–101, 102

Macocanaco, 59, 65–66

Maize. *See* Corn

Male rite of passage (Huskanaw), 45, 62, 176–77

Mallios, Seth, 17–18, 38

Mamanatowick (paramount chief), 1, 40, 62, 166, 178

Mandan dialect, 205n38

Mangoag community, 29

Manitou (spiritual power), 1–2, 40, 174

Mannahoac community, 29, 32–33, 64–65, 205n38

Manosquosick, 110

Map of Virginia (Smith), 79, 105, 145; colonialism and, 24–25, 26–29, 37; *Description of the Country, the Commodities, People, Government, and Religion*, 26, 27, 29, 32; icons, 47–48; place-names, 66; Smith and, 26–33, 61, 208n71

Maps, 75, 191; circles on, 4, 25, 29, 31, 39, 46, 47, 212n15; *Dartmouth Map of Virginia*, 157, 159, 176; in divination ceremonies, 25, 46; *Draught of Virginia*, 79, 145–46, 147–48; icons on, 47–48; Powhatan's Mantle as, 39; social space and, 20, 25, 53. *See also* Zuñiga Chart

Marriage: intermarriage, 21, 71, 102, 108, 113, 206n25; of Pocahontas, 111; politics and, 40, 41

"Massacres," 181–82

Massawomeck community, 29

Massinacack community, 65

Mattaponi community, 15, 143, 195, 201n71

Mattaponi Reservation, 194–96, 197

Maycock's Point: Abbott zone-decorated ceramics at, 94, 95, 96, 97, 98; aggregation events at, 94–95; fishing at, 94, 96; forager-fishers and, 73; midden deposits at, 93–94; Mockley ceramics and, 94, 96, 97, 98

McCary, Ben, 104

McKnight, Justine, 132

"Medieval Warm Period" (circa AD 600 to 950), 77

Memorials, places as, 184–90

Memory, 5, 9, 10, 184

Men: of fighting age, 29; with labor, division of, 32, 178

Merleau-Ponty, Maurice, 11

Mexico, ritual sites, 216n56

Midden deposits: at Maycock's Point, 93–94; Mockley ceramics, 73, 76–79, 91; Moysonec, 113, 116, 139–40; radiocarbon dates, 94; shell middens, 73, 76–79, 81, 82, 83, 84, 85, 86–87, 91, 149

Middle Woodland I centuries (500 BC–AD 200), 89, 90, 106

Middle Woodland II centuries (AD 200–900), 86, 87, 89, 91, 106

Middle Woodland period (500 BC–AD 900), 71, 73, 88, 92, 94, 95, 100, 125; archaeology of, 21, 68, 69, 74–75; ceramics, 76, 77; temperatures, 77–78

Mobility, 12, 21, 32, 68, 73, 207n36, 208n71. *See also* Pilgrimage

Mockley ceramics, 69, 70, 207n32; characteristics, 76, 77, 98, 208n50; forager-fishers and, 71–72, 77; Maycock's Point and, 94, 96, 97, 98; Moysonec Field F site and, 113; oyster-roasting platform and, 92; population movements and, 99; radiocarbon dates, 72; rim diameters, 97; shell middens with, 73, 76–79, 91; at Werowocomoco, 149, 152–53; Wilcox Neck site and, 120

Mohetan community, 32

Moieties, 41, 110, 203n63

Mollusks: clams, 73, 74, 77, 81, 92, 93, 165, 173; oysters, 85, 86–87, 92, 93, 149, 153, 173, 208n71; shell middens, 73, 76–77

Monacan community, 24, 29, 168, 169, 189–90, 201n71; burial practices, 125; federal recognition of, 143; language and, 32–33; place-name, 64–65, 205n38

Monuments. *See* Architecture

Mooney, James, 64–65, 205n38
Moretti-Langholtz, Danielle, 16, 41, 104, 110, 195
Mouer, Daniel, 141
Moysonec: midden deposits, 113, 116, 139–40; Moysonec Field F site, 113, *114*, *117*; settlement forms, 113–17; Smith and, 110, 116

NAGPRA. *See* Native American Graves Protection and Repatriation Act
Nansemond community, 15, 143, 201n71
Nanticoke community, 19, 99, 189–90
Nanticoke Lenni-Lanape community, 19
National Historic Preservation Act, 19, 105, 196
National Park Service, 197
National Science Foundation, 104
Native American Graves Protection and Repatriation Act (NAGPRA), 19, 105, 143–44, 215n39
Naval Weapons Station Yorktown (NWSY), 14, 21, 74, *75*, 76, 79
Necotowance (Powhatan leader), 112
Nepinough (earing of corn), 32
Newport, Christopher (Captain), 34, 40, 146, 167, 168
Nicholas, George, 143
Nipissing community, 118
Norwood, Henry, 25
Nottoway community, 201n71
Nutshell, 73
NWSY. *See* Naval Weapons Station Yorktown

Occaneechi community, 32
Okee (deity), 45, 174
Opechancanough (Pamunkey chief), 1, 2, 171; identity, controversy with, 79–80; revolts and, 112, 181–82; Second Anglo-Powhatan War and, 180; with Smith, capture of, 3–4, 50
Opperman, Tony, 93
Ossuaries (collective burials), 4; boxplot of minimum number of individuals in, *122*; Chickahominy River Survey and, 105, 117–25; Clark's Old Neck, 117, 126, 128–30; dogs in, *122*, *123*; Edgehill, 117, *121*, 122–23, *124*; at Potomac Creek, 184–85; radiocarbon dates, *121*, 211n35; Wilcox Neck site, 117, *119*, *120*, *121*, *124*

Ottawa community, 118
Outside, inside and, 4
Oysters, 93, 153, 173, 208n71; oyster-roasting platform, 92; shell middens, *85*, 86–87, 149

Paleoclimate, 77
Palisaded compounds, 130–32, 188
Pamunkey community, 15, 63, 201n71; federal recognition of, 143–44; Opechancanough, 1, 2, 3–4, 50, 79–80, 112, 171, 180–82; Pamunkey Museum and Cultural Center, 215n28; Pamunkey Reservation, 194–95; Pamunkey Tribal Museum, 197; treaties (1646 and 1677), 19
Paquinquineo, 79–80
Paramount chief. *See* Mamanatowick; Wahunsenacawh
Paspahegh community, 2, 28
Patawomeck community, 64, 185, 201n71; creation story, 52–53, 188–89; with memorialized places, 190
Peace treaties, 111, 112
Peirce, Charles, 47, 204n86
Percy, George, 28, 32, 46
Phenomenology, spatiality and, 11
Philip III (King of Spain), 33, 34
Pidgin syntax, 60
Piedmont sites, cultigens, *134–35*
Pigs, burials, 131, 188
Pilgrimage, 216n55, 216n56; objects, 193; Tsenacomacoh and, 184–90
Piscataway Conoy Confederacy and Subtribes, 201n72
Piscataway Conoy Tribe, 201n72
Piscataway Indian Nation, 201n72
Pissacoack, *58*, 63
Placemaking, 6, 9–10, 12, 68; creation story and, 52–53; in Tsenacomacoh, 20–23
Place-names: fishing and, 21, 54, 63; language with, *55–59*, 63, 205n38; Powhatan as, 60–61; rivers and, 21, 55, 62, 191; social space and, 53, 191; suffixes, 53–54, 63; travel and, 20–21, 55, 67; Virginia Algonquian, 60–67
"Place of the antler wearers." *See* Werowocomoco
Places: Chickahominy as meshwork of, 139–40; as memorials, 184–90
Plains Algonquian, 99

Plants: with dye or *puccoon*, 188, 216n50; faunal remains, *85*, 94; place-names and wetland, 21, 63; pollen, 87–88; radiocarbon dates, 132; Werowocomoco, botanical evidence, 163

Pocahontas (daughter of Wahunsenacawh), 3, 111, 167, 171–72

Politics: aggregation events and, 95; copper and political economy, 32; with "dual sovereignty," 17, 40; federal recognition of American Indians, 19, 22, 105, 143–44, 201n72; gift-giving and, 18, 37–38; marriage and, 40, 41; Smith and, 66; trade and warfare, 40; Werowocomoco as political center, 13, 22, 61, 62

Pollen, 87–89, *90*

Pope's Creek ceramics, 75

Populations, 206n25; of Algonquian speakers, 30; Chickahominy community, 112–13, *123*; population movements, 21, 73, 98–103, 113; weroances, 41–42; Werowocomoco, 164, 166

Post mold patterns, 157, 159–60, 161

Potomac Creek site, 64, 131, 165, 184–85

Potter, Stephen, 17

Pottery. *See* Ceramics

Poverty Point site, 213n26, 216n56

Powell, Nathaniel, 33–34

Powhatan (language). *See* Virginia Algonquian

Powhatan (name). *See* Wahunsenacawh

Powhatan (town), 60–61

Powhatan Lords of Life and Death (Williamson), 17

Powhatan's Mantle: circles and, 25, 41–42, 193; decorations on, 40–41; as map, *39*; sovereignty and, 25, 39–40, 49

Preucel, Robert, 47

Priests (quioccosuks), 109, 110, 174; divination ceremonies and, 4, 43–48, 50, 193; "dual sovereignty" with chiefs and, 17, 40; with Huskanaw or male rite of passage, 176–77; temples and, 4, 45, 46, 131

Prince George ceramics, 75

Protohistoric and Contact periods (AD 1500–1607), 89

Puccoon (dye), 188, 216n50

Pullins, Stevan, 77

Quioccosuks. *See* Chiefs; Priests

Quito, 9

Quiyoughcohannock site, 124, 176–77

Radiocarbon dates: animal burials, 188; ceramics, *72*; Chickahominy River Survey, *114–15*, 120, 130–31; corn, 153, 165; earthwork construction, 156–57; Indian Field Creek, Kiskiak community, 81, *83*; midden deposits, 94; ossuaries and paired burials, *121*, 211n35; plants, 132; Werowocomoco, *149*, *150–51*, 156–57, 159

Rappahannock community, 15, 142, 143, 201n71

Rassawek, 55, 65, 66

Relation of Virginia (Spelman), 161

Religion, 26, 27, 36, 38, 79, 118, 216n55

Reservoir. *See* King William Reservoir

Revolts, 22, 28, 112, 181–82, 183

Richardson, Anne (Rappahannock Chief), 142

Ripley, Bob, 141, 159

Ripley, Lynn, 141–42

Rituals: feasting as, 96, 118; Huskanaw or male rite of passage, 45, 62, 176–77; Mexico and ritual sites, 216n56; pilgrimage as rite of passage, 216n55

Rivers, *75*; Chickahominy River, 106, 110, *111*, *116*, *137*; place-names and, 21, 55, 62, 191; riverine settlements, 21. *See also* Chickahominy River Survey

Roanoke Colony, 26, 28, 36, 38, 47

Roanoke simple-stamped ceramics, 165

Rolfe, John, 3, 111

Rountree, Helen, 16, 171

Sacrifices, 118, 166, 183, 188, 189

Sanford, Doug, 18

Sapling-framed house (*yihakin*), 29

Saponi community, 32

Sea levels, rising, 207n30

Seasonal mobility, 32, 207n36, 208n71

Second Anglo-Powhatan War, 180

Secota (Secoton), 174, *175*

Selby Bay projectile points, 76

Seminole tribe, coalescence and, 108

Semiotics, 47–48, 204n86

Settlement forms, Chickahominy community and, 113–17

Settlement patterns: estuarine settings and, 76; houses, 30–31, 33

Shad. *See* Fish

Shakakonia community, 65

Shell beads, 33, 38, 40, 41, 49, 122

Shellfish, 92, 96, 136

Shell middens: Indian Field Creek, excavation area, *81, 82, 83, 84, 85,* 86–87, *91;* with Mockley ceramics, 73, 76–79, *91;* oysters, *85,* 86–87, 149; prevalence of, 86; with Varina ceramics, *91*

Shephard, Christopher, 131

Siebert, Frank, 60, 99, 100

Signs. *See* Icons; Indexical signs; Interpretants, signs and; Semiotics; Symbolism

Siouan community, 18, 206n25; clan system, 203n63; dialects, 32, 33, 64, 205n38

The Siouan Tribes of the East (Mooney), 64–65

Slavery, 28, 29, 108

Smith, John (Captain), 1, 2, 37, 48, 132; Captain John Smith Chesapeake National Historic Trail, 197; in captivity, 3–5, 29, 36, 50, 166–67, 172; divination ceremonies and, 43, *44, 45,* 46, 50; on gift-giving, 38; influence, 33–34, 36, 65; in Kiskiak, 80; Moysonec and, 110, 116; oysters and, 92–93, 208n71; places as memorials and, 184; politics and, 66; with Powhatan's Mantle, 38, 41; rescue of, 3, 15, 167, 171–72; with Virginia Algonquian, 29, 60; Wahunsenacawh and, 24, 25, 42, 61, 162–63, 166–68, 170, 172; as weroance, 172; Werowocomoco and, 29, 145, 164, 166–71. See also *Map of Virginia*

Snead, James, 12

Social change, 8–9

Social identity, 107–8

Social networks: Chickahominy community and, 110; feasting and, 21, 71, 93–98; role of, 106

Social space: divination ceremonies and, 45; Lefebvre and, 20, 212n9, 214n63; maps and, 20, 25, 53; with past, 10; place-names and, 53, 191; Werowocomoco as, 177–78

Sovereignty, 144; "dual sovereignty," 17, 40; Powhatan's Mantle and, 25, 39–40, 49

Space: defined, 9; phenomenology and, 11; social space, 10, 20, 25, 45, 53, 177–78, 191, 212n9, 214n63; space and place, 9–10; spatial imaginary, 20, 22, 144–45, 174–78, 183; spatial practices, 20, 21, 22; spatial representations, 20, 21, 190, 214n63; types, 20; Werowocomoco, spatial organization of,

173–74; Werowocomoco as space of colonial entanglements, 171–72

Spain, 33, 34–35

Spatial imaginary, 183; defined, 20; Werowocomoco and history of, 22, 144–45; Werowocomoco with Virginia Algonquian, 174–78

Spatial practices: Chickahominy community and, 22; of forager-fishers, 21

Spatial representations, 20, 21, 190, 214n63

Spelman, Henry, 32, 46, 118, 130, 161

Spiritual power. *See* Manitou

Spivey, Ashley, 144, 197–98

Starvation. *See* Jamestown Colony

Steadman, Laura, 96

Stereotypes, of American Indians, 14, 26

Stewart, Michael, 94–95

Story, creation. *See* Patawomeck community

Strachey, William, 30–31, 32, 41, 46, 145; dictionary by, 60, 61, 63, 65; oysters and, 93; places as memorials and, 184; with Virginia Algonquian, 60

Sturgeon. *See* Fish

Sturtevant, William, 108

Suffixes, place-names, 53–54, 63

Susquehannock community, 24, 29

Symbolism, 4, 47

Syntax, 60

Taquitock (corn harvest), 32

Taskscape, 12, 22, 173, 182

Temperatures: "Medieval Warm Period" (circa AD 600 to 950), 77; Middle Woodland period (500 BC–AD 900), 77–78; water temperature (200 BC–AD 1650), *78*

Temples, 5, 40, 50, 180; priests and, 4, 45, 46, 131; at Uttamussak, 173–74

Thomas, Julian, 9

Time, at Werowocomoco, 163–66

Tindall, Robert, 79, 145–48, 212n13

Tobacco, 28, 46, 88, 112, 181

Tokens, 186, 215n41

Tooker, William, 61

Tools: for ceramics, 69; earthwork construction, 157

Townsend, Camilla, 171–72

Townsend ceramics, 120, 152, 164

Trade, 40, 144, 159, *160,* 163

Travel, place-names and, 20–21, 55, 67

William and Mary Center for Archaeological Research (WMCAR), 14, 74
William and Mary Institute for Historical Biology, 13
Williamson, Margaret, 4, 17, 40, 172
"Willow Smoke and Dogs' Tails" (Binford), 207n36
Winsack, *58*, 62
WMCAR. *See* William and Mary Center for Archaeological Research
Wolf clan, 41

Women, 32, 69, 70, 178
Woodard, Buck, 41, 66, 110

Yihakin (sapling-framed house), 29
York River, *75*

Zuñiga, Pedro de (Don), 33–35
Zuñiga Chart, 33–38, 48, 79, 157, 176; Chickahominy River drainage, 110, *111*; role of, 50, 105; Werowocomoco and, 145

Martin D. Gallivan is professor of anthropology at the College of William and Mary. He is the author of various articles, reports, and books, including *James River Chiefdoms: The Rise of Social Inequality in the Chesapeake.*

www.ingramcontent.com/pod-product-compliance
Lightning Source LLC
Chambersburg PA
CBHW031437280326
41927CB00038B/473